BUILDING
A NEW
MAJORITY

9/19/16

BID
BAL

Synopsis

Building a New Majority weaves together the autobiographical recol-
lections of the political and professional life of the author, Michael P.
Balzano, with his seasoned analysis of several successful Republican
presidential campaigns. The combination provides the foundation
for recommendations for current and future Republican candidates
to follow in capturing a majority of the nation's working-class voters.
The narrative follows the author, the son of working-class Italian immigrants, from his boyhood in New Haven, Connecticut, through his
time as a high-school dropout and garbage collector to his return to
school, where he earned a doctoral degree at Georgetown University.

His story attracted the attention of staff members in the administration of President Richard M. Nixon. Brought on board to provide
insights and to coordinate efforts to reach ethnic and working-class
voters as part of Nixon's strategy to create a New Majority, he contributed to the winning 1972 campaign. He later performed similar
roles in President Ronald Reagan's 1980 and 1984 campaigns and in
President George H. W. Bush's 1988 campaign.

For any political party to win the White House, it must capture a
majority of working-class voters. *Building a New Majority* is a blueprint
for constructing a new Republican majority that can win elections.
Building upon those victories, they can govern in ways that invite
all people to share in a common future in which individuals may improve their social status and their economic well-being, living out the
American Dream.

BUILDING
A NEW
MAJORITY

MICHAEL P. BALZANO

BUILDING A NEW MAJORITY

iUniverse books may be ordered through booksellers or by contacting:

iUniverse
1663 Liberty Drive
Bloomington, IN 47403
www.iuniverse.com
1-800-Authors (1-800-288-4677)

ISBN: 978-1-4917-8590-4 (sc)
ISBN: 978-1-4917-8591-1 (hc)
ISBN: 978-1-4917-8592-8 (e)

Library of Congress Control Number: 2015920838

Print information available on the last page.

iUniverse rev. date: 1/22/2016

Book Dedication

My Grandmother Elinor Perrelli often said, "In America the streets are paved with gold, but you have to bend down to pick it up." In her own way, she was instilling in me the assurance of the foundational principle of our country – the achievement ethic – that rewards are based on merit, not on class or heritage or money or position of power, that all who come to this country have equal access to the American Dream.

This book is dedicated to all those who made this concept real in my life, beginning with my grandparents -

Pasquale and Elinor Perrelli

and especially my parents –

Michael and Jennie Balzano

who sacrificed daily so I could have a better life.

It is also dedicated to so many others in the Italian neighborhood where I grew up – the nuns, the teachers, the shopkeepers – everyone who told me over and over that it was possible to achieve success in America. One day I finally believed them and took up the challenge to change my life.

Finally, it is dedicated to my fellow travelers – working class and immigrant men and women who daily strive to make this concept real for themselves, their children and grandchildren, people whose hopes, dreams and aspirations are the foundation of the American success story and the story told in this book.

Contents

Preface

The election of 1972 represented a seismic shift in the American political landscape. In a landslide victory, Republican President Richard Nixon carried every state in the union except Massachusetts and the District of Columbia. This victory occurred because Nixon reached out beyond traditional Republican voters to win the support of working-class Democrats who were part of Franklin Roosevelt's electoral base.

As a Democrat with a working-class background, I was privileged to serve as Staff Assistant to President Nixon with the job of mobilizing outreach to ethnic, blue-collar, Democrat voters. Nixon's goal was to bring these Democrats into what he called a "New Majority." Later, during the presidential campaign of 1980, Ronald Reagan asked me to reconstruct Nixon's New Majority coalition. When Vice President George H. W. Bush began his run for the presidency, he, too, asked me to reassemble the coalition for his 1988 race.

Following the Nixon administration, I began to chronicle my experiences in the campaigns of Republican candidates in order to identify the essential variables that produced victory. My simple conclusion was that, from Nixon through Romney, those candidates who reached out to the working classes won elections, while those who did not lost. This book explains when and why working-class Democrats chose to abandon the Democratic Party to give Republicans a winning majority. It also explains why Republican administrations were unable to hold those majorities in successive elections. In these pages I have documented my experiences with Republican candidates from the 1972 Nixon race through Romney's campaign in 2012. I hope the reader will find this behind-the-scenes narrative both dramatic and engaging as well as instructive.

Much of the material in these pages was derived from White House memos, position papers, and interviews with officials who served in the Nixon, Reagan, and Bush campaigns and their administrations. Much was derived from the notes that I took over the years, along with newspaper accounts of the events I describe. Many of the quotes contained herein are sourced only from my memory. The reader will have to trust that from the disadvantage of my extreme dyslexia I developed a compensating near-perfect verbal recall. This was a blessing that allowed me, among other things, to record my professors' lectures on the hard drive of my mind instead of in indecipherable scrawls.

The story I tell and my observations are highly relevant for today's candidates. Working-class Americans now believe that neither party is concerned with their future. The Democratic Party is not interested in industrial-base workers, and the Republican Party has little or no relationship with working-class voters. Current and future candidates pursuing a New Majority strategy must listen to the cries of the working class. They want jobs, not entitlement programs. They want to be respected for the work they do and recognized for their contributions to the American Dream. This book chronicles how the long-term visions of Nixon, Reagan and Bush enabled them to capture the support of working-class Americans and provides a playbook for recreating their successes in the 21st century.

Acknowledgements

Three people central to the story told in this book – and of great consequence to my life – are Richard Nixon, Charles Colson, and Jesse Calhoon. Each not only took a risk in promoting and supporting my career but in catapulting me into the political drama that unfolds in these pages. I promised each I would someday tell the story of the New Majority, and it was that promise that provided a steady light at the end of the very long book-writing tunnel. Colson not only encouraged me up until the time of his death in 2012, but he also provided me with a trove of material from his personal archive.

Gratitude and thanks are owed to so many others who not only provided invaluable advice and encouragement but have been a rich source of insight and wisdom:

Jeane Kirkpatrick, my teacher, my academic mentor and surrogate mother;

Jose Sorzano, one-time fellow graduate student, classical scholar, political genius, and my close personal friend;

Jerry Jones, close friend and colleague, who tirelessly pursued the New Majority through the Nixon and Reagan administrations and continues to try to connect the Republican Party with America's working class;

My colleagues and great friends Jed Babbin and Dave Patterson who have invested decades in promoting America's working class.

Craig Fuller, my cohort in many adventures with Jesse Calhoon, Ronald Reagan and George H. W. Bush;

William "Bill" Gavin, advisor and speechwriter to Richard Nixon and Ronald Reagan, whose advice and encouragement came at a time when I needed it most;

Tom Duesterberg who not only advised and encouraged but coached me over a two-year period through many of the tough spots;

Charlie Walker, friend and three-time Space Shuttle veteran, whose insights about NASA's manned space program have been invaluable;

David Goodreau whose experience and insight into the industrial supplier chain has been a great help;

Audra Kincaid, archivist at the American Maritime Congress, who generously unearthed many documents vital to this project;

Jini Clare, Suzanne Bentz, Liz Prestridge, who gave generously of their time in providing editorial advice;

Martin Morse Wooster, my talented editor who measurably improved the quality of this work;

Ruthanne Goodman, my long-time colleague and friend, whose patience was tested at limits beyond mortal endurance. I would not have been able to start or finish this project without her and whatever thanks I can give her will be insufficient;

To my wife, Denise, my best friend, partner and confidante. During this three-year long project I suspect I was no less demanding of her time and attention and patience than I usually am and for that she has my deepest love and gratitude;

My sons Chris and Matt who have let their old man use them as sounding boards and who have never failed in their support and wise counsel, in addition to providing hands-on assistance with this entire project.

PART 1

CHAPTER 1

From Wooster Street to the White House (1935-1971)

October 1972

Like everything else I had done during the preceding six months in Richard Nixon's White House, this assignment, too, would be a high-wire act. Michael Rivisto, a prominent leader in the Order of the Sons of Italy on the West Coast, was able to get a meeting for me with San Francisco Mayor Joseph Alioto. Alioto had agreed to see me, an obscure White House aide, because Rivisto had asked him for a favor. I was overwhelmed as I entered Mayor Alioto's ornate ceremonial office. Expecting that Rivisto and I would be alone with the mayor, I was surprised to find three other people sitting in a circle of chairs that surrounded the front of the massive wooden desk behind which the mayor sat. The mayor smiled briefly, then stared at me coldly.

Rivisto made the introductions, telling the mayor that this was the young Italian boy he had spoken about who was very close to President Richard Nixon and who he had been helpful in getting West Coast Italians to meet with White House officials. He explained that the West Coast Chapter of the Sons of Italy had never been invited to the White House in the Nixon years prior to my joining the White House staff. Rivisto said that Nixon wanted a closer relationship with West Coast Italians. There was another reason why we asked for this meeting. Italian Americans were concerned about Alioto supporting a candidate, George McGovern, who championed abortion. There had

1

been public announcements on the East Coast that Mayor Alioto, a prominent Italian, would attend rallies in New York and New Jersey to endorse McGovern. Rivisto urged the Mayor not to do that.

Alioto had what appeared to be a polite half-smile on his face as he shifted his glance back and forth between Rivisto and me. I noticed a slight impatience in his manner as he drummed his fingers on the desk as if to say, "Yes, yes. Get on with it."

Suddenly, Alioto stood up and shouted, "Out!" I thought he meant me. He said, "Out!" and motioned to the group sitting in the room. He then pointed to me and said, "You. Out. Downstairs, in front of the building; I'll be there." I looked at Rivisto, who simply nodded.

Moments later Alioto came out of the building and said, "Come on, walk."

"Walk?" I said.

"Yes, walk," he said as he strode away, setting a pace so fast that I struggled to keep up with him as he started to walk around the entire city hall of San Francisco. There was a fairly strong wind that morning, and I was out of shape. But he was not. "Did Mitchell send you?" Alioto demanded.

"Who?" I was caught off guard.

"John Mitchell! You know who I am talking about, the attorney general."

"No," I said, "I don't know him. I came, as Mike Rivisto told you, to see if we could stop you from campaigning for McGovern in the Italian communities on the East Coast."

His pace was exhausting me. I asked, "Do you exercise like this?"

"Exercise?" he responded. "Hell, I want to make sure that if you're wearing a wire you're not going to be able to tape me."

"A wire?" I said, stopping to catch my breath.

"Yes. I don't trust Mitchell, or Nixon, for that matter," he said. "Mitchell has been spreading a rumor that I am the subject of a Justice Department strike force, alleging I have mafia connections."

By that time I could see that I was in way over my head. "I work for the president and Charles Colson, his special counsel," I said. "No one else. I don't know anything about the mafia. I am here to establish a relationship between you and the White House."

2

He stopped. "All right. I don't know you, but I trust Rivisto. Let me give you the benefit of the doubt. If you are really a White House aide, let me see if you have any clout. I want to be invited to the signing ceremony for the revenue sharing bill. I worked on that bill. I should be there, but for political reasons I was not invited."

We had come full circle to the front door of City Hall. Alioto looked at me, "Can you do that?" he asked. "If you can get that done and get me invited, I'll believe you, and I'll work with you on the McGovern issue privately. Wait here. I'll send Rivisto out."

Beaming, Rivisto emerged about a half hour later. "You sold him," he said. "Can you get him invited?" The event was less than three days away, but I said I would make it happen.

I was on the phone with Colson within the hour. He put me on hold for what seemed like an eternity, but it was far less than thirty minutes. "Do it," he said. "Invite him and get him there." And he hung up.

A few days later, on the day of the signing ceremony, Mayor Alioto and I met on the outskirts of the crowd surrounding Independence Hall in Philadelphia. Between police and Secret Service and other onlookers I made my way through the crowd, occasionally getting stopped at checkpoints where I used my White House pass to get me through.

The "mission impossible" parts of the assignment had gone well. Mayor Alioto had canceled his plans to campaign for McGovern in the Italian sections of New York and New Jersey. He had passed up opportunities to attack John Mitchell for the anti-Italian policies he had generated as attorney general; and the White House had agreed, at the last moment, to invite Mayor Alioto to the ceremony, in spite of the fear that his presence would add to his prestige and increase his chance to become governor of California.

Once inside the building, we climbed to the second floor and joined a receiving line where I had hoped he could be photographed laughing and joking with the president and vice president. My plan was to have pictures and a story that I would have distributed throughout the ethnic community, ending once and for all the rumor that Alioto was against the reelection of the president.

But now the plan was falling apart. Ron Ziegler, the press secretary, had never returned my phone calls. Jerry Warren, deputy press secretary, was not in the media booth as I had been told he would be. And none of the newsmen present were willing to follow an unknown White House aide to cover a story not assigned to them. It appeared there would be no television coverage, nor a UPI or AP story on Alioto and Nixon praising each other for their roles in the creation of revenue sharing, the touchstone of Nixon's New Federalism. With a little luck, White House photographer Ollie Atkins might get a shot of the three of us standing together, but I would never be able to get a print in time for the day's news deadlines.

"Oh hell," I thought, *"Chuck Colson had been right. The best one can hope for is a fifty percent success rating in this White House, and it's uphill all the way."*

We were inching our way along a receiving line of several hundred invited guests, including big city mayors and governors who were there on the occasion of President Nixon's signing the revenue sharing bill into law. Suddenly there was a tap on my arm. It was one of the president's personal aides. Over the noise of the multitude, he said in a discreet, low voice that was barely audible, "The president doesn't like staff people in receiving lines." Obviously, this aide had no knowledge of what I was up to, and this was no time to explain it to him. I made a half-hearted attempt to dismiss his order to me to step out of line. I whispered to the aide, hoping that Alioto could not hear me over the noise of the crowd, "I'm on a special assignment. I've got to get a picture to go along with a story for the ethnic press." As it turned out, Alioto had not heard me, but neither had the White House aide, whose Secret Service earphone was in the ear closest to me.

When he turned and walked away, I thought I had won, in spite of the fact that I was, once again, breaking a White House rule. We inched on, and as we approached the head of the line, I could hear camera ratchets rewinding and shutters clicking.

As we got within a couple feet of the vice president, I suddenly felt the pincer-like grip of a hand on my arm as an annoyed, red-faced aide said once again, "For Christ's sake, will you get out of this line! The old man is going to get pissed."

"Wait," I pleaded.

"Get out," he insisted.

A wave of defeat spread over me. "The hell with it," I said to myself and stepped out of line and was pushed into the moving crowd. I watched as Mayor Alioto went through the receiving line and shook hands with Vice President Spiro Agnew. As it turned out, Nixon had left the room and was preparing to make a speech outside in Independence Square. I had succeeded in getting Alioto to come and be seen at the event and to agree not to campaign for McGovern. But I did not get the photos with Alioto and Nixon that I would have circulated in the Italian neighborhoods in the Northeast and Midwest.

I left and went back downstairs and stood for about ten minutes as a group of VIPs pressed back into the building following Nixon's speech. I was so disappointed that I had not been able to personally introduce Alioto to President Nixon. If I had been permitted to leave the building, I would have gone to the airport and caught the next flight back to Washington. But there was no way of getting out of the building; the Secret Service now had both entrances blocked to cover the president's impending departure.

As I stood there, partially held up by the crowd that pressed against me from all sides, a path was cleared so that the president and Philadelphia Mayor Frank Rizzo could pass through. President Nixon was smiling as he walked along. I couldn't help thinking to myself that I was just another face in the crowd. I had worked my heart out to set up a photo event to prove that Alioto was partial to Nixon, and the president didn't even know who I was.

Suddenly, as if he had heard me, the president spotted me. His eyes visibly widened as he came through the crowd to pull me forward. "Frank," he said to Mayor Rizzo, "have you met Mike Balzano? He's the best staff man I have," he said touching my shoulder.

"Oh, I know Mike," Rizzo responded.

"Good man," the president said once again, this time striking my coat lapel with the edges of his fingertips. Then he turned and moved with his entourage through a door. "*He remembered me*," I thought to myself. "*He knows my name*." The crowd followed him, vanishing from around me like water on a beach receding around a seashell. I stood there, too happy to move.

Hours later I leaned back in my seat and stared through the clouds over the whirring propeller of the Allegheny propjet airplane taking me back to Washington. It occurred to me that it had all been worth it—the nights without sleep, the running around, even being in the air in this little plane, which I'm deathly afraid to fly in.

I thought to myself, *"Okay, I was taken out of the receiving line, but I did get Alioto into an event with Richard Nixon."* In that White House it was almost impossible to do anything good for the president. Everywhere I turned there were those who would say, "No, it can't be done, that's against the rules," or something like that. But having completed what many would call a mission impossible, I was lost in the pride I secretly enjoyed as I sat there. Nobody in my old Italian neighborhood, none of my friends on Wooster Street who still worked for New Haven's Department of Sanitation, not even my own family, would believe that the president of the United States really knew who I was and plucked me from a crowd of hundreds to introduce me to the mayor of Philadelphia. I didn't believe it myself.

How did Mike Balzano, a one-time high school dropout and garbage collector become a staff assistant to the President of the United States? Was it because I turned my life around, went back to school, and received a Ph.D. from Georgetown University? In truth, my academic credentials were not the determining factor in my presidential appointment. It was my knowledge of European-immigrant working-class communities with whom President Nixon sought to communicate. That knowledge came from a lifetime of experience living in the mosaic of an ethnic community.

Wooster Street 1935 - 1960

I grew up in an Italian section of New Haven, Connecticut, known as Wooster Square. Like other industrial cities in the Northeast, New Haven was populated by European immigrants who worked in the numerous factories and machine shops that made New England a magnet for a new generation of twentieth-century pilgrims. Whether they were Italians, Germans, Poles, Greeks or Lithuanians, all found employment in that rapidly growing part of the country. These immigrants shared a number of common characteristics. Some were entrepreneurs who came in search of business opportunities. Others were skilled tradesmen who were in short supply in America. The majority, however, were unskilled workers who left their native countries with less than a grade school education. They came to America in search of opportunities not to be found in their feudal societies. Regardless of their level of skills or the language they spoke, they came ready and willing to work and work hard.

This generation of new Americans grouped together in little neighborhoods, which took on the appearance of their native European communities. In many ways, the neighborhood in which I lived was a city unto itself. It was quite possible to meet all of the needs of the people who lived in the area without ever leaving a square mile. Wooster Street was the main artery; it ran some ten blocks in length. The street was dotted with small family-owned businesses of all varieties. The storefront windows of these little shops served as a first-floor pedestal upon which stood the remaining portions of three- and four-story brick apartment buildings.

At almost any hour of the day or night the sounds and smells announced the time of day more beautifully than the chimes of any timepiece. The dawn was filled with the scent of freshly baked bread. As the baker walked along in the pre-dawn darkness pulling his small wagon filled with bread, this little silver-haired man in his gleaming white pants, t-shirt and flour-covered shoes stood out against the backdrop of the asphalt streets and the dark red brick buildings which lined them. He filled the air with song. To see and hear him was to understand that Mr. Amendola approached his singing with the same intensity with which he baked his bread. He sang as though the streets and buildings were the stage props of an opera. At the top of his voice he sang to people he met scurrying to work in the murky light. As he pulled his wagon, he would pause to punctuate the high and low notes with his free hand. Each day when my mother was delivering me to my grandmother, the day care provider for her working children, we would meet Mr. Amendola who sang to us as we passed by. Early risers would watch from their second- and third-floor windows as he sang to the half-sleeping dogs and cats crouched in the doorways below. This urban rooster and his songs, coming as they did with the morning sun, signaled the start of the new day.

From early to mid-morning, Wooster Street residents could hear the rubbing of squeegees against shop windows and bristled brooms pushing water over the newly hosed-down sidewalks as the little stores opened for business. As the sun climbed the sky, the sounds and smells changed with the passing hours. As my grandmother and I walked along Wooster Street, we were met with a continuous mixture of odors, colors and sounds.

There was the fish market with its street-side tubs of codfish being rinsed with continuously running water. A few feet away a little store sold coffee and a variety of freshly roasted nuts. Everywhere the smell of roasting coffee beans filled the air. A few steps up the street in either direction were pastry shops that perfumed the air with the sweet fragrance of pastry shells, chocolate and vanilla cream, and rum-flavored yellow cake. Here, grandma always bought us a lemon ice.

Then there was the Italian Men's Club, where the smell of Italian cigars, both stale and fresh, mixed with beer and traces of wine, was ever-present. As long as I can remember, whenever we passed the Men's Club or went into the club to ask my grandfather for a nickel, men could be heard arguing violently, some shouting at each other at the top of their voices. As I grew older, I learned that they were not angry. That was their normal tone of voice.

A daily ritual with my grandmother was to visit St. Michael's Catholic Church, where she would stop to light a candle and pray. Built in 1889, the church had three entrances. Over the main entrance was a statue of St. Michael with sword in hand ready to vanquish Lucifer. My grandmother solemnly reminded me that I was named after St. Michael.

St. Michael's Catholic Church stood in stark contrast to the pristine, simply adorned Protestant churches just a few miles away that occupied places of prominence in what we Italians knew as the WASP area of the city, the New Haven Green. There were three main Protestant churches that stood behind a wrought iron fence that surrounded the park near Yale University. These churches pre-dated the American Revolution. One need only look at their congregations to know that they were part of the city's elite. Men wore suits to church and women wore large hats, always in harmony with the season. The parishioners of the Catholic churches, by contrast, were working-class immigrants—Italians, Poles, Slavs, and French, among others. St. Michael's on Wooster Square was the central gathering point for Italians and was the largest church in the state serving the Italian community.

From late afternoon into the night, the smells and sounds changed once again on Wooster Street. Numerous pizzerias emitted aromas from giant brick ovens. It was difficult to distinguish the odors, the sausage from the onions, the mushrooms from the bacon, the mozzarella from the tomatoes, or the dough itself. Nor was it possible to distinguish from which place of business the odors came; they seemed to float on the night air.

Wooster Street is nationally famous for its pizzerias, which were established in the early 1900s. Pizzas were baked in coal-fired brick ovens brought from Italy, leaving a residue of coal dust on one's hands when eating a slice of pizza. No one worried about carcinogens. Frank Sinatra was known to eat at Sally's. There were photos on the kitchen wall and newspaper articles documenting the Sinatra visits.

Then there was the music. From the alley between two buildings directly across the street from my grandmother's apartment came the sound of a full band—tuba, bass drum, and all. The band was the uniformed local "Banda de Roma," which rehearsed incessantly on the weeknights for the numerous concerts, feasts, and holy days that filled the summer weekends.

It was truly an international neighborhood. Fragrances from the different kinds of foods from the countries of origin of those doing the cooking emanated from the open apartment windows along the street. In addition to the fragrances, there was music from the different ethnic radio stations. You could tell the nationality of the residents by whether the music was Italian, Greek or Polish.

An Industrious People

Industrial New England lent its own set of sounds and smells to our area of New Haven, calling to memory the working-class people of

Wooster Street. The loud hoot of the seven o'clock whistle on the roof of Sargent's Hardware signaled the beginning of each workday for the residents of our Italian neighborhood, as well as the hundreds of Polish, Lithuanian and other ethnic enclaves in the surrounding area.

I recall the summer when I was just old enough to explore the cross streets that served to measure the blocks of Wooster Street. The area was filled with large and small machine shops that made and repaired all kinds of machine tools. As I walked along, once again the sounds and smells told about the community. There was the acrid smell of flux and the sound of high-pitched air from acetylene torches whose flashes, as well as the showers of sparks, warned that metal was being welded. Then there was the unsynchronized whirring sound of hundreds of sewing machines heard through the open windows of the Brewster Shirt Company.

Down at the end of most of the cross streets heading south, within two blocks, was the waterfront. The docks were always busy with coal and oil tankers unloading their cargoes. After 6:00 p.m., when the workers would leave the yards, the neighborhood kids had their chance to jump into the mountainous piles of coal. Whether we pretended that the cascading pieces of coal were shifting desert sands or crumbling icebergs, the scene was enough to mentally transport imaginative kids to far away places, images shattered only by the shouts of the watchman who came running to throw us out.

Along the Water Street area were the large manufacturing companies, which produced a wide variety of hard goods. On any side street in this part of the neighborhood one could get a vivid picture of industrial New England. On every block the sounds were similar and yet different. From just about every building came the sound of pounding drop-forges, the high pitched chatter of milling machines, the squeal of drill presses, and the screaming of grindstones. All these machines were powered by the ever-present hum of giant electric motors and the rumbling sound of belt-driven pulleys. The air on these streets was filled with the odors of atomized oil, burning grease, and rubber insulation from miles of overheated wiring.

My family lived in a three-room cold-water flat. There were two bedrooms, one that I shared with my older brother and one where my parents slept. There was no central heating system. Only the kitchen was heated with an oil stove, which was the central meeting place in the apartment. In addition to having no heat or hot water, no telephone or television, we had no bathing facility; only a toilet. To bathe, we heated water in a teakettle and took sponge baths. I couldn't wait to be old enough to go to the YMCA to take a *real* shower. We did not own a refrigerator. We were the only people I knew who still had an icebox. We had no car; my parents always walked to work or took public transportation, which throughout my childhood were trolley cars that were open in the summer and closed tight in the winter.

My father ran a milling machine at the Winchester Repeating Arms Company, one of the oldest rifle makers in the country. He was a highly skilled worker in an industry where precision was calculated to within thousandths of an inch. A proud member of the International Association of Machinists, my father worked six days a week, ten hours a day throughout World War II

My first experience in understanding that major corporations ignore front-line workers who know more about the manufacturing process than company managers came when my father told me about a problem that occurred when he was a drill press operator. He was drilling a piece of steel that was the receiver for the M-1 Garand rifle and was constantly burning out drills. His supervisor told him he was not operating the machine correctly. My father's response was, "The stock is too hard." The foreman laughed at him, basically saying, "You're just an Italian drill press operator. What the hell do you know about steel?" Then the milling machine operators began burning out cutters and they were being punished by management for not operating their machines correctly. The company brought in a metallurgist who said the stock was too hard.

My mother worked at Sargent & Company, one of the oldest manufacturers of locks and hardware in America. On two different occasions, she lost the tips of her fingers on her right hand on a power press without the proper protection. Later she worked on a foot press.

In 1941, all New England hardware companies, as well as all other large and small manufacturers, converted their operations to defense-related products. My mother made brass links that held bullets together for machine-gun belts and bomb shackles that released bombs under the wings of fighter aircraft. In the red brick factory buildings in which they worked, there was no air conditioning. Sometimes at dinner my parents would talk about people passing out in temperatures well above 100 degrees. In later life, I passed those buildings and remarked to myself they were right out of a Dickens novel.

My mother's company had no union and no benefits. There was a pension plan offered for years of service worked. When pregnant with me, my mother worked almost to delivery time when she was sent home for fear that a baby would be born on the shop floor. I was born at home a few days later. When my mother returned to work, she was told that her fifteen years of previously accrued service would not count for retirement. When Sargent's was finally unionized, the union contract did not cover her lost years of service. Between their collective ninety-five years of work experience, my mother and father had operated all manner of light machinery.

All during those summers in which I was old enough to wander alone, I worked my way through the different side streets peering into the basement and ground-floor factory windows to watch the various machines in operation. I watched rows of drill press operators who stood before their machines pressing down the arm that lowered the drill through the metal. I liked to watch the curling strips of hot brass, copper, and steel that rose smoking around the spinning drill.

Through other windows I would see huge tanks of water. Mounted on the tanks were large wire drums that turned like paddle wheels on a ferryboat, constantly submerging their tumbling contents of metal parts into the liquid. My mother told me that some of the tanks were used to chromium plate the parts, while other tanks were giant baths to wash them.

In still other windows, I watched large numbers of men and women sitting at bench-like tables. On the bench was a small machine that seemed to bend a flat piece of metal into a right angle each time the operator would kick forward a foot lever that hung beneath the bench. These workers were very busy. I watched with amazement as the woman closest to me, with one hand, picked up the small straight piece of metal piled on the bench in front of her and placed it into a pincher-like mouth. With her foot, she kicked the lever, which bent the metal into an angle. Then she removed the bent part with her other hand and threw it into a box and, with her left hand, placed a new flat metal piece into the pinchers—all in one motion. Insert, kick, remove; insert, kick, remove. All of those at the table did the same thing. No one spoke. They just sat there eyes focused on the pinchers and repeated the process. Insert, kick, remove; insert, kick, remove. My mother said that talking was not allowed in the shop. She said that if you were seen talking too often, the timekeeper would send you home.

One day, I was sitting crouched on my heels looking into the heavy, metal-screened windows at a huge machine, which to me seemed to be polishing brass doorknobs. There was a smell of burning grease, as well as tremendous heat, blowing in my face through the open window. Then a balding little man left the machine where he was standing and came to the window to look at me. Hair covered his burly arms, chest, and parts of his back, which gleamed with sweat. Atop his forehead was a large pair of clear, plastic goggles. He smiled at me through the window and said, "Hey, *guyo* ("boy"), you wanna work?" I just peered at him and he repeated, "You wanna work?" Above the odor of heat and grease and metal, I could smell his perspiration. Then he turned to face the machine once again.

During supper that night, when I told my father about the man's comments to me, he smiled but was visibly upset. "Not my honey boy," he said. "We want you to go to school, to learn. You don't want to be like the rest of us. We're working hard so you won't have to do what we're doing."

Before the age of fifteen, I was aware of the inescapable fact that the parents throughout the community worked a variety of menial jobs with the hope that their children would "go to school, learn and get a better start in life." What was clear to me, even at that age, was that these parents were sacrificing themselves so that their children could improve their lives.

Anyone looking at my educational history would know that my leaving school early in life was inevitable. Both my parents left school in their early teens. In the 1920s, children of working class families went to work to support the family. This was especially true during the Great Depression.

Teachers in the neighborhood public schools did their best to give their students a fighting chance. Parents who could pay the tuition sent their children to Catholic school in the community. These schools were all affiliated with local neighborhood churches. My parents sent me to St. Michael's School because we belonged to St. Michael's Parish. I was not a good student and most disruptive. By the third grade, I was asked to leave. I had stayed back in both first and second grade and simply couldn't keep up with even elementary school requirements. I was then moved to a public school in another neighborhood. That didn't help either. Officials there told my parents that I should move to a school nearer my home that could deal with my behavior problems. The third stop was a school that served the Italian community in our neighborhood. I did poorly there as well, but it was easier to survive.

Often I played hooky from school and engaged in mischief in the neighborhood. On one occasion, a friend and I smoked a pipe and accidentally set fire to a garage. The fire department came. The fire was put out. From then on I was deemed "Crazy Mikey" and children were prohibited from playing with me.

During those years I listened to evening radio programs. I was infatuated with them: "The Lone Ranger," "Tom Mix," "Superman," "Jack Armstrong, The All American Boy," "The Shadow," "The Green Hornet," "Terry and the Pirates," "Sky King," etc. I never missed a one. In fact, I began memorizing the stories as I listened to them, which increased my vocabulary tremendously. I now realize that I really learned English not from school but from the radio. My vocabulary, pronunciation and usage came from all of the different programs. Some of my teachers actually said they could not understand my ability to speak at a level above the others in the class and yet could not read or write a work assignment.

Today I know that I am dyslexic. That is why I could not read aloud in class or spell even the simplest words. But in the 1940s public school teachers were not trained to identify learning disabilities. Some of my teachers thought I was stupid, and why not? I thought I was stupid as well. Sitting as a non-participating student in class led to my laughing and joking with the other poor students, and more often than not, I spent the days sitting outside the principal's office. Later, not being watched, I simply left and went home.

At sixteen, I dropped out of school and began to wander from job to job. I soon realized that quitting school was a great mistake, but I recognized that the mistake was clearly of my own doing. During the years that I drifted, I accepted responsibility for failure. So it was with all of my friends who left school. I cannot remember any of my friends or their parents who blamed their inability to make a passing grade on the schools, the teachers, the books, economics, or cultural deprivation, discrimination, racism, or anything else. Failure, pure and simple, rested with *us*.

The willingness to accept success or failure as the individual's responsibility was the touchstone of our community. The young people in our area learned from their own parents and from the parents of others that, in America, opportunity was placed within our reach. But we had to reach for it. If we truly wanted to better ourselves, nothing would stop us. If we made only a half-hearted effort, or waited for someone else to do it for us, failure was guaranteed. Young people in our neighborhood were taught that, barring sickness or accident, hard work, sacrifice, and individual responsibility were the secrets of success.

From what has been said thus far, it should be apparent that, with respect to the work ethic, the philosophical overview of the neighborhood ethnic groups stood flatly in the tradition of the American experience. However, hard work and sacrifice were only part of the formula for success. To have the motivation for advancement was necessary, to be sure, but, beyond that, one also had to have a political system that afforded workers the opportunity for economic and social advancement. The ethnic groups in our neighborhood knew only too well that, in their native countries, that desire for economic and social mobility was meaningless, because the social and political systems in those countries did not provide for upward mobility.

When our parents came to America, they viewed the openness of the social system as inextricably intertwined in American political institutions. Because America's economic system provided for easy access to economic upward mobility and because the political system, i.e., democracy, permitted changes in social as well as economic status, immigrants in my community saw democracy and the achievement ethic as inseparable.

As immigrants poured into the Northeast urban centers they encountered the problems of the newly arrived. Ignorant of the language and the culture, they presented political parties with unlimited opportunity to build electoral majorities. Thus, from the early days of their arrival, they were constantly sought after by Democratic ward leaders who were eager to capture their vote.

In our community it was no different; ward leaders from both parties tried to outdo each other in delivering social services to the new residents in order to influence their party registration. The benefits received in exchange for pledges of political loyalty took on a variety of forms. In some cases, such as with the most recent immigrants, party leaders helped illiterate laborers fill out intricate forms to obtain citizenship. This was an act of great significance because it often resulted in immigrants crediting the party machine for positively affecting the outcome of their requests for citizenship. Once having received assistance, an immigrant family would immediately refer almost any government and nongovernmental written communications to these seemingly knowledgeable people for interpretation and clarification. The truth is that if a member of the party machine spent the time to help illiterate immigrants scale the paper obstacles to citizenship, it was quite natural for these humble people to be forever grateful. If that meant voting Democrat, it was a small price to pay to gain admittance into a utopia.

Beyond assisting in interpreting and processing the paperwork of everyday living, the ward leaders often took a major role in helping immigrants obtain employment. In some cases, this function took the form of accessing the ward leader's lists of contacts who knew of job openings around the city. In other cases, political patronage was unquestionably the vehicle used to obtain employment for constituents. In our community, the party workers who dispensed the greatest services and benefits for our people belonged to the Democratic Party, which was the party that demonstrated the greater understanding about the plight and needs of immigrants. Because the party workers were sensitive to the ethnic groups at a time when they were the most malleable politically, and, because they presented themselves as former immigrants themselves, the attraction to the Democratic Party was natural. From the perspective of non-English-speaking ethnics, the Republican Party was not as visible in our communities.

Another force largely responsible for moving ethnic groups in our community into the Democratic camp was the labor movement. The historical connection between labor and the Democratic Party is well known to students of American politics. In my neighborhood, all manner of blue-collar workers were influenced by union leaders to support Democratic candidates. Lacking either formal education or highly marketable skills, workers in our community were drawn naturally to union leaders who promised high wages and better working conditions.

One of the tactics used by union officials attempting to polarize employees and management was to paint a vivid picture of the Great Depression. Factory owners were portrayed as members of the well-to-do Republican class who shared the philosophy of government espoused by President Herbert Hoover and the Republican Party. Attempts to link the Republicans with the Depression, starvation and unemployment were less than subtle. In like manner, workers were told that salvation lay in organizing against management, against the owners of companies, and against the party that supported these groups, namely the Republicans. President Franklin Delano Roosevelt, on the other hand, was pictured as a modern-day saint. On countless occasions, I overheard my parents and other relatives castigating the Republican Party for its inhumanity. My father said that he and my mother supported the Democratic Party because it was the party of working people. "If it were not for Roosevelt, even today the Republicans would deny the poor people a slice of bread."

Whether or not they understood it, children in the neighborhood knew the political preference of their parents. Moreover, a character sketch of the typical Republican or Democrat was clearly drawn in the minds of the children. Republicans were portrayed as being totally different from us. They spoke English rather than a foreign language. They attended different churches, churches, it was said, that required less of them than those we attended. They wore jackets and ties even if it wasn't Sunday. They were not poor people, nor did they understand the plight of the poor. The word most often used to describe them was "cold."

On the other hand, the Democratic Party was seen as the party dedicated to helping poor people to better themselves. Voting Democratic, then, was seen as a key to success. As such, the link between the Democratic Party and the achievement ethic was easily established in the minds of those asking only for the opportunity to get to the ladder. To me, the Democratic Party symbolized the achievement ethic. To my family and all those around us, that proposition seemed universal. The achievement ethic orientation of my Italian community was reinforced by the public grammar schools in the neighborhood.

My Reentry into the System: Return to School 1955 - 1960

I can remember leaving the building the day I quit school. I walked alone down the street. I was fully conscious of what I had done. Upon leaving school, I went through dozens of jobs as I began searching for meaningful work. I failed at all of the jobs that were offered to me. I tried and failed at every attempt to learn a trade. Whether carpentry, masonry, plumbing, or electrical, I couldn't master the basics. Moreover, I was disruptive to all of the other workers who were serious about learning. I also did a two-year stint in the Connecticut National Guard, and was expelled.

My bad reputation in New Haven persisted. No one would hire me. I went through dozens of jobs. In 1972, the *Wall Street Journal* noted the fifty-six jobs that I had held in one year. I was desperate to find a job and the only option that seemed possible was as a garbage collector. I went to my Uncle Andrew who owned a bar and had contacts in city hall and asked for his help. He got me a job in the New Haven Sanitation Department picking up garbage every morning. My older brother was already working on a garbage truck, and I teamed up with him. My father was humiliated early one morning when we drove past him as he was on his way to work.

One day while working on a garbage truck I slipped on an icy street and suffered a severe back injury. I was unable to work for month.

My doctor said I would no longer be able to earn a living by physical labor. By chance, an old friend of mine named Ray Boffa, who was an optician, said he had the authority to hire an apprentice lens grinder. He told me that I could learn a trade. I thanked him for his offer and confessed that I was stupid and had failed at every trade I tried. He persisted, and I agreed to take the entry-level job as an apprentice lens grinder for the American Optical Company. That was a turning point in my life. Ray's belief in me, and his training and guidance helped me begin to believe I could be successful. For the first time, I found something at which I could excel.

Over the next four years, I continued my optical apprenticeship and also attended high school in the evening division of the public school system. In 1960, I graduated from high school, passed the Connecticut exam to become a licensed optician, and became the branch manager of a small optical company in Darien, Connecticut.

The experience of returning to high school had opened up a whole new world to me and I wanted to continue learning by enrolling in college. I decided to take a history course at the University of Bridgeport. I received an A. I then took a course in psychology. I received another A. And so it was to continue through three semesters totaling almost one year of college with a straight A average. I was encouraged by the Bridgeport faculty to attend the university full time and offered a scholarship. I left the optical business and entered the University of Bridgeport as a full-time student.

Bridgeport and Georgetown University 1961 – 1971

At the end of four years, I graduated *magna cum laude* and was urged by the faculty and the deans to go on to graduate school. I was awarded a fellowship to study for a Ph.D. at Georgetown University in Washington, D. C. There I met Jeane Kirkpatrick who became my mentor and life-long friend.

With the exception of my experience in Connecticut's blue-collar community, I was not involved in partisan politics. When I voted, I always voted the way my parents did: Democrat. My relationship with Jeane Kirkpatrick was, initially, politically neutral. As I got to know her and took courses from her, it became clear to me that, philosophically, Jeane was an ardent Democrat; but she never pushed her views on her students. Jeane and her husband, Kirk, worked for their friend Hubert Humphrey in his race against Richard Nixon in 1968. Following the defeat of Humphrey, the Democratic Party began moving further to the left.

It was at this time that the Kirkpatricks began to view Richard Nixon as a president who supported America's traditional values. At a memorable dinner in the Kirkpatricks' home there was a conversation that included Max Kampelman, Richard M. Scammon and Irving Kristol, all of whom seemed in agreement that the Democratic Party had left its conservative anti-communist constituency to embrace the radical agenda of the protest movement. Along with the Kirkpatricks, these men were conservative Democrats who now saw Richard Nixon as standing against a communist takeover in Southeast Asia. They were also disturbed by a rise of leftist professors who were encouraging their students to join a national protest movement against the Vietnam War. These lifelong Democrats began to view Nixon as the only check against Soviet mischief. Thus, the Republican Party was seen as a viable alternative to the next candidate who sought to capture the Democratic nomination, George McGovern of South Dakota who openly advocated what some people said amounted to surrender in Vietnam and leaving American prisoners behind.

I entered Georgetown as a Democrat who had voted against Nixon in 1960, against Goldwater in 1964, and against Nixon in 1968. I thought I knew what the Democratic Party stood for. Like the Kirkpatricks and their stalwart, traditional Democratic allies, I too began to feel that the Democratic Party was moving away from its traditional values and was leaving me behind.

A Call from the White House

Following the award of my doctorate, Georgetown University notified the local press of the unusual nature of my candidacy. On June 9, 1971, the *Evening Star* carried a front-page story entitled "Garbage Man to Ph.D." that focused on my background as a former high-school dropout and garbage collector. [1] The story centered on my working class background as well as my knowledge and understanding of immigrant communities. The article also focused on my belief in the achievement ethic and my fear that it was under attack. Most importantly, I cited President Nixon as an exponent of the achievement ethic and envisioned him as the one man in a position to restore America's faith in that traditional value.

Ironically, two weeks before the *Evening Star* article appeared, Charles Colson, the special counsel to President Nixon, held a meeting with Jerry Jones, who ran the White House personnel office. Colson said that the president was moved by a *New York Times* photo of an American flag atop the boom of a construction crane. The president believed that the administration had to find a way to communicate with the kind of blue-collar patriotic Americans who put that flag on the top of that crane. Nixon reasoned that such workers supported his anti-communist foreign policy and especially his Vietnam strategy. Colson asked Jones trecruit a person capable of creating a blue-collar outreach for the 1972 campaign.

Jones was overwhelmed. He had an M.B.A. from Harvard, had held a senior position at McKinsey and Company, and was brought into the White House personnel office by Fred Malek, another Harvard M.B.A., to recruit senior executives from the business world to fill top positions in government agencies and departments in the Nixon Administration. Searching for a blue-collar expert who could operate a national campaign to reach Middle America was well beyond his experience. He told Colson that he did not have a clue where to start.

Weeks later, Jones came across the *Evening Star* article about the garbage collector who received a Ph.D. He showed the article to Colson who, according to Jones, responded, "No, this can't be true. It would probably never work." Jones told Colson he would like to pursue the Balzano story. Colson was clearly skeptical but gave Jones approval to check it out.

Subsequently, Jones invited me to the White House to talk with him. He appeared to me to be the epitome of the proverbial Texan: tall, broad-shouldered, good-looking man. I was most impressed by the smile emanating from his eyes, a smile that seemed to radiate from the small, clear-rimmed eyeglasses he wore. At first he asked questions about my work experience, which led me to suspect he had a job in mind to offer me. Then he began probing me about my personal philosophy, especially the work ethic and my thesis that it was disappearing in America. All through the conversation he leaned way back on his swivel chair, taking studied drags on a long cigar. At times, the clouds of silver gray smoke blurred my view of his smiling eyes, which seemed glued on me.

I met with Jerry Jones on at least three occasions when we discussed my ideas on the conditions in the country and what the president could do to address them. Over and over again the questions turned to my knowledge of ethnic groups around the country. The size, location, concentration, and political profile of these groups were the focus of the inquiries.

Finally, about two and a half months after the process began, Jones said that I was the leading candidate for what was going to be the ethnic voter bloc coordinator for the Committee to Re-elect the President (CRP). For that position I had to be interviewed by Fred Malek. During my meeting with Malek, he focused on my understanding of working class ethnic groups and seemed impressed with my background.

When I returned from my meeting with Malek, Jones said I had done fine and that I had one final interview, which would be with Charles Colson. A few days later, Colson called to meet with me. I was anxious when I entered Colson's office that first time. He was sitting behind a large oval-shaped, highly polished rosewood desk, the top of which was supported by a thin set of chrome legs which emerged from a single centered point beneath the desk, a design which gave the appearance of a desktop floating on air. To the right was a long white telephone bank covered with dozens of periodically blinking lights. Colson was talking on the phone when I entered the room and, without interrupting his conversation, he motioned for me to sit down. On the desk before him was a sheet of paper, which seemed to consist of two columns of figures.

As he spoke, I glanced around the room so as not to appear to be staring at him. From the corners of my eyes, I looked very carefully at this man about whom I had heard so much. From the immaculate, neatly pressed white shirt to the gleaming shine on his brown wing-tip shoes, he was impeccably dressed. Despite his title, reputation, and dress, there was something very informal about him.

Colson slowly swung back and forth in his huge black leather swivel chair. He wore no jacket, so as he turned his profile to me I could see his gold cufflinks bearing the seal of the president. I looked very carefully at his face. There was something very personable about it. His lips were somewhat large and slightly turned upward at the corners of his mouth; they seemed to form a natural smile even when his face relaxed. From behind his tortoiseshell glasses his eyes, too, reflected the same soft smile. To look at his non-threatening face and relaxed body I could not help but mentally juxtapose his reputation with his appearance. I expected Colson would be stern. Everything that I had heard about him focused on how tough he was. He had the reputation for being ruthless. Instead, the overall impression Colson gave me was completely opposite of his reputation.

Still on his call, Colson periodically answered, "Yes. Yeah. I see." Then, propping the phone between his shoulder and his neck, he reached down behind the desk and pulled out a large loose-leaf note-book, which contained pages of figures similar to that he had on his desk. After referring to the notebook for a moment, he said, "Good. Okay, Al, that's a considerable change. Let's look at it again in two weeks and see how it's going." In what seemed like one smooth motion he placed the paper into the notebook, closed it, put it back in the drawer, hung up the phone, and turned the chair to face me.

"Mike Balzano, I've heard a lot of good things about you," he said as he lit a cigar. "I understand that a lot of people think you are the guy we need to set up our ethnic voter bloc over at 1701," the nickname for the president's reelection committee. He said that I had done a lot of incredible things in my life but that he did not see anything in my background which would indicate that I could build a mechanism to go after a voter bloc in a presidential election. He took a puff on the cigar and asked, "What do you say to that?"

I answered very slowly, "Well, I never said I could. I have some ideas about people, about ethnics, and about social movements." I told him that I thought the president was in a position to exert some leadership in a direction that the country needed. I said that Middle America was looking for someone to restore and preserve the time-honored traditions which made our country great, traditions which were being undermined every day.

I began telling him how I felt about a number of volatile social issues and that I believed those with backgrounds similar to mine felt the same. After about ten minutes he interrupted me and, with a distant look in his eyes, said, "That's interesting." Pointing at the phone, he said, "I was just talking with a national pollster who is doing some private polls for the White House. Everything you just said is exactly what the pollster told me. You've got a pretty good nose. But I still don't see that you have the knowledge or experience to set up the kind of mechanism they need over at 1701."

We then talked at length about the belief in the achievement ethic commonly held in working class communities and how it was important that the president approach these communities from that perspective. Colson said I had some good ideas, but unless I could find a way to put them into motion, they would be useless. "Balzano," he said raising his voice, "are you a doer or just another idea man?" His words were challenging, but his face was still smiling. His lips were still in that half smile but his eyes meant business.

"This has all been very interesting," Colson said as he stood up to shake my hand.

In my subsequent debriefing with Jones, he advised that the campaign operation was still in transition, but he added that he had several conversations with Colson and noted that he was very impressed with me. He said that Colson admired my life story and bootstrap philosophy along with my belief that a way had to be found to restore the achievement ethic in our society. Jones also said Colson believed that no one at the campaign would know how to use my talent.

About a week later I sat in Colson's office, talking with him about life in my ethnic neighborhood. I shared with him some of the ideas I had about the achievement ethic and its importance to the future of our country. Colson bemoaned the fact that, although the president truly believed in the importance of the achievement ethic, his messages never seemed to reach the American people.

Colson asked, "How can we take this concept and get the country behind it? What's more important, how can we tie the achievement ethic to the president?"

"Well," I responded, "the president is not saying it with words that the average man can understand. To me, the president has the right ideas, and I know what he stands for. But I have to pull it out of what he says. His ideas are hidden behind impressive words."

I told Colson that that it seemed to me the president didn't understand the kind of people he was trying to reach. To reach these people the message had to be basic, almost simple.

"Be specific," he said.

"All right," I replied, "the Labor Day speech."

"The Labor Day speech?" he repeated slowly, then paused momentarily as he identified the passages that stood out in his mind. "It was a great speech," he said with an air of confidence. I disagreed. I argued that, while the speech praised American workers, it also criticized people on welfare, which made the president sound cold-hearted. Colson was moved. He asked me to rewrite the speech, inserting the symbols needed to convey the president's message. I accepted his challenge and submitted my draft later that day. A few days later we met again.

"I read your Labor Day speech," Colson began. "I see what you meant. It's a hell of a lot clearer in this speech." He then said that my arguments were in harmony with his polling data and that he believed that my Italian community was a microcosm of other working-class ethnic minorities throughout the country. He continued by stating that the president needed to reach out to those working class people, and he believed I could make a significant difference in that outreach. Colson then said that he had come to the conclusion that no one at 1701 would understand me and that I would be wasted there. He said, "I've decided that you really belong over here."

Colson then said he wanted me to talk with ethnic groups around the country to start collecting information about what the people out there wanted to hear the president say. He added that I would be the White House liaison with a group that did not exist in his operation: ethnic and blue-collar Americans. Colson continued by stating that the president would be going to China and that things would be quieter in the White House for a few weeks. He said that I would need to talk to his administrative assistant, Dick Howard, who would give me an overview of his operation. He stood up with a smile on his face and said, "OK, Mike?" I couldn't wait to get out of there for fear that he would change his mind. I ran down what seemed like a two-hundred-yard-long hallway leading down to Pennsylvania Avenue and raced home to tell my wife a story that I could barely believe myself.

CHAPTER 2

Inside the Nixon White House, 1971-1973

Colson's Office of Public Liaison

The Office of Public Liaison (OPL) was the nerve center of the Nixon White House. It was the radar, the sonar, the antenna, and the satellite dish that picked up and responded to every constituent issue no matter how remote from the White House.

After that last meeting with Colson, weeks passed before I saw him again. Colson was always busy, so much so that most communication between him and the staff was either done in formal memos or by questions passed through Dick Howard, his administrative assistant. Except for Monday morning staff meetings, which were sometimes canceled, few of the staff members ever met with Colson one-on-one.

My first meeting with Howard, for my orientation to the White House, was memorable. He sat behind his desk writing on a yellow pad a list of questions I wanted to ask Colson. Then he explained in very general terms the various offices in the White House. "John Ehrlichman heads the Domestic Council," he said in a monotone voice. "He's got people working for him all over the building. The Domestic Council guys have more square feet of office space than anybody else in here."

"Herb Klein handles Communications, but we usually work with Ken Clawson." His face was expressionless as he talked. One of his hands was flat on the edge of the desk so that his long thin fingers were stretched across the desktop. As he spoke, he drummed his fingers on the desk in periodic ripples. His other hand held a felt-tip pen, the back of which he constantly put back into his mouth between sentences.

He began to tell me about the other members of Colson's staff and how important it was for me to become familiar with their respective functions; suddenly his interoffice line buzzed. He barely put the phone to his ear when he said, "Yup!" He sprang to his feet, still holding the pen in his mouth and quickly slipped into his suit jacket. He grabbed a plastic clipboard with a pad clipped to it and, with long strides, synchronized with his swinging arms, his thin legs carried him toward the door. Looking over his shoulder as he disappeared into the hall, he blurted out, "Talk to some of the other staff people. I'll get back to you."

While the president was off to China, the White House was virtually empty. Workmen were busy cleaning, painting, and tending to repairs that were necessary. For those first few weeks, I sat in the large empty office next to Dick Howard.

Eventually I was moved to a very small office on the fourth floor of the Old Executive Office Building, which I shared with two people who seldom were in the office. I once ran into one of them, a man with gray hair who wore a Panama hat. I remarked to myself, he seemed like an old guy, but at thirty-seven, anyone with gray hair appeared old to me. I asked Colson about him and he responded, "Well, he's a White House Fellow."

Years later I would be asked by a grand jury about my relationship with this White House Fellow who, I later learned, was E. Howard Hunt and who played a major role in the Watergate break-in.

Colson's staff was constantly expanding during 1972. The staff was divided by subject matter. At the Monday morning staff meeting each person would give a progress report on the activities they were pursuing. There were a number of people on the staff who attended these meetings: Henry Cashen, Pat O'Donnell, Steve Karalekas, Bill Rhatican, Don Rodgers, Kathleen Balsdon, and Bud Evans. While all of these people were important and played key roles in the structure that Colson had created, some members of his staff were clearly principals.

Among the principals was former ABC newsman John A. Scali who, because of his extensive foreign policy experience during the Kennedy years, became a foreign policy advisor on Colson's staff. Scali's history was impressive. In 1959 Scali covered the Kitchen Cabinet debates between Vice President Nixon and Soviet Premier Nikita Khrushchev. During John F. Kennedy's presidency, Soviet agent Alexander Feklisov warned Scali that a shipment of intercontinental ballistic missiles was heading for Cuba on a Soviet ship. Scali contacted President Kennedy's foreign policy team at the White House and told them about the call that he had received. Kennedy appointed Scali as his secret go-between with the Soviet Union, with the goal of avoiding a nuclear confrontation. Most of Scali's day-to-day interaction was with Colson and President Nixon. While he did not deal with the other staff members except when attending an occasional Monday meeting, he and I became very close friends because of our common Italian heritage.

The Office of Public Liaison's outreach was divided into as many segments as there were components of the American public: business, labor, seniors, women, Hispanics, blacks, ethnics, and many from the Captive Nations that fell under Soviet rule following World War II. Outreach also included religious groups: Catholics, Jews, and Protestants of all denominations. Other groups included sportsmen, hunters, gun owners, shooters, collectors, and all of the special interest publications that catered to them. There were trade, business and professional associations whose executive directors regularly met with Colson or one of the constituent liaison officers assigned to that group,. When Colson's staff members met with constituent groups, we transmitted their issues to Colson, who, in turn, brought all constituent concerns directly to the president. The Nixon administration was pro-business, and it was also pro-labor. Nixon's attention was equally divided among all these groups and he meant to serve all their needs. No other president that I would ever serve had such an elaborate field structure.

Acknowledging and understanding constituent demands from all of these voter bloc groups was only the first step in making government responsive. It required control over a bureaucracy predominantly staffed with Democrats who, for the most part, totally opposed anything that the administration sought to accomplish. These entrenched bureaucrats did not want to serve any constituency important to the president, no matter how urgent the national need. Their motive was purely political. They did not want to give a Republican administration access to constituencies that were predominately Democratic.

For instance, when the Nixon administration attempted to provide grants for economic development in minority communities, grand juries were convened to investigate what prosecutors called the administration's "responsiveness program," charging that the White House was giving community grants to obtain votes. Democratic administrations have helped minorities since the mid-1930s. When Democrats engaged in this activity, it was described as social justice. When Republicans supported minority communities, it was deemed a federal crime. This was the beginning of the criminalization of policy differences that went beyond the federal bureaucracy into the Justice Department.

In Nixon's second term, Jerry Jones became director of the White House personnel office. Jones worked with Colson, tying the personnel function to policy objectives. Public policy and personnel selection were inseparable. Nixon appointees in the second term were selected not only for their knowledge of the subject matter which their agencies oversaw, but also for their commitment to follow the public policy direction set by the president. Part of Colson's responsibility was to weed out administration appointees pursuing their own agenda and grandstanding to the anti-Nixon press. Some members of the press took great delight in covering appointees who publicly declared their independence from the president. Colson removed these appointees whenever they surfaced.

Late in the campaign, Colson's staff expanded to over twenty-five people, a staff larger than any other in the White House. Colson's staff loved working for him. First, there was the pride derived from working with a controversial figure who was close to the president. Second, Colson was a man with a great sense of humor. He would say anything to get a laugh and was constantly playing practical jokes.

For example, the Colsons had been invited to Dick and Marcia Howard's home for dinner, and were served a dinner of spicy Mexican food. All during dinner Colson commented on how "hot and spicy" it was. The next morning, which was a Sunday, Marcia received a call from a "Nurse Wheelwright," allegedly a nurse at Bethesda Naval Hospital. In very professional terms she told Marcia that Colson had been rushed to the hospital at 4:30 a.m. with acute stomach pain. The nurse said that the hospital was calling to determine the contents of the dinner in order to prepare antidotes for possible ptomaine poisoning. The Howards were horrified. Dick insisted that this had to be a joke and, through the White House switchboard, tried to call Colson at his home. Colson, anticipating the call, had gotten the White House operators to tell Howard that there was no answer at the Colson residence. It took a string of phone calls to Bethesda Hospital to determine that neither the Colsons nor Nurse Wheelwright was there.

Then there was the memo addressed to me on the occasion of my speaking at an Italian rally in New York's Central Park. That spring a noted Italian mobster had been murdered in broad daylight outside a New York City restaurant. With the attempted assassination of George Wallace in May 1972 still fresh in everyone's mind, Colson spread a rumor that I was going to be assassinated and that the president would attend my funeral, making me the Italian martyr of the 1972 campaign. One of Agnew's top aides said without laughing, "I'd be careful if I were you. I wouldn't put it past him." Colson even went so far as calling Al Snyder, the White House Communications Director, to insist that the Central Park speech be covered live on all networks because I was going to be assassinated. I'll never forget the look on Snyder's face when I went to his office to get information on press contacts in New York. When I told him Colson sent me down to see him about an event, Snyder stared at me and said, "Yeah, I know." When Colson heard that I was really concerned, he sent me a memo that was circulated around the White House. The memo, obviously tongue-in-cheek, stated, "By the way, don't for a moment miss the theatrical opportunity that this could present. If you are going down for the count anyway, you should go down in a blaze of glory. Regardless of where the bullet enters, you should always clutch your left side over your heart. That makes a much more dramatic photograph. Be sure also that reporters are within earshot so you can say 'long live Richard Nixon, the greatest President in history.' Remember down through the years, dying words have always been those the longest remembered."[2]

In August 1972, the now-infamous "walk over my own grandmother" memo[3] for which Colson will be forever remembered, was written to his staff as a joke when it became apparent that people had been taking vacations or long weekends. A few days before he wrote the memo Colson said at a staff meeting how frustrating it was to see other presidential aides playing tennis, or exercising in the gym. He commented, "Oh, I got a nice card from so and so, vacationing in the Catskills. The Catskills are beautiful this time of year. He's probably sitting by a lake thinking of ways to help the president get reelected. I ought to get the president to send him some words of inspiration." Colson's August memo also contained an apology for not returning our calls, let alone seeing us. The "walk over my own grandmother" memo was written tongue-in-cheek and it was received in that sense by his staff. By contrast, the national news media did not see Colson's memo as a joke and, instead, used it to characterize him as ruthless.

From Captive Nations to Industrial Unions

One of my roles on Colson's staff was to create an outreach to ethnic organizations in the Northeast and Midwest. Jerry Jones was keenly aware of the importance of the ethnic community, but at the same time realized that the Republican National Committee (RNC) tolerated, rather than making wise use of, the nationalities groups at their headquarters. He often spoke with Colson about the need to expand ethnic participation in Republican policy formation. It was one of the reasons Jones wanted me on Colson's staff. Jones expanded my relationship beyond the White House staff directly to the RNC and to George H. W. Bush, the Chairman of the Party. In our meeting, Bush expressed his frustration with Laszlo Pasztor, the director of the Nationalities Division. "No one here knows how to work with them. They have trouble staying on the message we all agree on," he said. "They constantly go to the Hill and try to create policy on their own."

Staff members in what was sometimes referred to as the Heritage Division were mainly people whose countries of origin were known as Captive Nations, those that had come under the effective control of the Soviet Union following World War II. In February 1945, at Yalta, the so-called Big Three, Franklin D. Roosevelt, Winston Churchill and Joseph Stalin, agreed to partition post-World War II Europe by annexing such nations as Lithuania, Latvia, Estonia, Czechoslovakia, Hungary, Bulgaria, Romania and parts of Poland to the Soviet Union. Collectively, these countries became known throughout the Cold War as the Captive Nations.

What happened at Yalta was critically important to Americans who had emigrated from Central Europe. It was the reason they supported Republicans over the Democrats for the next fifty years. Understanding Yalta was the key to understanding Captive Nations ethnics. Prior to Yalta, these countries were independent nations. They were horrified at being forced into domination by an atheist Soviet Union notorious for having starved to death forty million of its own citizens through centralized planning and collectivist social policies that placed its citizens in gulags and slave labor camps. Most egregious of all was the placement of Poland behind what Churchill would later term the "Iron Curtain," a geographic line separating the free world from Soviet-enslaved populations.

Russia continued its oppressive control of the Captive Nations from the beginning of the Cold War through the suppression of the Hungarian Revolt of 1956 and the Czechoslovakian Revolt of 1968, and until the Berlin Wall came down in 1989. There were secret police raids, midnight arrests, and the disappearance of anyone complaining about food shortages, forced labor, church attendance, or free speech. American relatives of people living in the Captive Nations religiously followed events in their homeland via shortwave radio and other smuggled information.

The Heritage Groups, as Republicans called them, were decidedly anti-communist. Roosevelt's involvement in allowing the atheist Soviet Union to annex Christian nations propelled their American relatives toward the Republican Party. At the same time, these ethnic Americans were ardent admirers of Richard Nixon because he devoted his life to fighting the evils of communism. The Republican Party championed Radio Free Europe, a system of broadcasting news from the Free World to those behind the Iron Curtain.

Laszlo Pasztor, director of Heritage Groups at the RNC, had been a Hungarian freedom fighter. He had a long history of opposing communism and had been hunted by the Hungarian secret police. When

Hungary revolted in 1956 the Freedom Fighters could not overcome Soviet tanks and thousands of troops. Pasztor, who was marked for death, fled the country with his six-year-old son. He came to America and started an ethnic organization dedicated to freeing Hungary. Pasztor linked up with Anna Chennault, an émigré from China. Her husband, General Claire Lee Chennault, led the famous Flying Tigers who fought the Japanese during their invasion of China in World War II. Ultimately, the Captive Nations groups became part of my portfolio.

Colson's staff members were both researchers and liaison assistants. Through information provided by his staff, and his own personal contacts with the leaders of national organizations, Colson was able to effectively inform and position the president on the key social issues affecting these powerful constituencies. From early 1971 through mid-1972, Colson added new categories to his core staff, increasing the number of interest groups that fell under his sphere of responsibility. Colson knew that these new groups would significantly affect the 1972 election.

The Committee to Re-elect the President vs. Colson's Staff

As the structure of the campaign at 1701 began to emerge, it bore a striking resemblance to the makeup of Colson's staff. That is, at 1701 the electorate was also divided into a series of interest groups or voter blocs: blacks, Hispanics, women, and ethnics being the major categories. Under this arrangement, each target constituency became the sole concern of a voter bloc director responsible for designing and monitoring all campaign appeals to their designated group.

It has been argued that Colson had neither input nor control over the design and operation of the Committee to Re-elect the President. Three considerations would suggest otherwise. First, the division of the electorate at 1701 into voter bloc groups resembled the division of Colson's staff, which predated the 1701 operation by more than two years. Second, as Colson added new categories to his staff in mid-1972, these categories *also* were added to the 1701 structure. Third, no one could be hired as a voter bloc director at 1701 unless Colson personally approved.

Deputy Campaign Director Jeb Magruder did not like the idea of Colson's separate White House operation, especially one in which the president placed such confidence. Seeing Colson as a rival, Magruder tried to outdo Colson through mobilizing a record turnout for Nixon at the polls. But in short order, the campaign staff began seeking ways to demonstrate their ability to outperform Colson's organization. This escalating competition was at the root of Magruder's engaging in tactics later termed "dirty tricks." Ultimately, Magruder's tactics brought in federal prosecutors and resulted in jail terms for some of the organizers who lied under oath. The Washington press corps tried for years to pin the dirty tricks operation on Colson and his staff, but all the investigations before several grand juries proved that Colson's Office of Public Liaison was not involved in dirty tricks.

The essential difference between the White House voter bloc group directors and their counterparts at 1701 was that we were able to affect presidential policy while their voter bloc group directors were limited to communication designed to mobilize voters. Colson's White House operation performed a legitimate function of the Executive Branch. The reelection voter bloc groups at 1701 went out of existence on November 7, 1972.

Colson was viewed as the political czar of the White House; therefore, *anything* he did appeared "political." To everyone at 1701 we at the Office of Public Liaison were part of the reelection effort, and an uncontrollable part at that. However, it was this basic difference between the rogue operation at 1701 and Colson's White House operation, among other things, that caused great friction between the two.

Fred Malek went out of his way to establish some form of harmony and coordination between the two units. He requested that the White House voter bloc directors meet weekly at 1701. This did not occur, mainly because our own assignments often conflicted with the meetings. Additionally, Colson did not want the White House staff seen as part of the reelection machine. In hindsight, this was especially fortunate because of 1701's involvement in the dirty tricks allegations. Instead of weekly meetings, Colson agreed to have 1701 staff members send copies of their weekly reports to Malek. But these reports, too, had to be watered down because of the confidential nature of the information. Hence, they turned out to be absolutely useless to Malek. Finally, Malek requested that some of his key staff members be allowed to sit in on Colson's staff meetings. This met with mixed success. It was like the Marines and the Army meeting for a joint briefing. We were the Marines.

With respect to coordinating all activity aimed at capturing the ethnic vote in 1972, one loose end had to be secured, the Heritage Division of the Republican National Committee. As early as 1967 a sizable portion of the Republican rank and file began to identify it-self along lines of national origin. During the 1968 election, the RNC encouraged these groups to coalesce into ethnic categories, such as "Poles for Nixon," "Czechs for Nixon," etc. Their success in both 1968 and the off-year elections of 1970 demonstrated enough political clout to warrant the creation of a Heritage Division at the RNC.

Expecting to have total sovereignty over the ethnic strategy and its implementation in the 1972 campaign, the leaders of the Heritage Division of the Republican National Committee created the Nationalities Council, which was composed of representatives of the various Heritage Divisions within the state party structures through-out the country. More than mobilizing support and giving that sup-port some structure, the Heritage Division had raised its own funds. Pasztor expected that additional funds from the campaign war chest would be channeled into the Heritage Division for use in mobilizing still more ethnics. All this would have been fine if the RNC were go-ing to control the campaign. But since ethnic voter blocs had been established at the Committee to Re-elect the President, the question of control over the ethnic voter bloc effort emerged. Initially, the ad-dition of an ethnic counterpart on Colson's staff further complicated matters, because my functions evolved into a direct channel for ethnic demands to reach the president, cutting out the nationalities group at the RNC altogether.

At the RNC, Pasztor saw himself as an advocate for the Heritage Division cause, which, by right, he should have been. Promoting that cause meant Laszlo was forever beseeching the White House for pres-idential stroking of his constituency. Primarily, Laszlo sought three things: patronage for ethnics, federal programs to deal with their social needs, and interaction with the president to bestow honors upon this group. Laszlo constantly met with frustration. Senior White House officials regularly ignored Pasztor's entreaties and paid little or no attention to this important voter bloc. Being an activist, Laszlo never knew when to stop. With each failure to obtain any of his goals, Laszlo persisted and intensified the noise he and the Heritage Groups made.

When Jerry and I met with RNC Chairman Bush in the spring of 1972, I assured Bush that, when I was fully ensconced in the White House, I would meet with Laszlo and try to promote some ethnic events where the Nationalities Council would be in charge. He was delighted. I also told Laszlo I would help connect him to the campaign structure at 1701 before it was finalized. Unfortunately, Magruder had a different thought in mind as he set up the operation at 1701. He insisted that Laszlo would not have any input beyond getting out the vote of his own people. Correctly perceiving that his operation was going to have trouble with 1701, Laszlo began pounding on my door trying to get Colson to give his operation full control. Colson refused to get involved.

The issue was further complicated because Colson, who had to approve the person who would serve as group director for the ethnic voter bloc at 1701, simply had not had time to do so. Magruder and Malek pushed Colson to hire Jack Burgess, a young man who had worked in the 1968 campaign.

During that time, Colson assigned to me the job of mediating differences between the Heritage Division and 1701. This proved to be an impossible task while the ethnic voter bloc position at 1701 remained unfilled, since Laszlo insisted that he or at least one of his people fill that slot. Finally, Secretary of Transportation John Volpe, who had been governor of Massachusetts, appealed to Colson to resolve the matter. I was called by Colson to join the two men at midpoint in their meeting.

"Mike, the secretary and I have been talking about some way of coordinating Malek's ethnic operation with the RNC Heritage groups," Colson said, removing his glasses and rubbing his eyes. "The Secretary thinks that the operations can work together, but there is a need to clarify the respective roles to be played by each."

"That's right, Mike," Volpe concurred. "The last thing we want to have is a slip in our own ranks. You know Laszlo," Volpe smiled. "He's upset because Malek is setting up an ethnic operation without even consulting with him, let alone allowing Laszlo to run the ethnic operation himself."

"Yes," Colson agreed. He added, "As soon as we get that ethnic slot filled, I think Laszlo will settle down."

"I told Chuck," Volpe continued, "that I will host a luncheon, inviting all the parties, and see if we can't iron this thing out to everyone's satisfaction. I'll see that Tony also comes."

"Tony?" I questioned.

"Yeah, you know, Tony. Tony DeFalco from Boston."

"No, I don't know him," I replied, thinking to myself, *"Oh, boy, wait until Laszlo hears that he will not be the one to pick the ethnic director."*

"You'll like him," Volpe said.

Reading the uncertainty in my eyes, Colson injected, "Tony is a friend of Volpe's. He's got a real nose for politics. From what I've seen of that operation over there, I want to be sure there are some old hands mixed in with some of the people that Malek is bringing in."

A luncheon was held in the secretary's private dining room at the Department of Transportation. Volpe made an admirable attempt at praising Malek and Pasztor and their respective styles.

"Fred, with your management ability and your organizational insights, I just know everything will be just fine," the Secretary said to Malek who, without blinking an eye, replied, "Thank you, Mr. Secretary."

"And, you, Laszlo," Volpe continued, "you've got real clout," he said, pushing his clenched fist forward as though he was delivering a quick punch. "Why, with your ethnic contacts throughout the country and Fred's management ability, the president will have the best of both worlds going for him."

"Oh, yes, Mr. Secretary," Laszlo replied, "and the ethnic groups all over the country are waiting. You know they have raised their own money. They have all of the state party mechanisms ready to go, and the Nationalities Council is so excited, and you know . . . ."

Volpe interrupted, "That's right, Laszlo, and what we have to do is to coordinate with Fred here."

"Oh, yes," Laszlo once again started, "we are all ready to go. We are waiting for our operation to be called upon at the national level."

"Yes, well, you see," Volpe interrupted, pointing to the gray-haired man sitting in the meeting. "That's why Tony is here. Tony is going to be working with Fred. He's going to see to it that your operation really delivers the punch." Volpe's short arm was thrust forward with a clenched fist.

"Yes," Laszlo continued, "we are ready to deliver the punch, but Congressman Derwinski said we were going to control the ethnic operations." Ed Derwinski was the congressional patron saint of the Captive Nations groups in Chicago. He, along with Congressman Henry Hyde, another Republican from Illinois, had large numbers of Captive Nations constituencies in their districts.

Malek spoke up at this point. "The control has to be centralized for management purposes. There is an enormous problem in coordinating fifty different state operations."

"Oh, yes," Laszlo responded, "that is why we now have the Nationalities Council."

"Yes, but," Malek injected, "it has to be coordinated with the total national effort."

"But of course," Laszlo concurred, "we will coordinate everything."

"That's right," Volpe said, blotting his napkin against his lips. "That's why Tony is with us. He's going to coordinate."

I watched the verbal ping-pong match, getting pains in my stomach from holding in the laughter. Tony, a chain smoker, must have gone through a pack of cigarettes. His massive chest accented every exhalation, which increased in strength as the luncheon went on. Finally, both men focused on the word "coordination," each thinking the other understood how the term was being used. But anyone in the room could see that they were in total disagreement and yet both were nodding and saying yes, thinking that the other man understood him. Tony grabbed me aside as the luncheon ended.

"Listen," he said, "are those guys for real? I don't know about you, but to me this meeting hasn't settled a damn thing."

I agreed, reassuring Tony that we would straighten it out, but added that it might be better if the meeting could continue without him. He agreed and promptly left. I pulled Malek aside and told him that I did not think that the issue had been resolved.

Malek whispered, "You heard the guy agree that things had to be coordinated. Tony was sitting right there. Volpe told him Tony would coordinate. Tony works for me, so the issue is settled."

Volpe had to leave, but Malek insisted the meeting go on, so the three of us returned to Malek's office where it continued. After another hour of trying to define the word "coordinate," Malek told Laszlo that Tony was going to coordinate all ethnic activities from 1701.

As Laszlo and I returned to my office, he was very somber. "Oh, this is very bad," Laszlo said. "I think it is a bad idea to bring in this man Tony. He's not even a member of the Nationalities Council. Nobody knows who he is. How will I explain? If we had Jack Burgess, at least I could say they selected one of ours. But who is this Tony?"

I reported all this to Colson who was mildly interested. "Tony will handle everything," Colson said. "You've done your part. Now stay the hell out of it."

But the fight was by no means over for Tony. The entire 1701 operation had as many problems in communicating with each other as Laszlo would have had if he had been the voter bloc director. As Colson said earlier, Tony was a seasoned campaign veteran, a real political animal. He had not been at the Committee a week when he contacted me to give me his impressions of the staff at 1701.

"First of all," said Tony, "the place is filled with kids who don't know a damn thing. Second, which is worse, they think they know everything. Third, all that kid Magruder talks about are systems, management and diagrams. What diagrams?" Tony said, raising his voice. "Just give me some bread and turn me loose around the country. I'll show you how you get votes. These guys want diagrams, not votes."

Having already gone through the systems analysis approach in use at 1701, I was sympathetic to Tony's argument. I tried to reassure him that once things got underway, these preliminary differences would pass. As weeks went by, however, the conflict between Tony and the management style of 1701 took its toll.

Also working for 1701 heading up the Hispanic voter bloc group was Alex Armendaris. He and I had much in common. He, too, came up from the lower rungs of the social and economic ladder, having been born into a large, impoverished Mexican-American family in Chicago. It was as if we had grown up together.

I spoke with Alex Armendaris to see what might be done to salvage the situation. Alex shook his head. "Michael," he said in his usual modest tone of voice, "these people insult you all the time, and they don't even know they're insulting you. The other day Magruder suggested that the best way to identify the president with Spanish-speaking Americans would be to take his picture eating a taco. You know, Michael, I tried to tell these guys that all Mexicans and all Cubans are not poor people. But these guys don't know that. What's more, they won't listen. Magruder talked to me like I'm wearing a sombrero and a shawl. That guy Tony won't last. He sits there smoking those cigarettes and he's burning, you know? They're always reminding him he's Italian. Michael, I don't pay attention to it. I know they're dumb, but Tony gets mad. He's not going to last."

I caught Colson later that night and explained the situation. As usual, he was very much in a hurry and did not want to hear about it. I predicted that Tony would quit. Two days later one of Malek's people called to tell me, "Hey, that ethnic guy you sent over here quit this morning." Once again the search was on.

From my perspective, the personnel problems at 1701 were rooted in the cultural differences between the managers and the staff. The ethnics were not looked upon as people who fell into a social continuum. Rather they were lumped together under separate headings: Poles, Italians, Mexicans, etc. All were stereotyped as recent immigrants who had not distinguished themselves by climbing high enough on the economic and social ladder. This issue later became a problem when the White House personnel system was considering ethnic presidential appointments.

A few days after DeFalco resigned from 1701, I received a call from Dick Howard, who said, "Colson wants to move quickly to fill that ethnic slot at 1701. Do you have any candidates?" The only candidate on the horizon who understood both the Captive Nations mentality and the second- and third-generation urban ethnic was Taras "Terry" Szmagala. I had heard he was vaguely interested in the position, but was reluctant to leave Cleveland as he was serving as a senior aide to Senator Robert Taft. I worked through Cleveland Mayor Ralph Perk, a longtime friend of Szmagala, and was successful in getting Terry to interview for the post.

The skids were already greased as far as Colson's approval was concerned, and, having established some credibility with Malek's people, I knew Terry would be offered the job. I spent a good six hours with Terry, both in my office, then over dinner at my house. He was very close to Laszlo and understood that operation very well. He was a mild-mannered fellow who, I knew, would serve as a bridge between Laszlo and Malek. I then went through the business of management and systems, which Malek's people would undoubtedly throw at him.

Then we moved to the most sensitive part of our discussion: the insensitivity of the senior staff at 1701 to ethnics that at times bordered on insult. Being a man with excellent perception and someone who had worked in the hierarchy of the Republican ranks before, Terry was aware of the problem and had long since lost his sensitivity to their unconscious but offensive mannerisms. From his comments, I knew he could handle the job.

After the last collision between John Volpe, Laszlo and Congressman Derwinski, all the parties were finally content with a new arrangement in which Colson would assume responsibility for coordinating the activities between the nationalities and the White House. Colson transferred that responsibility to me. Jerry Jones told me that I was the clear choice of all of these parties. Jerry said Colson was particularly pleased and saw me as a problem solver. This was important, because he began increasing my responsibilities. Colson said he wanted me to meet with two Italian labor leaders from Pittsburgh who would introduce me to unions in Ohio.

A short time later, I traveled to Pittsburgh to meet with key leaders in the steelworkers union and was met at the airport by Francis "Lefty" Scumaci, a representative of I. W. Abel, president of the United Steelworkers, and the business agent for the boilermakers, Fred Gualtieri. We were driven to a labor union hall outside Steubenville,

Ohio, where locals from Ohio, Pennsylvania, and West Virginia were gathered for a meeting.

Lefty walked me through the room to be sure that I shook hands with everyone there. The Italian union leaders were impressed that Nixon would have an Italian on his staff. The Polish leaders were equally impressed that Nixon would bring aboard an ethnic to make contact with them. On the drive back to Pittsburgh, Lefty asked if I would come back again to meet with union leaders in Pittsburgh. Colson was pleased with my Steubenville report and said he was thinking of expanding my constituency to include the industrial-base unions in Ohio, Pennsylvania, and West Virginia, whose leadership was dominated by Italians, Poles, and Slavs. Colson added that the president already had a relationship with New York's building trades unions through Peter Brennan, but thus far we had no relationship with unions in the industrial sector.

Shortly after my trip to Pittsburgh and Steubenville, I received a call from Lefty Scumaci asking me to visit workplace sites around Allegheny County. When I went to Dick Howard to find out about travel arrangements, he said that the staff did not travel. If there was any business I had to conduct, I should do it by phone call or letters. This was a problem for me because labor leaders wanted to talk to me in person. I didn't dare bring up this subject in a staff meeting, so I waited to meet Colson in the hallway.

To me, the most frustrating thing about being on Colson's staff was not being able to see him when I felt it necessary. Both Joan Hall, his secretary, and Dick Howard were experts at keeping me out of Colson's office. This was their job. Ultimately, I shadowed Colson in the hallway. I explained that I needed his approval to travel to Pennsylvania to meet with union leaders, in particular the international president of the steelworkers, and that Dick Howard had said there was a restriction on staff travel.

"Okay, okay. Come back to the office," Colson replied. Howard was called in and Colson told him that I had struck up a relationship with key union leaders in Pennsylvania and that he wanted to give me approval to make a few trips. In practically no time at all I was meeting with union and ethnic leaders in Massachusetts, Connecticut, Rhode

Island, New York, New Jersey, Pennsylvania, Ohio, West Virginia, and Missouri.

By far my greatest opportunity came when Scumaci arranged for me to meet with his boss, the president of the International Steelworkers, I. W. Abel, who had a reputation of being a statesman. He was a pleasant, soft-spoken, gray-haired man. "So you're Nixon's labor man. I've heard a lot about you. You're a Democrat, is that right?" He asked questions about my family. I was eager to tell him that my mother and father were union members. I told him how my mother lost the tips of her fingers when she worked on a power press at the age of fifteen.

He listened with great interest, never taking his eyes off me. When I told him that my mother had worked eighteen years at Sargent & Company and had had to take time off when I was born, which resulted in her losing all the time she had accrued towards her pension, he responded, "You see, my boy, that's why there are unions. Your mother would have been protected from that kind of abuse."

Abel motioned to the chair beside his desk and said, "Come here." I sat close to him. He drew his chair closer to me, then pulled on my necktie, drawing me within inches of his face, and asked, "Are you somebody in this White House, or just window dressing?" I froze in place, thinking how I should answer him. I blurted out, "Well, I do work for the president."

He replied, "Let me be open with you. You told me how your mother lost her accrued time for her pension, so I want to tell you what's happening to my members." He then explained that the steel industry was undergoing hard times. He envisioned a time when large companies would be declaring bankruptcy. In fact, it was already happening. He had tens of thousands of members who were terrified that they would all lose their pensions. He told me how large and small steel companies were working at the margin and were not making the contributions to their pension plans. He feared a disaster coming.

"I want you to tell Dick Nixon that the nation needs a law to protect the pensions of hard-working Americans. Can you tell him that?" he asked. "Can he do anything to help these people?" I told him I would tell the president what he said, but I had no idea how I was going to do that. Abel said that he had broached this issue with Governor Nelson Rockefeller, with whom he sat on the National Council on Productivity. He said that Rockefeller seemed friendly to the idea, but he thought that, as a liberal Republican, Rockefeller would not have the clout within the Nixon administration to effect a major policy change for union workers.

When the meeting was over, Scumaci took me to dinner. Lefty said he could not believe the impression I had made on Abel. "In half an hour he trusted you with his highest priority. We have been having secret meetings about this for a year. Only a handful of union leaders know how bad things are. You gotta do something, Mike!"

The next day I told Colson about my meeting with Abel. Colson leaned back in his chair and said, "This is a policy issue that would have to be reviewed by the Domestic Council, the Office of Management and Budget, and would have to be enacted into law by Congress. I don't think we can deliver this." He jotted some notes on a pad and then said, "I'm going to need to talk to the president about this. I have worked policy issues before, but I had to work them back-channel and get the president to issue executive orders rather than run the public policy gauntlet I just mentioned. Not only will I have to get around the Domestic Council, but I will also have to get around all of the anti-labor forces in the Republican Party as well."

Then Colson said, "But there is a precedent for this. About a year ago, the president needed something, and the only one who could help him was the president of MEBA."

"MEBA?" I asked.

"Yes, the Marine Engineers' Beneficial Association," Colson replied. "Jesse Calhoon, the president of MEBA, helped Nixon accomplish a major foreign policy goal and, in doing so, established a precedent. We had to secretly go around the entire White House staff and the State Department to get it done." When I asked what it was, he said he would tell me about it later. He needed to think about how to approach the president regarding Abel's request. He called me the next day.

"I talked with the president about your conversation with Abel and about the pension issue. He wants you to pursue it," Colson said.

"Me?" I almost choked.

"You," he said firmly, nodding his head. "Your role in the White House is about to change. We want you to be more visible out in the states and communities important to the reelection of the president." He directed me to stay close to Lefty, saying that Lefty was the kind of labor leader Nixon admired. He was a salt-of-the-earth type of person who believed in God and country.

I talked with Scumaci, who agreed to set up meetings with union presidents in Ohio, Pennsylvania, West Virginia, and New York. I toured steel mills in all those states. I toured freight yards and warehouses. I even toured the assembly lines in the Chrysler and GM plants in Detroit. Before I left Detroit, I appeared on a morning television talk show and discussed the president's commitment to working people.

Upon my return from Detroit, Colson phoned to tell me I would receive a call from a reporter at the *Wall Street Journal*. A reporter also would call me from *Life* magazine. I was to grant both of them interviews in my White House office.

Shortly thereafter I gave an interview to James P. Gannon of the *Wall Street Journal* and to Hugh Sidey of *Life* magazine. I told both reporters what I had been doing in the industrial states. Later, the *Wall Street Journal* ran a front-page story tracing my activities,[4] the groups I addressed, the companies I visited, and the ethnic fraternal organization with which I met. The article, with a caricature sketch photo, surprised me. Without my having given Gannon a single specific as to where I had gone, he cited most of the places I had visited. The article also traced the history of my youth, including dropping out of high school, my inability to hold dozens of jobs, returning to high school, entering college and receiving a Ph.D.

As a result of the Sidey interview, Nixon's outreach to ethnics and blue collar workers was highlighted in Sidey's column on "The Presidency" that appeared in every issue of *Life* magazine. The first, entitled "Tying Up the Lasagna Network," which appeared in the September 29, 1972, issue, discussed Nixon's outreach to ethnic communities. The second article[5] included a drawing of the president wearing coveralls and a hardhat and building a wooden throne. The story noted that Nixon was building the throne with the support of the blue-collar workers who identified with him on the merits of the work ethic. National news professionals recognized that Nixon was making inroads into the blue-collar communities that, by tradition, were Democratic voters. Hugh Sidey saw the essence of the achievement ethic movement and stated so in his articles. Both articles clearly indicated that a major theme of the Nixon reelection campaign was the achievement ethic.

CHAPTER 3

Birth of the New Majority (1971)

Shortly after the June 1972 *Wall Street Journal* article [6] appeared, Colson's secretary asked me to meet him outside his office at noon. I accompanied Colson as he emerged from his office and walked at a fast pace down the Old Executive Office Building stairs. As we entered the basement of the West Wing, I asked, "Where are we going?"

"To lunch," he replied.

We were ushered into the West Wing and escorted into the private dining room adjacent to the larger dining area reserved for the West Wing staff. The smaller, private dining room allowed senior staff to dine apart from the others. I was overwhelmed. A Filipino steward handed me a White House menu. There were only two other tables located some distance from ours. Not wanting to spill soup or appear awkward eating a salad, I ordered a sandwich. My hand trembled as I drank coffee from a china cup and saucer.

Colson began by saying that the president was extremely pleased with the media coverage of my activities at the White House. He said that the president had read the Jim Gannon and Hugh Sidey articles in their entirety rather than a brief description in the president's Daily News Brief. "The president wants to increase your visibility," Colson said. "He wants to make you the White House ambassador to Middle America." Colson waited for my reaction. I couldn't move. "Are you up to it?" he continued.

"What would I do?" I asked.

"The same thing you've been doing, but more of it. The president and I both think your background makes you a natural to carry the message of restoring the achievement ethic to America," he replied.

My lunch with Colson turned out to be a series of revelations on Nixon's strategy to build a New Majority. It was a complicated, multi-layered, multi-faceted story. Colson began with a history of how he came to the White House and why he was chosen. He said that early in the first presidential term, Nixon was frustrated by administration appointees, as well as his own White House staff, who followed their own agendas instead of his. A trusted friend of the president, Bryce Harlow, who had been an advisor to Dwight Eisenhower and Barry Goldwater, recommended that Nixon hire Charles Colson, a person who would be completely loyal to him and who was capable of reshaping the White House. Harlow later recalled that he told Nixon that Colson would fix the loyalty problem in the White House but would probably break all the china doing it.

The president gave Colson total authority to do whatever he thought necessary to bring the White House under control. He was then given a series of "mission impossible" jobs. Each time he solved a problem, his authority increased. He set up shop in the Office of Public Liaison and reached out to the business community. The assignment subsequently expanded to include organized labor. Colson launched a series of off-the-screen meetings with a few labor leaders and met with success.

Colson then described to me two major breakthroughs that changed the president's relationship with organized labor. The first involved Colson's outreach to Jesse Calhoon, president of the Marine Engineers' Beneficial Association (MEBA). The second breakthrough happened as a result of the "Hard Hat Riots" in 1970.

Colson began by describing his relationship with Calhoon as the most important of his "off-screen" connections with labor leaders. As he reviewed with me his history with Calhoon, Colson noted that Jesse Calhoon was one of the most astute labor leaders in America. Calhoon first went to sea as a coal passer in 1939 at age 16. By 1949 he had worked his way up to chief engineer, and in 1954, he began his climb up the political ladder at MEBA, ultimately rising to become president of the union. He spent the next decade consolidating the various maritime locals into a powerful national organization. A brilliant financial strategist, Calhoon consolidated all of the maritime union pension funds into one and managed it himself. His investments grew so fast and so large that soon every financial house on Wall Street wanted to manage his account. Colson noted that Jesse was an ardent Democrat and an even stronger anti-communist. Ironically, it was a foreign policy issue that first linked Nixon to this union.

During the late 1960s, the United States and the Soviet Union were engaged in negotiations known as SALT, the Strategic Arms Limitation Talks. The cost of the arms race between the two superpowers was motivation for both parties to seek caps on the escalation of both nuclear weapons and their delivery systems, which were draining the treasuries of both countries.

President Nixon, whom the Russians knew was a fervent anti-communist, was both a hardliner and a tough negotiator. He entered the debate, publicly stating that any agreement "had to limit offensive weapons." In 1971 Nixon modified his stand to include limitations on both offensive and defensive systems, noting, "To limit only one side of the offense-defense equation could re-channel the arms race rather than curtail it." [7]

An additional complication in the SALT negotiations was the fact that the United States had the benefit of a new antiballistic missile program (ABM). Author Seymour Hersh, in his book, *The Price of Power*, argues that the memoirs of both Nixon and Henry Kissinger indicate that both men had less interest in the ABM system than in seeking a freeze on the number of launchers each side would be permitted to build. American missile technology was more advanced than that of the Soviets, and incorporated multiple warheads in a single missile, in effect multiplying the number of targets that could be hit from one missile launcher. So, when the Soviets agreed to a freeze on *their* missile launchers, they were agreeing to a unilateral freeze because they knew that the United States could increase the number of warheads on their missiles using fewer launch sites.

According to Hersh, the night before the May 20, 1971, press conference in which Nixon was to announce his major breakthrough in the stalemate over nuclear arms talks, Nixon, Kissinger, Colson, H. R.

(Bob) Haldeman, and John Erlichman were celebrating on the pres-idential yacht, *Sequoia*. The agreement that Nixon would announce in the joint statement the next day would be "the beginning of a new era in US–Soviet cooperation." This agreement was reached through back-channel communications completely outside the arms control agency and the professional diplomats at the State Department. This back-channel tactic was similarly deployed in the ping-pong and panda diplomacies that ultimately led to Nixon's trip to China and the opening of diplomatic relations with the Chinese.

But why were the Soviets so cooperative in making concessions to the United States on SALT? The reason, according to Hersh, was that the Soviets were facing a problem that the United States could help them solve: starvation. Nixon knew that poor harvests in the Soviet Union had created food shortages in Moscow and had triggered riots in Poland. To feed 240 million people, the Soviets needed grain, but that grain would have to be imported. Hence, behind the Soviet willingness to make concessions was a guarantee that Nixon would liberalize US trade policy to allow the Soviets to buy the grain they needed. The SALT agreement was linked to the sale of grain. This, too, was achieved through Kissinger's back-channel diplomacy.

However, a problem arose when the White House discovered that US maritime unions would not load the grain onto Soviet ships. The unions demanded to carry at least fifty percent of this cargo on American ships, which the Soviets would not allow. This situation once again required back-channel communications that Kissinger could not handle. Kissinger called Jay Lovestone, the AFL-CIO Director of International Affairs, who set up a White House meeting with Teddy Gleason, then-president of the International Longshoremen's Association. In an earlier attempt to ship grain to the Soviets in 1964, Gleason had said, "Let the Russians go to hell. Let 'em starve." Gleason was again telling the US government that the longshoremen would not load the grain unless fifty percent of it went on US ships. On June 9, 1971, Kissinger implored Gleason to load the grain on Soviet ships. Gleason responded, "Dr. Kissinger, I want to tell you something. We won't let you sell the American people down the Volga or down the Yangtze." [8]

According to Hersh's retelling of these events, Nixon turned to Colson to help win over the unions and save the SALT agreement. Colson pointed out that President Kennedy had tried unsuccessfully to get the longshoremen to assist when he negotiated with the Soviets. If Kennedy had been unable to get the maritime unions to load Soviet vessels, why would they load them for Nixon, a Republican? Colson credited his cordial relationship with Jesse Calhoon as the reason the logjam was broken.

Jesse Calhoon did not want to deny Nixon a foreign policy victory. At the same time, he wanted to move at least some of the wheat, if only to show the American flag in Soviet ports bringing food to the starving Russian people. However, he saw two long-term opportunities that would be advantageous to the maritime unions and to MEBA. The first involved the air traffic controllers who participated in a June 1969 and a March 1970 sick-out, many of whom were fired. The second opportunity was a way to create jobs for the entire merchant marine industry.

Using his close relationship with presidents of other maritime unions, Calhoon convinced them that Nixon was ready to rehire all of the controllers who had been dismissed. By helping Nixon on an issue of such importance to his foreign policy agenda, the maritime unions would be in a position to gain some advantages in encouraging Nixon to help the maritime industry, which had been losing cargo to other nations that exported their trade goods on their own ships.

To accomplish this, Jesse brought the air traffic controllers under MEBA's umbrella. Affiliation with MEBA would allow the air traffic controllers membership in the AFL-CIO, instead of being a stand-alone public sector union. On its face, it appeared that Calhoon had pulled off a coup—expanding the ranks of MEBA by capturing what he saw as a new high-tech membership. But Jesse's move was far more sagacious. Jesse was solving a minor problem for Nixon with respect to rehiring the fired air traffic controllers in order to obtain a different objective: the opportunity to carry Alaskan oil on American flagships.

Oil industry interest in drilling on public lands had surged as wells operated in the early half of the 20th century began to decline. The possibility of drilling on the North Slope of Alaska held out a way of reducing America's dependence on oil from the Arab states, which were both unstable and increasingly hostile to the United States.

Calhoon monitored the debates over the desirability of opening the North Slope and saw a greater possibility to create maritime jobs by carrying Alaskan oil, not across the Pacific to other countries but from Alaska to the lower 48 states. Three things were needed: First, a presidential decision to open the North Slope to drilling, along with the creation of a pipeline to carry the crude oil from the North Slope to the Port of Valdez; second, a fleet of modern tankers known as Very Large Crude Carriers (VLCCs) to transport the oil (which Nixon secretly promised Calhoon he would build); third, a presidential order requiring the Alaskan oil to be Jones Act cargo—that is, the ships had to be built in US shipyards, registered in the U.S., crewed by American seamen, and repaired in US shipyards.

Jesse had discussed this opportunity with Chuck Colson as he brokered the wheat deal and convinced the other unions to support Nixon and give up the demand to carry fifty percent of the wheat. Calhoon convinced the unions that even if they were successful in moving the grain, the operation would be of short duration and only provide a small number of jobs. Hence, when Jesse agreed to help deliver union acceptance to load the wheat on Soviet ships, the visible quid pro quo was that Nixon would rehire the air traffic controllers. Jesse's unspoken objective was to get Nixon to declare Alaskan oil Jones Act trade. Carrying Alaskan oil would require a new tanker fleet. As Jones Act trade, the tankers would have to be built with American steel in American shipyards. Calhoon was pre-positioned to give the president what he needed and achieve a greater objective for the union, the industry, and the country.

Recent labor historians and students of labor issues have written books and articles pointing to Calhoon's desire to expand his small union by seizing the opportunity to bring what became the Professional Air Traffic Controllers Organization (PATCO) under MEBA.[9] None of these analysts understood Calhoon's *real* objective was the expansion of the US merchant fleet.

In 1969, Nixon signed the Export Administration Act to ban the transport of Alaskan oil to anywhere but the continental United States for ten years. Nixon hosted a meeting at the White House at which Calhoon presented him with a model of the first new tanker. The door between the unions and a Republican president was now open. Nixon, Colson, and Calhoon had secretly accomplished a major foreign policy objective for the president and at the same time created a new industry for the country: a US tanker fleet. Building a relationship with Jesse Calhoon and the Marine Engineers was the first step in the creation of the New Majority.

Colson then described the second breakthrough for Nixon's creation of a New Majority, which occurred in 1970 when an antiwar protest in New York's lower Manhattan turned violent. Students from local New York universities marched on Wall Street to demand the withdrawal of American troops from Vietnam and Cambodia. They blamed Wall Street for war profiteering. The students, unshaved and looking like rabble, were carrying Viet Cong flags.

At that time, there was a major construction project taking place adjacent to where the protestors were gathered. Some of the construction workers were veterans of World War II, Korea and Vietnam. Many wore American flag stickers on their hard hats. Catcalls increased back and forth. When some of the students climbed atop the statue of George Washington that commemorated his taking the oath of office and urinated on the statue, construction workers came off the scaffolding and began punching the protestors. Television coverage of the event showed students atop the statue being pulled off by burly hard hats; some were knocked unconscious, while other were sent running for their lives. This incident was dubbed by historians as the "Hard Hat Riot."

As reported in the media, New York Mayor John Lindsay was justifiably concerned that if the clash between construction workers and university students persisted, someone could be seriously injured, if not killed. [10] Mayor Lindsay asked Peter J. Brennan, the president of the Building and Construction Trades Council of Greater New York, to meet with him in City Hall to seek solutions to the conflict and to stop his workers from resorting to violence. Brennan offered to get the unions to participate in a peaceful demonstration. The mayor agreed. A full-page ad appeared in some of the major New York dailies inviting all construction workers to participate in a march in front of City Hall to demonstrate their support for the nation's commander in chief.

According to media accounts of that march, it was one of the largest demonstrations in New York history. The number of marchers, according to newspaper estimates, was between 60,000 and 150,000 men and women. Offices in Manhattan began emptying their document shredders and created an impromptu ticker tape salute to the marchers. The parade line passing City Hall lasted six hours.

At our luncheon meeting, Colson shared with me a description of what happened when Peter Brennan and his executive board returned to the union office at about 7:30 in the evening. While they were celebrating a victory, the office secretary announced that Charles Colson from the White House was on the phone and wanted to talk to Brennan. Instead, it was the President of the United States on the phone. He shared with Brennan a list of weapons captured and destroyed during the Cambodian raid. He then asked Brennan and his board to come to Washington so he could personally thank them. On May 26, 1970, all twenty-two union leaders met with Richard Nixon and presented him with a hard hat inscribed "Commander in Chief." Brennan told the president, "The hard hat will stand as a symbol along with our great flag, for freedom and patriotism to our beloved country." With that hard hat, the bond between Nixon and the Building Trades was sealed. The second major component of the New Majority was now in place.

Colson's background briefing during my lunch with him in the West Wing was thorough and insightful. He said he wanted to establish a third component of the New Majority: Democratic mayors in cities with large ethnic populations such as Rizzo in Philadelphia and Alioto in San Francisco. He also wanted to include powerful labor leaders of industrial unions. Here he focused on my relationship with I. W. Abel as a way to begin outreach to industrial unions. He then announced that I was to be the contact between the White House and Abel. I was to let Abel know that Nixon was seriously considering his request to create a government guarantee to insure the pensions of working men and women. Colson said that creating a pension guarantee program would be much harder than creating a US tanker fleet.

He said to caution Abel that he was not to tell anyone in the union movement what we were attempting so as not to create opposition.

Our discussion then turned to a wider issue. Colson said that the president believed that the Republican Party was filled with silk-stocking types, wealthy country club Republicans with Ivy League credentials that ran the Republican Party like an exclusive society. Colson had been asked to join the staff, not only to ensure the loyalty of the staff, but also to devise ways to expand the party's base. He noted that he had talked to Jerry Jones about this and that the president believed that blue-collar Democrats like me were the future of the Republican Party. Colson said, "The president believes that the man who drives to church on Sunday in a pickup truck with a rifle rack on the back window philosophically is a Republican, but he doesn't know he's a Republican, and the Republican Party has no mechanism for communicating that message to him or the rest of Middle America." Colson concluded that he had not worked out all of the details but assured me that my appointment to the White House staff was a step in that direction.

When I left the luncheon, several things were clear. Colson wanted to expand the contacts between the president and Middle America. He already had a benchmark with the maritime unions and the building trades unions in New York and now wanted to encompass steel workers and other crafts in America's industrial base. It was clear that Nixon wanted to unite major elements of the Roosevelt coalition with the Republican Party to create a New Majority. Like Republicans, members of the Roosevelt coalition believed that rewards are distributed by merit and that opportunity in America is available to anyone who accepts that success is tied to hard work and sacrifice.

The basis for a New Majority was, and is today, belief in the achievement ethic. This belief was already a part of my DNA. An appeal to Americans on the need to adhere to the achievement ethic would be attractive to all Americans whether American-born or immigrant. Building a New Majority became the driving force behind the election of 1972, and helping to build that New Majority became my chief responsibility.

In 1972 I was thrust into dealing with the major unions that constituted the nation's industrial base. I met the families of union leaders, their parish priests, and the leaders of their fraternal organizations. I was accepted into their communities as one of them. They were family. They knew that I understood them; they trusted me to convey their issues to the White House. There is no way that I could have been successful in my new role had I not been raised in a union household and a working-class community.

The Big City Mayors

In the short time I had been on the White House staff, I was being given increased responsibility. It began with urban ethnics, expanded to the Captive Nations and nationalities, and was broadened to include the leadership of industrial unions. Then, quite by accident or a stroke of luck, my responsibilities expanded to include big city mayors with large ethnic constituencies.

My relationship with the mayors of major cities began with Ralph J. Perk, the Republican Mayor of Cleveland. Perk's election in 1971 was widely recognized as the first victory for ethnic mayors in large urban cities. Philadelphia Mayor Frank Rizzo also organized the ethnics to support him. Rizzo, a former chief of police and a hardliner on criminal justice issues, was a Democrat whom the party would not support because of his tough stance on street crime. Like all of the other Democrats with whom I talked, Rizzo believed the Democratic Party had abandoned the core principles that made them Democrats. He first campaigned as a Democrat for Nixon, then switched parties to the thunderous applause of Philadelphia's ethnic communities.

As described in the introduction, San Francisco Mayor Alioto had agreed to campaign for McGovern. He did not change parties as Rizzo did but his absence on the campaign trail as an Italian mayor hurt McGovern.

The most influential mayor with whom I had contact was Mayor Richard Daley of Chicago. Our association began as the result of an incident that occurred during the 1972 Democratic Convention when the Chicago delegates were refused their seats. These disenfranchised delegates, backers of Hubert Humphrey, were sent home, and other delegates who endorsed McGovern were seated in their place.

When the Chicago delegates were unseated, there was primetime television coverage of Chicago's 25th Ward Alderman, Vito Marzullo, storming out of the convention with his entire delegation as the hand-picked McGovern delegates were seated. Marzullo did not leave quietly. He said that the delegates McGovern picked were half-naked women and welfare recipients who had no ward organization and no constituency capable of electing anybody.

The Monday following the convention I asked my assistant, Dagnija Kreslins, to call Chicago City Hall and put Marzullo through to me. I introduced myself as an assistant to President Nixon and said that I was calling from the White House. Before I could say anything further, he repeated, "You are in the White House?" I said yes, and he hung up.

The phone rang ten minutes later. Dagnija ran in saying Marzullo was on the line for me. I told Marzullo that I was sorry I had disconnected him. He interrupted, "You didn't disconnect me. I hung up. How the hell did I know who you were? I had my girl call the White House and ask for you so I knew you weren't some crackpot."

I told Marzullo I had watched the news show that covered his reaction to being unseated at the convention and that I was most interested in McGovern's answer to the moderator's question about why Marzullo was not supporting McGovern. McGovern's response was that he didn't know Marzullo.

"Yeah, but he's going to know who I am on Election Day!" Marzullo exclaimed. He tossed off a series of epithets in Italian, using words to describe, among other things, women with no moral character. Bearded young men who smelled like they slept in their clothes also outraged him, he said. We then spent time talking about his ward, and he asked about my role in the White House. I recounted for him my work with ethnics. He asked if I knew Al Mazewski, president of the Polish National Alliance. I said I had met with him. He added, "He's a good friend of mine. He is a Republican, but we're friends."

Our conversation was in both English and Italian. He said that when the credentials committee told him that he needed more minorities and women in the delegation, he replied, "In Chicago the delegates are selected in the wards. However, if you told me that you wanted certain people represented, we would have seen to it that you had minorities and women, etc." He said their response was, "Yes, but they would have been your people, not ours."

"*Your people?*" Marzullo questioned. "What the hell are you saying? You want delegates that will vote your way and not in tune with the people of Chicago? The hell with all of you; I'm taking my delegation home." Marzullo said they didn't try to stop him. The next anyone heard from Vito was on television as he stormed out of the auditorium.

Marzullo then asked, "When will you come to Chicago?"

"Well," I said, "I'll get there."

At that point, in Italian, he said, "No, you will come now. There are some people I want you to meet."

Colson was ecstatic. "Go, go, go now!" he said.

A few days later I was in Vito's office. We talked about the convention again. Then he said, "I want you to meet someone." We climbed two flights of stairs and suddenly I was in the office of one of the most powerful mayors in American politics, Mayor Richard J. Daley.

This was the man I had seen on television at the riot-torn Chicago Convention, red face and all. Vito introduced me as "my friend in Washington that I told you about." He told the mayor that I had called him after the Chicago delegation was unseated. Mayor Daley said nothing. As Vito talked, he sat motionless. Finally Vito said, "Mr. Mayor, do you have a message for the President?" Mayor Daley waited for what seemed like forever. Was he going to tell me to go downstairs and walk around the block, as Alioto had during my first meeting with him?

Finally, he spoke. "You tell Dick Nixon that I am going to support the Democratic ticket."

Well, I said to myself. *What else could I have expected. This was Mr. Democrat.* Unexpectedly, Vito became excited. He jumped up and thanked the mayor profusely. "Thank you. Thank you, Mr. Mayor. I knew you wouldn't let me down."

As we walked down the stairs, Vito was jubilant. "Did you hear him? Did you hear him? He is going to support McGovern and the whole Democratic ticket."

"Vito," I said shyly, "I don't get it. That's not good news. How am I going to tell Nixon this?"

Marzullo responded in Italian, *"Guyo, no capisce?"* (Don't you get it, kid?) *We're going to help Nixon!"*

Marzullo said that by supporting the ticket they would control the election machines in every ward throughout the city, and that if the mayor didn't support the ticket, Jesse Jackson and Alderman Bill Singer would take over the voting machines. Apparently, the delegates that were *not seated* at the Democratic convention would be running the voting machines during the presidential election.

Marzullo laughed, pinching his fingers together in an Italian gesture, and said, "See, the mayor helped Kennedy the same way by controlling the machines, and we cost Nixon the 1960 election. Now we're going to cost McGovern the election."

Before I left for Washington, I met with Aloysius Mazewski, president of the Polish National Alliance, and told him what Marzullo had said. Al responded, "This is a revolution. Never has there been an election in Chicago where the Democratic Party was splitting a ticket. This is the first time in history that Cook County Democrats will allow precinct captains to instruct voters on how to split a ticket. They will vote for local Democratic candidates and a Republican president." Al went on to say, "Party organizations are like the Army. You do as you are told. You vote Democrat or you get nothing!" It was now clear that Daley was supporting Nixon.

I called Colson from O'Hare Airport before boarding my flight back to DC. He was exuberant. "Mike, I'm going to tell the president right now. See me first thing tomorrow morning."

The next morning Colson was waiting for me. "Do you know what you've accomplished, Mike?" he said. "The president is ecstatic. Stay close to Marzullo. Give him anything he wants. Wow! The president is very pleased with your performance," he said.

A few weeks later, the Marzullos invited my wife and me to spend a weekend with them. Marzullo set up a meeting for me with Frank Annunzio, who represented the 11th congressional district in Chicago. The three of us talked about the possibility of Nixon marching in the Columbus Day parade, a major event. Marzullo told me it would be very important for Nixon to be identified with the Columbus Day event. It would solidify Nixon's support from the Italian community.

I spoke with Colson about this, and he said he would get back to me. Later that day, Colson said that the president could not attend himself, but would send Mrs. Nixon. Annunzio was delighted with the news. On Columbus Day, I accompanied Mrs. Nixon as we walked in the Columbus Day parade with thousands of Italians. She was warmly received at the reception prior to the parade and went a long way to solidifying the relationship between Italians and the president.

The drumbeat for Nixon was beginning to build as Democrats deserted McGovern in every state normally associated with the Roosevelt coalition. Former Texas Governor John Connally formed "Democrats For Nixon." Mayor Rizzo organized a similar group in Philadelphia.

Steelworker Lefty Scumaci, lifelong Democrat, took the bold step of supporting his son Ross's decision to speak in support of the president at the Republican Convention. Throughout the campaign, I had worked with Lefty Scumaci to bring Nixon's messages to the steelworkers. As a senior union official, Scumaci technically could not endorse Nixon. Yet, later that year, Lefty had little choice but to become linked to the election of 1972. Stan Anderson, a White House aide and one of the strongest advocates for bringing the New Majority into the Republican Party, arranged for Lefty's son Ross to address the Republican National Convention in Miami. Ross Scumaci had founded a community group called "Working Youth for Nixon." Anderson worked with convention officials to enable a teenager, who had never given a speech in his life, to address the convention in prime time.

This presented Lefty with a dilemma. Because of his visible position on Abel's staff and the union's declaration of neutrality, Scumaci at first tried to distance himself from his son's decision to address the convention. But fortified by neighborhood residents and Abel's comments that Lefty "looked pale and needed a few days in the sun," the Scumacis threw political caution to the wind and flew to Miami to attend the convention. Unfortunately, they were unable to reach the convention hall because the demonstrators had ice-picked the tires of the buses in the streets approaching the causeways. In fact, the antiwar protesters and the Miami Beach police clashed in front of Scumaci's hotel, filling the lobby with fleeing demonstrators and tear gas.

With eyes red from tear gas, the Scumacis had to watch their son on television. Scumaci's neighborhood precinct wards also watched as Walter Cronkite announced Ross Scumaci's speech, noting the significance of working-class participation in a Republican forum. Pittsburgh's workers beamed with pride as they heard the young man's opening remarks: "By trade, I am a boilermaker." Pride turned to fury when, in the middle of the address, CBS switched its coverage to police attempts to clear the traffic jams resulting from the protesters' assault on vehicles approaching the convention hall. The protesters, police, and tear gas filled the TV screens. Coverage of Ross Scumaci's speech was over.

The event galvanized Pittsburgh's ethnic and labor Democrats to back Richard Nixon. A short time later, Mike Sam, the Lebanese-born director of the National Wage Office for the United Steelworkers, told me, "Protestors? When I get into that voting booth, I'm going to register *my* protest! I'm going to ring that chime for Nixon so hard that my vote will break the machine!"

Three days before the election, Nixon called the Scumacis and personally thanked Lefty and Ross for the stand they had taken on his behalf.

Aside from the insult to the Democratic Party of having Chicago's Humphrey delegates unseated, Mayor Daley was morally offended by McGovern's positions on amnesty for deserters, abortion, and liberalization of the nation's drug policies. He was not alone in this sentiment. George Meany, president of the AFL-CIO, shared Daley's view. Knowing that union members who made up Middle America would support Nixon in the 1972 election, Meany declared that the Federation would not endorse any candidate. The AFL-CIO declared neutrality. This was permission for the entire labor movement to go with Nixon when they entered the voting booth.

McGovern went to Chicago in an attempt to demonstrate to party stalwarts that he was still close to Mayor Daley but here, too, he met with problems. Abe Mernick, a supporter of Mayor Daley, carried a large sign outside City Hall charging that McGovern "double-crossed the mayor." Mernick then carried his sign into the building, walking behind the presidential candidate through the halls. There is no way that Mernick would have been allowed access to the building if Daley had not approved it.

Even before the Inauguration, Nixon was making personal phone calls to labor and ethnic leaders, thanking them for their support and telling them he wanted to maintain their support in the coming years of his second term. According to Colson, who urged the calls, the president did not say, "I want you to switch parties and become a Republican," but it was clear that this Republican president wanted them to be a part of a permanent New Majority.

Before I came to the White House, Nixon had already made great strides in opening a relationship with labor unions. He had approved a fleet of oil tankers to move Alaskan oil and, thanks to Peter Brennan and Don Rodgers, the New York hard-hat march had opened a relationship with the building trades. Two months before I arrived in 1972, Nixon had pardoned Jimmy Hoffa, the imprisoned former head of the International Brotherhood of Teamsters, on the condition that Hoffa stay out of union politics until 1980. Collectively, all these decisions made the labor unions take more than a second look at Nixon.

Ultimately, the New Majority encompassed a broad spectrum of groups: Captive Nations groups, ethnic and fraternal organizations, maritime unions, the building and construction trades, industrial base unions, religious groups, as well as mayors of the cities with large ethnic populations. Although most of these groups were considered part of the Roosevelt coalition and traditionally voted Democrat, all of these people shared a belief that rewards are distributed by merit and that opportunity in America is available to anyone who accepts that success is tied to hard work and sacrifice.

Conflicts in the White House (1972-73)

The Office of Public Liaison (OPL), by its very nature, created conflicts within the White House. The job of the staff was to serve constituencies: Each OPL staff member was to be an advocate for a particular voter bloc group. Pursuing these constituencies and the issues that were important to them was not easy. To do so, we had to get federal agencies to listen to the concerns of our voter bloc groups. Some cabinet officers had their own bureaucratic obstacle courses to negotiate; others had agendas of their own. Since every federal agency had a counterpart in the Office of Management and Budget or on the Domestic Council, collisions between OPL and any of those White House operations frequently occurred. People in these offices cried foul each time they believed that a member of Colson's staff intruded on their territory. I ran into this problem early in my tenure.

Almost every issue we dealt with required policy information from other White House offices. That information generally was not easily obtained from the Domestic Council or the Office of Management and Budget. Admittedly, in my case, the issues that affected my constituencies evoked impassioned responses. For instance, I needed information on the persecution of Jews and Christians in Russia and the need to continue funding for Radio Free Europe and Radio Liberty. Other volatile issues included gun control proposals that affected sportsmen, school busing, the legalization of drugs such as marijuana and LSD, as well as policies generated by the Department of Health Education and Welfare promoting sex education in neighborhood schools.

A simple request for policy information often revealed that offices within the White House held very different positions than did the president. The Domestic Council, for example, sponsored a bill to ban "cheap, easily concealed handguns" that were said to be readily available in crime-ridden inner cities throughout America. As it turned out, the Domestic Council had advised Nixon that the "Saturday Night Special" bill would help alleviate crime. In no time, Ash Halsey, the editor of *American Rifleman,* a publication of the National Rifle Association, was in my office arguing that any handgun was "easily concealable" and asking for the definition of "cheap." He said, "You are going to negatively impact legitimate shooters and hunters who also live in the inner city."

I approached Colson with this problem. He said Nixon was concerned about the availability of handguns to lunatics; that Arthur Bremer had stalked him and Hubert Humphrey before he shot George Wallace. Colson told the president that there were more guns in the United States than people and that guns were part of American history. Moreover, Colson told the president that it was impossible to totally prevent bad people from obtaining guns. He advised Nixon that the Saturday Night Special bill would prevent only law-abiding citizens from obtaining handguns.

With Nixon's permission, Colson convened a task force that included Jerris Leonard, Donald Santarelli, Gordon Liddy, Egil "Bud" Krogh, and me to pull together the facts on this issue. Santarelli, who was associate deputy attorney general of the United States, went to the National Rifle Association annual meeting in New Orleans to brief the NRA leadership on the implications of the gun bill. Also involved was the White House general counsel, Ed Morgan. Morgan advised the NRA members that the Saturday Night Special bill was Nixon's bill and that the White House supported it. He argued that the bill was being debated, had moved through both houses of Congress, and it was near passage.

Colson's team quickly gathered definitions of "cheap and concealable" handguns. With definitions in hand, we mired the bill down with so much detail that the president threatened to veto his own bill. All of the sporting magazines carried articles crediting Nixon with saving their guns. One of the nation's leading gun magazines had a photo of a handgun being melted down with a blowtorch. The Saturday Night Special bill was dead. Many people on the Domestic Council who had supported the bill were outraged.

Just about every social policy issue I dealt with in the White House involved someone else's office. Turf battles were a constant. Unquestionably, the most controversial of all issues was court-ordered school busing. Courts were ordering inner-city students to attend schools in the wealthier suburbs outside inner-city limits. They were also ordering suburban children to be bused out of their neighborhood school districts into the inner city. A national explosion erupted over this issue. Ethnic and labor union people who lived in the suburbs said they had worked hard to leave the inner city and that they were being punished for their success.

In order to get information about court-ordered busing, I called the Domestic Council. Council staff said they had no control over busing and that the issue was in the hands of the Office of Education. I went there and got no information. But the tom-tom drums were beating throughout the White House proclaiming that Colson's staff—and particularly me—was fomenting trouble over busing.

The assistant secretary for the Justice Department's Civil Rights Division contacted the Domestic Council to alert them about my calls seeking information. An Ehrlichman aide, trying to defend his boss from another embarrassment and seeking to curb my tendency to go around government agencies with impunity, sent a January 5, 1973, memo to Ken Cole, a White House principal. While the aide's memo ostensibly focused on the fact that there was little the president could do to stop court-ordered busing, in fact it was mainly designed to demonstrate the Domestic Council's frustration with my activities circumventing the system, as noted in the last lines of the memo:

> I want to take this opportunity to wish you every luck in your effort to control Balzano's activities. If this becomes a problem I think it would be appropriate for you to draft a memorandum to Ehrlichman that he can go drop on Haldeman's desk. Haldeman and the president think Balzano is the greatest thing since sliced bread. Unfortunately, only those of us who have watched him closely know that he's an accident looking for a place to happen. [11]

I am sure that when the aide wrote the memo to Ken Cole, he thought it would end up on Haldeman's desk. Instead, Cole wrote to Colson [12] who called me in and gave me the memo. I asked Colson if I had created a problem for him. "No," he said, "I'll answer this memo later. You keep doing everything you're doing." Colson's response to Ken Cole read as follows:

> Despite his impulsive nature, I might say that there are few people around who did more to rack up votes for us during the campaign than Mike. Just the symbolism that Mike represented was enormously significant to us all over the country.

> You have to understand about Balzano that he is
> an activist. If he discovers the gate is locked, he simply
> kicks down the fence. He has many admirable quali-
> ties but patience is not one. His instincts are right, his
> heart is right, and I defy anyone to find anyone more
> loyal than Balzano.

Colson later gave me a copy of his memo, and told me to do whatever I needed to do for my constituencies and he would authorize my
activity later. He said, "There are no sins of commission; only sins of
omission. Don't tell me why you didn't do something; tell me how you
succeeded." It should be understood that, in the White House, aides do
whatever they can to assist the principal they work for. Ehrlichman's
aide and I did what we had to do to further the mission each of us had.
To serve my constituency, I needed to take every shortcut around the
White House bureaucracy. That usually meant crossing boundaries
that separated the various offices of the White House, which inevitably
led to collisions with White House staff.

Perhaps the best example of these dust-ups occurred over Nixon's
trip to the Statue of Liberty in September 1972 to dedicate the opening
of its museum. The museum commemorates the history of America
as a nation of diverse nationalities that immigrated to our shores. By
this time, I would have thought that Colson's office would have been
informed, if not involved, in any event with the president that included
ethnics, heritage groups, or nationalities. But we were not.

Four days before the museum was to open, I received a call from
Colonel Casimir Lenard, director of the Washington office of the
Polish American Congress. He advised that the president was about
to engage in an event that would insult not only Polish Americans, but
all other nationalities as well, and I had to stop it. He said that I had to
call ethnic leader Mitch Kristalovich at once. I called Mitch who said
in a very excited voice (he was always excited): "The president is going
to New York to make a speech at the Statue of Liberty that will insult
all of the ethnics in America. The museum has exhibits that denigrate
Polish Americans."

Rather than admit that the president's ethnic advisor knew nothing about a presidential visit, I let him tell me what he knew. My assistant, Dagnija Kreslins, came in while I was still on the phone and told me I had to take a call from Terry Szmagala right now. Terry was getting calls from members of nationality groups saying they were going to the Statue of Liberty en masse to demonstrate against the president. Since I felt comfortable with Terry, I confessed to him that I didn't know what the hell he was talking about and that I would get on it.

I called Al Mazewski, president of the Polish National Alliance, to see if he had heard anything. As usual, Al was a real gentleman. Apparently, Leonard Walentynowicz told him that people working on the exhibit advised Mitch Kristalovich that Eastern Europeans, who were the a significant portion of the immigrants in the early part of the century, were not represented in a large statistical chart depicting the people who immigrated to America. He said there were no references to Poles, Italians and Catholics. Most troubling to Al was a talking statue of Polish General and American Revolutionary War hero Tadeusz Kosciuszko, referring to himself as stupid! Al added a very reasonable question: "How can you have a major event depicting the flow of immigrants into the United States without inviting ethnic leaders to at least be represented on the platform?" This was enough for me to start looking through the White House to find out which office knew about the event.

I started with the Domestic Council, which, except for knowing of the president's participation, knew nothing about the event. They said that since the Statue of Liberty was on public property, I should talk to someone at the National Park Service. The National Park Service told me the event was under control of the state of New York. The state officials said it was a city event, not a state event. Someone from city hall told me I should contact the National Park Service. Finally, I called the White House Press Office to see what they knew. Deputy Press Secretary Jerry Warren said the event was on the schedule and that presidential advance was now in charge. "Who?" I asked.

"Presidential advance," Warren repeated. "You know, Ron Walker's shop."

Until that day, I had never heard of Ron Walker, let alone presidential advance. Walker, a former military officer, was a tough, take-charge, no-nonsense person whose staff responded to his orders as if he were a drill sergeant. In later years I would come to know Walker very well when we both worked for Ronald Reagan, but at the moment I could not get through to him. I had to climb up the staff ladder to get the information I needed. Knowing that I was getting a reputation in the White House for being a bull in a china shop, I approached Walker's office very gingerly.

I spoke with Karen Hart, a lovely young woman in Walker's office, who was clearly cautious, if not nervous, about my questions. "Mr. Walker is not in," she said.

I traced the steps that I had already taken, telling her that Jerry Warren had referred me to Walker's office.

"Mr. Walker is out on an advance," she said. "Can you tell me what you want?"

I asked about an event at the Statue of Liberty to be held later in the week.

She responded, "The presidential advance is on top of that event."

I asked if there was anyone I could talk to about the event. She responded that all of the staff members were out advancing other events. Then I clearly got one of those "I've heard about you" looks. So I thought it best not to tell her about the ethnic protest that I was trying to stop.

I told all of this to Colson who said that I should go to New York and find out what the hell is wrong and what we needed to do to fix it.

The next morning I was on the Eastern shuttle to La Guardia. When I arrived at the Battery Park Ferry, I discovered that, in preparation for the president's visit, all ferry transportation to Liberty Island had been stopped. I stood at the waters edge, looking at the statue, trying to figure out how I would get to Liberty Island.

Then I saw a tugboat moored at a pier several hundred yards away. It was an old tugboat with automobile tires hanging off its sides and a large, reddish-brown stack of manila hemp covering its bow. As I walked up to the tugboat, I told myself I had to get that boat to take me to the island. What would I say? I kept repeating Chuck's words in my mind, "There are no sins of commission." An inner voice spoke to me, "You can take a kid out of Wooster Street, but you can't take Wooster Street out of the man."

I held up my White House pass and yelled to a red-bearded man on the deck, "I am representing the president of the United States, and I need this boat to take me to that island."

In semi-shock the man waved me to come aboard. Someone from the wheelhouse shouted, "Who is this guy?" The red-bearded man shouted back that I was from the White House and that I needed to get to the island. In a scene reminiscent of Barbra Streisand commandeering a tugboat in *Funny Girl,* I stood on the bow of that tugboat, bouncing over the waves through New York harbor and arrived at the foot of the Statue of Liberty thirty minutes later. I told the captain of the tugboat to wait for me. He agreed to do so.

The main entrance to the building was closed. I walked around the base of the statue and fortunately found a door that was open. I entered and began touring the museum by myself. A distinguished man who looked like a museum curator appeared and nervously asked who I was, how I got there, and what I was doing in the museum. I showed him my White House pass and told him that I was there to preview the exhibits.

He said, "But the White House has been here for almost a week. Why do you have to approve the exhibits?"

I told him that apparently there had been some cultural issues that were unknown to the advance team, issues that could conceivably be a problem for the president. I told him that the White House had been besieged with calls from angry ethnic leaders and that I had been sent to resolve their issues. I needed to tour the exhibit. He was quite put out, but we were at the entrance to the exhibit so I entered with him still behind me, still protesting.

A huge panel identifying the waves of immigrants who had come to our shores confronted me. The chart identified Irish, English, and Jewish immigrants, but none from Eastern Europe. Other exhibits dealt with the opening of the West. There were photos of covered wagons, Spanish shawls, exotic fans, etc, but not one crucifix to show that most of these immigrants were Catholics. I asked the curator if he had any talking statues.

"Talking statues?" he responded. "Well, there is an exhibit dealing with the American Revolution that has figurines in revolutionary dress that also have recordings attached to them." He took me to a large exhibit where mannequins about two feet high were encircled in a glass enclosure. As I stood in front of each doll-like figure, I triggered an automatic tape, which played a recording that told of that statue's role in the Revolutionary War. The George Washington statue spoke of his command as general of the Continental Army. Paul Revere talked about his midnight ride. At the statue of General Tadeusz Kosciuszko, the recorded message said that the General knew that people questioned his judgment and his intelligence, but nobody questioned his patriotism. The recording made it seem like Gen. Kosciuszko was telling a stupid Polish joke.

Before I told the curator what needed to be changed, I asked for a list of dignitaries who would be on the podium. The list showed twenty dignitaries from the state of New York and the five boroughs of New York City. The invocation was to be given by a rabbi. Without saying anything about adding ethnic and fraternal dignitaries to the platform, I told the museum curator of all the changes that needed to be made before the White House would approve of the president's participation in the event.

"Are you serious? We can't change these things in forty-eight hours," he said.

"Sure you can," I said, "if you cover up the following exhibits with drop cloths, hang some crucifixes near the Spanish shawls and shut off the recordings so that no one has to hear Kosciuszko's speech."

"I can't change the soundtrack," he said.

"No," I replied, "but you can disconnect the soundtrack from the entire exhibit during the opening tour and change the recording later."

His protests were eloquent. But I told him that I had just spoken to the special counsel to the president, who had responsibility for the president's participation, and that I was ordered to tell the curator that if these changes were not made by the time I returned the next day, the president would not be there for the opening of the museum. He was stunned and frightened but pledged he would do as I asked.

I did not return the next day, but when he watched me leave on that tugboat, he surely believed I would return. I called Dagnija from the airport and told her to call Terry Szmagala and ask him for a list of ethnic leaders who should fly to New York immediately to attend the event the next day. I also asked that he find a Polish or Italian Catholic priest to address the crowd. I called Al Mazewski in Chicago to invite him and at least two other Polish leaders from New York to the ceremony.

Dagnija, Jack Burgess, Terry Szmagala and I met at the ferry the morning of the event. Terry had assembled a group of young children dressed in native Italian, Polish and Ukrainian attire, to give a large bouquet of flowers to Mrs. Nixon when the helicopter landed. I used my White House pass to get five ethnic leaders and one priest past the Secret Service detail to the podium. There I encountered the first of three advance men who were managing the event. The lead advance man was on me like a hawk. "Who are you, and where are you going?" he asked.

Over the noise of the crowd, aircraft flying overhead, and the incessant sound of the wind blowing in from the harbor, he strained to hear what I was saying. His face changed from an inquisitive look to one of horror when I told him I had to get this ethnic delegation to the platform.

"Whoa, whoa, does Ron Walker know about this?" he asked. I said I didn't think so, but the White House had approved what I was doing.

I told him not to worry, because these men were going to be *on* the platform and that one of them would be speaking. The gray-haired Italian priest, who obviously didn't know what we were talking about, simply smiled, nodded approvingly, holding the paper with his prepared remarks while holding his hat in place so that it would not be swept away in the wind.

Suddenly the whirl of chopper blades could be heard, and I left the platform to see Terry Szmagala place the girls at the landing site. The scene was beautiful. Mrs. Nixon was thrilled. The president was pleased, and the picture of those girls presenting flowers ended up on the front page of newspapers nationwide. The ethnic papers would now say that ethnic and fraternal order leaders came to praise Nixon, not to demonstrate against him. President and Mrs. Nixon, who had been to Poland in May of 1972, were happy that the Polish leadership had come to this event. Haldeman was pleased; Colson was ecstatic that the event went well.

However, with some of the White House staff, a lot of china was broken. Nonetheless, what would have happened if the president had been drawn into a demonstration against him? No one in the White House was sensitive to this issue. The president got the credit from the ethnics, which is what I wanted. I was convinced that I had to continue to endure my White House reputation as "an accident looking for a place to happen."

Nixon's relationship with the Polish community was solid, since, as vice president, he had visited Poland in 1959 and had the highest respect for the Polish people. Before Nixon's 1972 trip to Poland, Henry Cashen, who was in charge of Catholic constituencies, arranged for John Joseph Cardinal Krol, Archbishop of Philadelphia, which had a significant Polish Catholic community, to join the president on his yacht, the *Sequoia,* and to brief him about Catholic issues. I cannot think of any other ethnic group that Nixon talked about more than the Polish people.

When I learned of the president's impending trip to Poland, I saw an opportunity to involve the entire Polish-American community. At the suggestion of Al Mazewski, I proposed to Colson that John Krawiec, the editor of *Zgoda,* a Polish daily paper read by Polish-speaking residents of Illinois, should accompany the president as part of the press corps. Krawiec would send his daily copy to the editors of other Polish newspapers. Everything went well until the White House could not clear the uncredentialed Krawiec to be part of the White House press corps. The press plane took off without him. This was another example of the inner office struggle between the Office of Public Liaison and Ron Ziegler's press office.

When Colson found out Krawiec was not on the plane carrying the White House press corps, he told me to get Krawiec on the trip. I went to deputy press secretary Jerry Warren who was sympathetic and told me to call J. Bruce Whelihan, staff assistant in the White House press office. Whelihan was extremely helpful and got Krawiec put on a second plane leaving for Poland the following day.

As a result, Polish language newspapers throughout the Northeast and Midwest were extremely grateful to President Nixon for providing Polish Americans with information about their relatives behind the

Iron Curtain. Additionally, film clips taken during the president's trip were spliced together to create a documentary that Polish leaders of fraternal organizations distributed to theaters in Polish-American communities. Polish Americans in communities throughout the Northeast and Midwest viewed the film looking for their relatives in the crowds.

These White House staff conflicts are cited to demonstrate how the staff was, at times, polarized over territorial disputes. But the conflicts were deeper than simply turf battles. To get a broader sense of White House conflicts, one must read Colson's memoir, *Born Again*. While it is the story of Colson's conversion to Christianity, it is also the story of how Colson approached dealing with other White House principals and resolved power struggles. One manifestation of the competition was brought about by Colson's staff pursuing legitimate functions to serve constituencies. But another form of competition was more serious. It became a contest between White House principals who perceived the addition of Colson to the White House staff as a threat to their power.

One can only imagine the impact of Nixon calling Colson several times a day to seek his advice in the presence of an Oval Office meeting of assembled senior staff members. Eventually, Colson was called to meet with the president alone. The president expressed his dissatisfaction with the staff even before the establishment of the Committee to Re-elect the President was formed. Once the committee was in place, Colson's influence was expanded to oversee that operation as well.

Perhaps the two principals most upset with Colson's expanding portfolio were Henry Kissinger and John Ehrlichman. The tension between Kissinger and Colson over the SALT agreement was ably described by Seymour Hersh in *The Price of Power*. When Kissinger revealed that there was an insurmountable problem getting the unions to load the wheat to Soviet ships to consummate the deal, Nixon turned to Colson and Colson made it happen, leaving both Ehrlichman and Kissinger out of the process. Everything changed after that. The lines were clearly drawn. From then on, it was Colson versus all of the other major White House principals.

Tensions escalated further when Colson took over responsibility for White House functions that involved the Committee to Re-elect the President. This decision resulted in White House principals seeking ways to demonstrate to the president that they, too, could devise ingenious schemes to prove their importance. The desire to impress the president propelled some of the younger staff members, including Jeb Magruder, deputy campaign director at the campaign, and Dwight Chapin, assistant to the president in the White House, to initiate activities that eventually resulted in jail terms for them and the people they hired to engage in high-risk tactics, later deemed illegal. Much of this activity was rooted in competition gone awry.

In *Born Again,* Colson recounts the unintended consequences of his "walk over my own grandmother to elect the president" memo. "Not surprisingly, the furor the memo kicked up served only to reinforce Nixon's respect for my loyalty. 'Colson—he'll do anything, he'll walk right through doors,' the President would brag to others.

"In our small White House circle, machismo and toughness were equated with trust and loyalty; these were keys to the cherished kingdom guaranteeing continued closeness to the throne."

Colson then lamented, "We had set in motion forces that would sooner or later make Watergate, or something like it, inevitable." [13]

Watergate ended Nixon's goal of creating a New Majority. In retrospect, the Watergate break-in was an attempt to obtain salacious information on Democrats that would put them in a compromising position with their voters. The fact is that Democratic constituencies probably would not have cared. Those responsible for planning the break-in and the cover-up kept Colson in the dark on the entire caper. Colson was simply too smart to be involved in anything that stupid and would have counseled the president against it.

CHAPTER 4
Forging an Alliance (1972-74)

Nixon won reelection in 1972 in a landslide carrying all but one state, Massachusetts, and the District of Columbia. McGovern did not even win his own state of South Dakota. Following the election, Colson told me that Nixon never believed that the American people would elect someone who ran against the values of the nation. Colson said that even the media pundits did not recognize that throughout the entire election cycle of 1972, Nixon never campaigned against McGovern. He just went about the business of being President. He opened China. He went to Poland. He obtained a settlement in the Vietnam War by initiating the Paris Peace Accords, but not before the Vietnamese released all of the American prisoners.

The proof of Nixon's popularity with the people was evidenced in ethnic and blue-collar communities throughout Middle America. Big city working-class districts, whether Democrat- or Republican-controlled, went for Nixon. The labor unions, freed by AFL-CIO President George Meany's declaration of neutrality, went for Nixon. In those cities controlled by Democratic machines, the Nixon victory was even more resounding. Chicago Democratic Alderman Vito Marzullo said, after our meeting with Mayor Daley that Chicago had cost Nixon the presidency in 1960 but that Chicago gave him the presidency in 1972. The *Chicago Tribune* reported that Marzullo was one of three Democratic aldermen in Chicago to endorse Nixon.[14] The *Tribune* later reported that federal investigators were harassing Marzullo on

Election Day, and Marzullo responded, "What are you trying to do to me? I'm out here getting the vote out for Nixon."[15]

Shortly after the election, Colson asked me to prepare a list of key people in my New Majority constituencies, stating that the president wanted to have a New Majority Christmas Party. I produced a list of more than a thousand people who would be invited. The list included auto mechanics, steelworkers, boilermakers, janitors, salesmen, and many people who never dreamed they would see the White House, let alone be invited to attend a Christmas party with the President in the White House. Even Abe Mernick, the man who followed McGovern all over Chicago City Hall with a sign calling McGovern a double-crosser of Mayor Daley, was invited to the event.

During the party the Nixons greeted everyone in a two-hour receiving line. When he came to Mitchell Kobelinski, the President patted him on the shoulder and, in front of at least a dozen other Poles, said loudly, "Hey, I want you in my administration. I need you; you can't say no." Before Kobelinski could respond, I interrupted and said, "You see, Mitch, I told you he wants you."

As we approached the Inauguration, Colson told me that Nixon wanted to do something special for the Marzullos. The night before the Inauguration there would be a series of concerts at the Kennedy Center, followed by a black tie, candlelight dinner on the roof terrace level of the Kennedy Center. My wife and I would escort Mr. and Mrs. Marzullo to the concert and dinner as the President Nixon's guests. The Marzullos were delighted.

I was provided with a limousine to transport the President's guests to the dinner. We were to meet at my home and proceed first to the concert. When the Marzullos arrived, they were dressed for a cocktail party. Vito was wearing a pinstripe blue suit. Mrs. Marzullo was wearing an attractive, short cocktail dress. Denise and I were in formal attire, tuxedo and floor-length gown. Denise, the daughter of a State Department official and a diplomat herself, said to the Marzullos (who recognized that we were formally dressed), that we had just returned from a formal event at the White House and needed to change for this evening's event. She pulled me into the bedroom and quietly said, "These are the President's guests and we cannot embarrass them. We will dress as they have." Moments later Denise and I emerged from the bedroom dressed in a blue suit and cocktail dress. The Marzullos were none the wiser.

Of all of the many events that my wife and I were privileged to attend during the Nixon administration, the candlelight dinner was one of the most spectacular. Following the concert, a musical salute to the states, we were guided to an elevator that took us to the roof of the Kennedy Center. When we arrived we were met by a small group of musicians dressed in American Revolutionary garb equipped with fifes and snare drums. We were escorted by a fife and drum corps from the elevator foyer to the center's main dining room where our presence was announced as "Dr. and Mrs. Michael Balzano of the White House Staff, and Alderman and Mrs. Vito Marzullo representing the Honorable William Daley, Mayor of Chicago."

The room was filled with luminaries. There were also the most prominent officials from the Nixon Cabinet. Colson and Attorney General John Mitchell introduced themselves to the Marzullos and told him how pleased and honored they were to meet such an important political icon. Their handshakes conveyed their respect and admiration to one who wrote the book on big city political machines.

As these individuals greeted Marzullo, they looked into his face and especially his eyes. No one gazed at his business suit in an atmosphere where formality was paramount. The only exception was John Ehrlichman. As he shook Marzullo's hand he could not help but gaze at the suit that Vito was wearing. After thanking Marzullo for all he had done for Nixon, Ehrlichman turned to me, deliberately gazing from my head to my toes as if to say, "Balzano, this is a formal event and you are not dressed!" He looked at both of us and said, "Mike has done an excellent job for the President."

When he walked away, Marzullo, a man whose knowledge of people would impress a clinical psychiatrist, said to me in Italian, "He looks at you like he's measuring you for the box."

I responded, "He is." [16]

During the dinner Colson told me that the president wanted Vito and his wife to view the Inaugural Parade the next day with him from the glass-enclosed reviewing stand in front of the White House.

Alderman Vito Marzullo, standing with the president reviewing the inaugural parade, visibly demonstrated the president's desire to solidify his relationship with the New Majority in his second term.

After the election, Colson handed me a file of memos from Pasztor and Volpe, both of whom expressed their discontent with the administration on hiring ethnics. The job fell to me to canvas ethnic fraternal groups around the country and to provide Colson with a strategy to present to the president.

My list contained three categories of names: first, the traditional Republican representatives in Washington, i.e., the Republican National Committee Heritage Division; second, group members who came to my office representing candidates they proposed to assist; third, qualified people I met while traveling around the country. Many of these groups believed that the administration preferred to hire people with similar backgrounds in business, Ivy League schools, and a host of other secondary characteristics, which placed them high in the economic and social strata of society. Elitism was believed to be typical of the Republican Party at the national level.

While there was a dearth of ethnic representation in the Nixon administration in general, the group that was singled out as most in need of representation in the administration was the Polish Americans. Not one Polish cabinet member or agency head could be found in the Nixon administration. While they were the least represented in the administration, they contributed heavily to the 1972 landslide. Both Democrats and Republicans saw the ethnics as a prize target of opportunity. Indeed, early in 1972 when Edmund Muskie appeared to be the front-runner, his campaign staff pointed out with pride that Muskie was the son of Polish immigrants.

From a historical perspective, Nixon should easily have captured the Polish vote, both because of his long-standing support for Poland and because of his strong anti-communist stance. The only real hurdle to bringing them into permanent alignment with the Republican Party was settling the ruffled feathers over the lack of Polish appointments. Colson immediately turned his attention to these supporters who felt abandoned and convinced the president that these Democrats should be given access to top positions in the second administration, thereby making a New Majority party a real possibility.

The President found particularly attractive the opportunity to bring some old-line Democrats into the administration. The president had respect for the old-line Democrats and felt that their experience and strength would enable him to move the federal bureaucracy more than his current managers. In short, Colson assured all of his staff that access to top-level positions in the second Nixon term for ethnics was guaranteed by the President himself. With this promise in hand, I struck out across the country to shake hands with leaders of ethnic groups, sealing the bond in the name of the President.

On election day 1972, I was in California when I received a call from Colson ordering me back to Washington, noting that Fred Malek had been assigned the job of staffing the new administration. Colson then said that in the next sixty days most high level government positions were going to be filled. He noted that if we wanted the New Majority to have a place in this administration, we needed to guarantee that they at least get in the door. He said that if everything worked the way it was supposed to, New Majority appointments would be sewn up by the middle of December 1972. A memo clearly outlining Colson's plans for bringing the New Majority into the Republican Party followed his call: [17]

> I am particularly anxious that we bring key labor leaders, Democrats, ethnic leaders into the new Administration.... We must not ignore them; we must bring them in, not only to ceremonial events like the Inauguration, but put them on committees, boards and in some cases to see that they are placed in full-time Administration positions.

I had already worked with White House Office of Personnel. They were good people but I feared that, with two exceptions, they would not be able to handle the cultural sensitivities required in dealing with members of the New Majority. The two exceptions were Jerry Jones and Stan Anderson. Jones was a natural when it came to understanding Middle Americans. He genuinely liked them. Jones had met with Lefty

Scumaci and Michael Rivisto from the Sons of Italy, and other union and ethnic leaders as well. Jones cautioned me not to alienate Malek's recruiters. They were professionals and had to be dealt with as such. He urged me to be patient and try to educate them concerning the sensitivities of ethnic candidates. Jerry said that in the long run we would secure ethnic appointments, perhaps not at cabinet level, but he was certain we would get some agency heads.

I began making lists of those New Majority members who we felt were worthy of cabinet-level posts. Then the trouble started. Cabinet appointments were made without our knowledge. It was apparent that the cabinet posts had already been promised and were being filled without input from the lists we were compiling. We were submitting New Majority candidates for positions that had already been filled.

By late November 1972, complaints began rolling into my office from leaders of my constituent groups inquiring about presidential appointments. I assured everyone that all was well, that it took time to process people for such high-level positions. But then came the weekly announcements from the White House of still more top-level positions being filled. By early December, my constituents were saying that the President had no intention of keeping his word. The moment I received that message, I warned Colson that the situation now called for his immediate action. On December 8, I sent the following memo to Colson: [18]

> Ethnic leaders are quite disturbed because the cabinet positions now announced reveal no ethnic representation . . . . It is essential that the agency directorships be given to ethnics. . . The New Majority was promised 'meaningful' participation in the Nixon Administration. Bureaucratic level jobs will do little for the President's image.

Colson gave me the memo he sent to Malek and told me to go back to Anderson and Jones and see if they could break the deadlock. [19]

> The cabinet positions are gone, but agency directorships remain. It is essential that we move with dispatch

to appoint highly visible recognized ethnics with clout
to direct a federal agency.

I met with Stan Anderson. He was sincerely trying to get ethnic appointments but told me that the recruiters were telling him that our candidates were just not strong enough for executive-level positions. He said that perhaps we could place them in civil service jobs. I explained that our candidates were fairly well off and were not looking for permanent jobs in the government.

Colson assured me that all was well. "We've lost a few cabinet posts to in-house people, but then some internal shifting around was to be expected. The president personally asked some of the cabinet people to shift to other cabinet posts. The important thing now is to focus on those under-secretary positions and agency heads. We'll be all right; don't worry."

Weeks went by and more appointments were announced. Still no ethnic names appeared. I took it upon myself to investigate the process, thinking that, like the cabinet posts, some other office was dealing with the remaining presidential appointments. I was wrong. White House personnel were assigned the action. The problem was that our New Majority candidates were competing with traditional candidates with the odds stacked in favor of the mainline Republicans. Our candidates admittedly did not have pedigrees comparable to the Ivy League, corporate management class. Our candidates were being thrown into the reject file marked, "good, but not heavy enough."

I talked with Rob Davison, one of the recruiters, asking him to explain why our candidates were unsatisfactory. I was specifically interested in one Polish vice president from a fairly large midwestern bank whose file was returned "good, but unsatisfactory."

"Well, I don't know what to tell you, Mike, other than he's just not heavy enough," Rob said with a pleasant smile.

"What do you mean 'not heavy?'" I asked. "He's a banker. He's handled millions of dollars. What do you want?"

Rob responded, "Well, it's the whole package, Mike. Sure, he's handled millions but other candidates have handled billions. The guy's history doesn't indicate a facility to function at the level required in this kind of a position."

The more we talked, the more I realized the importance placed on secondary considerations. Our candidate had not attended a prestigious academic institution. Moreover, he had gone to night school. I asked if his record didn't show that he was indeed an achiever. The response was that he showed promise but was not quite mature enough for a prestigious appointment.

Ethnics tended to view the most prestigious appointments as those made to the judicial branch, whether federal, circuit, district, or the Supreme Court. The one ethnic group absent from the federal bench was Polish Americans. The Polish lobby had great ambitions. Al Mazewski sent me a drawing he ran in the newspaper of his ethnic fraternal organization, the Polish National Alliance: [20]

By January of 1973 it was clear that our ethnic candidates were not being seriously considered regardless of their qualifications. There was no better example than the case of a West Coast Italian-American judge who had been offered as a candidate for a federal judgeship by the

Sons of Italy. As early as May of 1972, Michael Rivisto, the same man who helped us with San Francisco Mayor Alioto, came to my office claiming that qualified ethnics were excluded from high-level judicial appointments.

During the campaign, ethnic and prominent labor leaders from Washington, Oregon and California lobbied for a federal appointment for a sitting judge who served with distinction for eighteen years as a trial judge on the State Circuit Court of Oregon. He had been a faculty member of the National College of the State Judiciary, a graduate institution open only to judges with three or more years of trial experience.

Aside from his widespread knowledge and experience as a trial judge, he further distinguished himself by solving two major problems confronting the contemporary judiciary at all levels: trial disruptions and court management.

Given his background and given the number of influential supporters petitioning the White House on his behalf, we thought that he was an excellent candidate for the next federal judicial opening in his region. We assured the judge's supporters that the President would strongly consider the judge to fill the next vacancy, which turned out to be on the US Court of Appeals for the Ninth Circuit. We submitted the judge's name as a candidate.

In late January 1973, I received a call from Stan Anderson who informed me that the judge was disqualified because of his age. There was an unwritten law, Anderson continued, that a federal judge should be no more than sixty years old because of the mandatory retirement at age seventy, therefore our judicial candidate would only be able to serve for nine years instead of ten.

Without checking, I stupidly reported this to Michael Rivisto who was acting as a liaison for me with the judge's sponsors. Rivisto soon turned up in my office with a list of federal judicial appointments made over the past ten years, which clearly revealed that judges older than our candidate had been appointed.

Anderson told me that he was only empowered to offer the judge the Military Court of Appeals. I asked Stan, "What happened to the opening on the Ninth Circuit?" He responded that it was not in the cards.

I called the judge to make the offer. He was most polite in his refusal but stressed his desire to remain on the West Coast. Ultimately, he was appointed to serve on a presidential commission to revise the federal appellate court system. The commission was indeed prestigious and it gave the judge's supporters some satisfaction that they had secured something significant for a judge with an ethnic name. But it was in no way a fulfillment of the president's promise as articulated before the election.

By late December 1972, I could no longer answer my phone. Ethnics from across the country were pounding on my door crying, "Sell out!" Colson, realizing that we were up against an unseen palace guard, decided to go around the system and tell the president what was happening. According to Colson, the president listened with great interest and then asked to see a list of all appointments that had been made over the past weeks since the election. As he reviewed the list, he came across the name of a young lawyer who was quite active in the antiwar movement. The president remembered the man from earlier dealings with him when both men worked as lawyers in New York.

Colson used the opportunity to tell the president that White House recruiters had devised a scale that weighed the odds against the New Majority candidates. According to Colson, the president ordered that Colson meet with Malek and his entire staff immediately.

Twenty minutes later Colson's secretary called telling me to get my list of rejected ethnic candidates and be outside Colson's door in five minutes. To my surprise, Colson did not want to see me. Instead, he was taking me to what was to become a famous meeting between Colson and Malek's personnel operation. As we walked down the hall with hurried steps, Colson explained.

"There has just been an explosion in the Oval Office. The president is livid," he said. "I can assure you that after today we will have no further trouble with New Majority appointments."

The room was filled with Malek's staff. For a fraction of a second I felt somewhat embarrassed. I could see the look on the faces of lower-level staff members. They had that "Mike squealed on us" look in their eyes. The group sat in a horseshoe formation. Colson sat at the open end, Malek sat opposite him, and I sat next to Colson. Jerry Jones sat a few seats over from Malek. Anderson was on Malek's other side.

Malek opened up the meeting by saying, "We are here to talk about ethnic appointments." The mood was light and friendly. Staff members took notes. Colson opened the conversation by saying, "The president is very disturbed by the lack of cooperation from the personnel office with respect to appointing New Majority candidates to high-level positions in his administration."

Malek began talking about the procedures that were put in place to see that the most qualified people were selected to fill those positions. "We are looking at education and proven track records of all candidates and selecting only the best," he said.

Colson told the group that the president thought the criteria for selection was wrong and that he would be giving the staff new criteria. Colson posed a hypothetical case in which two candidates were being reviewed for a presidential appointment. One was a typical Republican heavyweight who had attended Princeton or Harvard Law School, had the right family and the right connections. He was probably worth a few bucks. The other one was different. He could not get into one of the Ivy League schools. In fact, he couldn't afford to go to school fulltime because he was busy working to support a family. Instead, he got his degree by working days and going to school at night, and had a position as vice president of a small but up-and-coming bank.

"Now," he said, pausing again to relight his pipe, "the president feels that our candidate is the kind of man he wants in the job because he is a hard worker and has not had the world handed to him on a silver platter. The president wants to see some new names and new faces in his administration. He wants to see names like Kobelinski, Walentynovicz, Sulmonetti; some ethnic names."

At this point Malek inserted, "You'll get ethnic names. But why do they have to be the names you submitted? We can find people with ethnic last names as well as anyone. There are lots of people who have ethnic last names who have made it in business, industry and in this administration—Germans, Italians, Poles, you name it. Why can't we take the credit for the ethnics already in government?"

"Fred," Colson said, "I didn't call this meeting. It's immaterial what either of us wants. I'm only delivering a message. The president wants ethnics in his second administration. But, what's more, he wants *these* ethnics," Colson said holding up our list of candidates, "because these are the people who supported the president." He noted that some of these people were lifelong Democrats who hurt themselves in their own party because they supported Richard Nixon. He said, "They were loyal to us. They kept their promises, and we are going to keep ours. We have presidential appointments to give out. These people are perfectly qualified to fill them."

"You know," Colson added, obviously remembering still another example, "we're not even keeping our own people on in the administration. I got a call from Don Santarelli the other day. He's returning to private life. I asked the guy why he wasn't staying on to help. He tells me he handed in his pro forma resignation like everybody else. Here it is December and the guy hasn't heard anything. He sees other people in the administration being given high-level posts. What would you think?" Colson noted that Santarelli was a brilliant and loyal and that the president, "needs him, wants him, and where is he? Out! Instead of loyal guys we get people who lead marches against the president!"

Colson repeated that the New Majority rallied around the work ethic and gave the president the largest political victory in history. "Now is the time for us to keep our promises to the New Majority," he said.

Malek then said, "Give your list to Jones, and we will reconsider all the candidates." He folded his notebook and whipped out the door. Both Colson and I believed that the issue of the New Majority appointments had been settled.

One day late in December, I received a call from another member of the White House personnel office who read a list of candidates for presidential appointments that was being sent to Haldeman for approval. Not one of our candidates was on the list. When I pressed him for their candidates' relationship with the Nixon campaign, he volunteered that he could not truly say whether or not these people had even voted for the president. He also said that he had been told that our list had been exhausted and that there were no qualifying ethnics among them. I wrote Colson a memo relating my conversation with the caller who was apparently new and was working in the personnel office over the Christmas holiday.

On January 2, 1973, Colson wrote a detailed memo [21] to Malek's entire staff, again spelling out the president's desire to bring the New Majority into the Republican Party during his second term, focusing on the achievements of individuals, not their social or academic credentials:

1) We are interested in placing members of the New Majority in visible high level government positions.

2) We are going to place those ethnics who are sponsored by organizations which have returned the

President to power, because the President promised to do so.

3) We will break with the past tendency to view
competence in terms of demonstrated manage-
rial capability and Ivy League credentials as the
chief indicator of a person's potential worth to
the President. We will substitute instead 'achievement' viewed in terms of a person's successful attainment of modest but impressive objectives in
the economic and social world. The idea here is
to give a successful small businessman and successful graduate of a less prestigious institution
of higher learning a chance to become corporate
giant material. In other words, instead of finding
'heavy weights,' we will take members of the New
Majority who show great potential and make them
'heavy weights.'

It is only through acts of good faith that we will retain
the New Majority in our camp. Hence, we are fulfilling
the President's promise to involve the New Majority in
his Administration at the highest level possible.

Colson sent a memo to Haldeman that was clearly designed to jam
the appointment mechanism. "It seems that from our list of some forty
odd names of prominent, loyal members of the New Majority, only two
are being considered for appointments and to date none have been
appointed." [22]

Apparently not getting the message, Malek wrote to Haldeman on
January 4, 1973, recommending two people for presidential appointments who had not come from the New Majority list.[23] The Malek
memo indicated that these people were highly qualified Italians.
Haldeman, still trying to get New Majority candidates from our list,
channeled the memo to Colson for comment. Colson was once again
horrified.

On January 8, 1973, Colson sent a memo to Larry Higby, Haldeman's chief of staff. In his memo to Higby Colson stressed that with a successful election behind us, now was the time to appoint people who would support the president's objectives. The names Malek submitted to Haldeman were people who were *not* on our list; in fact, no one could vouch for them as being loyal to the president. Colson ended his memo this way: [24]

> The kind of guys I would recommend to do it are the Balzanos, the Don Rodgers, the Don Santarellis, the Wally Johnsons; these are the guys who are just dying to do something with the second four years, not just to fill a box on an organizational chart.

I do not believe that Fred Malek or any of his staff of professional recruiters were deliberately trying to undermine the president's desire to appoint qualified ethnics into the Nixon administration. At the same time, Colson was approaching presidential appointments from Nixon's goal of broadening the Republican Party by bringing in those ethnic groups that did not have a seat at the table. Since I was caught up in this struggle, I was in Colson's corner. But I think that both Colson and Malek were doing their best to serve the president from their different vantage points.

While I have not worked with Malek in the private sector, I am aware of his reputation for being one of the best managers in America. Malek was probably doing what he does best, finding the best people to assume top positions of authority to run the government. His staff of recruiters was doing the same thing.

Jerry Jones understood the difficulty of trying to find qualified candidates to work in government. He was on board with Colson's mandate to identify people who could be built into heavyweights and was doing all he could to pursue Nixon's goals. Jones, who had run the personnel shop while Fred Malek was on leave to the campaign, was trying to bridge the gap between traditional recruiting and the importance of giving New Majority candidates an opportunity to participate in the administration at the highest level. He was trying to balance the mandate to build the New Majority and the need to have capable people running federal agencies and departments.

The struggle over presidential appointments that took place in the personnel office had a major impact in determining two appointments: Peter Brennan, the man most associated with the New York Hard Hat Demonstration in support of President Nixon's Vietnam policies, for Secretary of Labor, and my appointment to direct ACTION, the federal agency for volunteer service. Nixon made both of these appointments personally. Nixon's senior staff opposed the Brennan appointment because the position required someone with experience in managing a large bureaucracy. Brennan's experience was limited to the New York building trades. Nixon overrode his senior staff. Jerry Jones believed that if Brennan were supported with a cadre of seasoned people, he would be able to manage just fine. But it was clear from the beginning that the senior people in the White House did not want Brennan to be Secretary of Labor.

In the midst of my struggle with the White House personnel office, Colson told me that he would be leaving sometime after the Inauguration. He also said he had already spoken with the president and suggested that I would serve him best at the White House as the liaison with the New Majority. I was quite comfortable staying at the White House.

While at Key Biscayne with the president Colson formalized what was to be my new White House position. I was to stay in the Office of Public Liaison under the leadership of William J. Baroody, Jr., an assistant to Defense Secretary Melvin Laird who had agreed to become counsel to the president in the new administration. Many years later Colson told me that in a November 19, 1972, taped conversation with Nixon[25] the president had said that he was considering me, at one point, for the cabinet and that Colson had made a fervent appeal that I stay in the White House because I was the key contact that the president needed for all the ethnic groups and the Democrats. Out of the blue, John Ehrlichman proposed that I move over to the Labor Department as Brennan's right hand. Colson understood full well what Ehrlichman was up to and told the president.

Colson took me to lunch in the private White House executive dining room and told me that Ehrlichman was determined to push me out and did I want to reconsider a cabinet post. He said he had talked to Jerry Jones who told him I would be an excellent candidate for Director of ACTION. Again, I repeated my desire to stay in the White House. There were still some in the administration who preferred that I take a federal agency post, Caspar "Cap" Weinberger among them.

About two weeks later, Colson left the White House, and I was busy trying to set up a mechanism in-house to work with the New Majority. I soon began hearing rumors that John Ehrlichman was moving to clean out the rest of Colson's staff. At first I did not pay attention to this. But then from a very reliable source I heard that I was going to go to the Labor Department.

I called Secretary of Labor Peter Brennan late one night to talk over what I had heard. He acknowledged that he was making plans, as he put it, "to take you with me, Mike." I asked him where he got the idea. He said that he heard that was what I wanted. I told him that, with all due respect, my situation at the White House had been resolved and that the president had agreed that I was supposed to stay on and work with the New Majority. Brennan then began to express his frustration because he, too, was having trouble trying to get his own appointments through the White House personnel system. He said, "I need under secretaries and I want to pick them myself."

I spoke with Jerry Jones, who acknowledged that he was holding up Brennan's appointments. "Mike," he said, "he's going to need experienced people but he won't listen. He won't survive." I told Brennan I would work with Jerry Jones on his behalf. I then tried to find out who started the rumor that I wanted to leave the White House. The only one who knew anything about it was Dick Howard. Dick told me that there was a move on, by Ehrlichman, to get all of Colson's guys out and that the only thing we could do was to fight back and try to survive. I didn't want to tell Dick what was going on in my mind, but I could see the writing on the wall. Colson was gone and John Ehrlichman was housecleaning. I was convinced that Dick was not going to survive himself, let alone hold a staff together. Bill Baroody, Chuck Colson's replacement, had just come on board. He was trying to assess where things stood with the New Majority and how he should go about so-lidifying outreach to New Majority constituents.

As the days passed and the pressure built, I decided that no one in the White House Office of Public Liaison would survive without Colson. So the only thing for me to do was to go back to the earlier position, that is, to run a federal agency, using that agency as a vehicle to promote the president's policies. Jerry Jones told me that a great deal of groundwork had been laid for my appointment to ACTION weeks ago and that it would not be too difficult to get the ball rolling again. However, he let me know that John Ehrlichman had a candidate in mind for the position named Patricia Hitt, who was an assistant sec-retary at the Department of Health, Education, and Welfare and the highest-ranking woman in the Nixon Administration.

I told Jerry that if I could not stay at the White House I wanted the position at ACTION. He then threw my name back in the hat. The name was given to Stan Anderson and the whole process for a White House clearance began.

A few days later Jones heard from Stan Anderson that Patricia Hitt's name had been placed high up on the list as an active candidate for the job. The rumor once again began circulating around the White House that Balzano was going to be sent to the Labor Department.

The next day I got a call from Jerry Jones who said that Ehrlichman was now pressing to get Pat Hitt appointed. Ehrlichman called Jones and told him to rush the paperwork and the FBI clearances because he wanted to announce the appointment of a woman as an agency head. Ehrlichman told Jones that he thought they should go ahead and announce the appointment without the clearances. Jones responded that it was his understanding that Balzano was the administration's candidate for the ACTION agency and that he would not move forward on a clearance process without a memo from Haldeman. At that point Ehrlichman must have been desperate because someone, and no one knows who, leaked to the press the news that Pat Hitt was about to be named director of ACTION. The rumor circulated that it was Ehrlichman. When I saw the article about Pat Hitt, I knew what had happened. Ehrlichman was determined to send me over to the Labor Department.

Jerry Jones called me at about midnight that night and told me that Ehrlichman was now moving to nominate Pat Hitt because she had already been announced in the newspapers, she was an old friend of the president's, she represented a high-level woman appointment, and that it would be too embarrassing for the president to withdraw her name. Jerry agreed with me that Ehrlichman had leaked it to the press to create precisely the situation that he now claimed existed. Jerry told me whatever move I was going to make that it was now or never.

Early the next morning, after quite a bit of deliberation, I decided to create a crisis. I resigned. I wrote a letter to Bob Haldeman outlining all the reasons why I was resigning. I retraced all of my dealings with the White House staff, my inability to get even one ethnic appointment out of the White House personnel office, and my battles with the Domestic Council to obtain information on policies and appointments important to my constituency. I told Haldeman I was being pushed out of the White House even after the president told Colson and Ehrlichman that he wanted me there to continue my work with the New Majority.

Shortly after firing off my resignation, I called Peter Brennan, who was in Miami with Nixon. I told Peter that I had just resigned and told him the whole story. Peter, in turn, told the president that there had been a palace revolt at the White House, Balzano had resigned, and that the promises the president had made were being reneged on by the men around him.

The president called Haldeman and told him that he had learned that Balzano had resigned and ordered Haldeman to fix it. Haldeman, who was in Atlanta, called me saying that he was on his way back to Andrews Air Force Base and not to do anything until he got back. He said that he and John Ehrlichman were returning to Washington and that I was to leave the evening free for a meeting with them.

We met in Haldeman's West Wing office. Ehrlichman was all smiles. Haldeman was all business. He had a yellow pad that clearly had a line drawn down the middle separating what appeared to be pros and cons. "John," Haldeman said, "you want to deal with the ACTION agency issue first?"

Ehrlichman was very friendly. "Mike, a federal agency is a major corporation," he said. "What makes you think you are qualified to run ACTION?"

Good question, I thought, but Ehrlichman obviously did not know anything about my history other than at one time I had been a garbage man. "Well," I said. "First of all, I wrote my Ph.D. dissertation on the largest component of that agency and traced its history from the origin to the President's executive order creating it. Then the current director, Joe Blatchford hired me, to examine the structural changes that were required to bring all the different volunteer programs together into a single agency."

As I went on, Ehrlichman's face dropped. He realized he had asked the wrong question. Haldeman smiled and shook his head and said, "John, I think we've heard enough on this topic. Let's deal with Mike's relationship with the White House staff."

"Mike," Haldeman continued, "why do you say that the White House is working against your constituency?"

I had an indexed file on my lap and turned to the section dealing with ethnic appointments. I began to walk through each of the arguments the White House personnel office used to disqualify the ethnic candidates. I also detailed the meetings Colson had with the personnel staff, stating, restating and restating in meetings and follow-on memos to Haldeman the president's desire for ethnic appointments. I handed Haldeman the file. Ehrlichman was not smiling. Haldeman was again shaking his head. "Interesting," he said, marking his yellow pad.

"Mike," Haldeman said, "you think it's personal between you and John, don't you?"

"Yes," I answered. "John told Jerry Jones that he wanted to appoint Pat Hitt without first doing the required clearances. Then someone leaked her name to the press as the next director. It wasn't Jones."

I then turned to Ehrlichman and said, "Jerry asked you not to make that announcement but you did." I knew that I was way out on a limb making this accusation.

"Mike," Haldeman injected, "you claim to have had trouble getting information from John's staff on issues. Tell me about that."

Again I went to my file and spoke about the gun control and busing issues I was ordered to deal with by Colson. Haldeman nodded approvingly, then interrupted. "You seem to think that the opposition you encountered was personal," he said.

"Well, yes," I said, going to the middle of my file and pulling out the memo discussing my gathering information on the busing and gun control issues and concluding that something had to be done to reel me in. I offered Haldeman the memo from Ehrlichman's staffer criticizing my activity and referring to me as "an accident looking for a place to happen." Haldeman read the memo out loud. [26] He then laughed and said, "Oh, John. This is really sloppy."

Ehrlichman had his head down and was obviously defeated. I then went to the section of my file dealing with the president's intent to create a New Majority. Ehrlichman interrupted arguing that the New Majority strategy was just a campaign gimmick. "You think we're going to allow these people to come in and take over the Republican Party? These people are not our kind of people; they don't belong here."

Haldeman looked at Ehrlichman. "John," he said, "what are you saying? The president wants a New Majority to be a major part of the Republican Party. He says this all the time. Are you not listening to him?"

Haldeman closed the portfolio. "Mike," he said, "I appreciate your being so candid. We'll call you."

I was embarrassed for Haldeman, who finally understood how Ehrlichman, and probably others in the White House, really felt about the people that made up the New Majority.

When the president returned the following week, Jerry Jones called and told me that Haldeman approved my appointment to direct ACTION and that he was making a list of all the jobs available in the administration including ambassadorships for Pat Hitt. She told Haldeman that if she could not head ACTION, she would leave the administration. Believing that Nixon would never deny the request of a close personal friend of thirty years, and one who had been involved in his first congressional campaign, Hitt requested a meeting with the president. At that meeting Nixon explained that the ACTION appointment involved major considerations concerning promises he had made to a constituency that he sought to make a permanent part of the Republican Party. Nixon told her that she could have anything she wanted except that agency. She chose to leave the administration. All this was confirmed to me in a later conversation with Haldeman.

The more I have thought about that week over the years, the more I realize the seriousness of Nixon's commitment to the concept of the New Majority. His commitment to the New Majority was the focus of a presentation that I made at a Symposium on the Nixon Presidency sponsored by Hofstra University in 1987. The Hosftra event was the first time any of Colson's staff had spoken publicly about our work in the Office of Public Liaison. Following the Symposium I was invited to provide a written record of my oral presentation, which I subsequently shared with former President Nixon. Julie Eisenhower told me that her father read the chapter in one sitting. After completing it he wrote me a letter on that day. [27] His brief 1989 letter was prophetic. After thanking me for all the work I did in helping to build the New Majority, he lamented, "Had Watergate not aborted our efforts, we would have changed the political balance of power in the second term."

The New Majority and Watergate

On August 8, 1974, President Nixon resigned and Gerald Ford became president. I was still Director of ACTION, and remained so until January 20, 1977, when Jimmy Carter was inaugurated. In the Nixon White House the New Majority had been pursued primarily by two people, President Nixon and Charles Colson. Yes, there were others, Jerry Jones, Bill Baroody, who followed Colson as director of the Office of Public Liaison (OPL), and me. We all believed that the New Majority was the future of the Republican Party. But Watergate and the hearings aimed at impeaching the president as well as a special prosecutor bent on indicting all of Nixon's White House staff inevitably led to the loss of focus on solidifying the massive inroads we had made into Democratic strongholds throughout the Northeast and Midwest. The Watergate scandal destroyed any hope of achieving a political realignment of America's electoral landscape.

Bill Baroody clearly understood the potential of OPL and, following in Colson's footsteps, kept the structure of the Office of Public Liaison essentially the same. He had a good relationship with President Ford, but he did not have the access to Ford that Colson had had to Nixon. Moreover, the senior staff that Ford assembled, with the exception of Don Rumsfeld, did not fully understand what had to be done to continue to reach out to these new voter groups. I impressed upon Baroody the need for Ford not to veto the pension reform bill that Nixon agreed to sign in his promise to I. W. Abel, President of the United Steelworkers of America.

During the first month of his presidency, Ford appointed Leonard F. Walentynowicz to the head of consular affairs in the State Department. But almost immediately Ford's attention shifted to more pressing business.

There were three essential reasons why President Ford did not pursue the political opportunity Nixon had left behind. First, after the departure of Richard Nixon, the Ford Administration did not make pursuit of the New Majority a priority. This may in part have been due to Ford's enduring so much heat after the Nixon pardon. But Ford visibly moved away from most of the unions who had endorsed Nixon.

Second, even if Ford might have wanted to pursue the New Majority, some Republican congressmen and senators urged Ford officials to clean house of all Nixon appointees, including the most recent New Majority appointments. Secretary Peter Brennan was pressured to leave and did so in 1975. I was pressured to leave and did not.

Third, visible spokesmen of the New Majority at both the national and the state levels were being both persecuted and prosecuted. Watergate provided not only the opportunity for the Democrats to reverse the political gains made in 1968 and 1972, but also gave Democratic operatives license to attempt to criminalize policy differences. During the 1987 Hofstra University Conference on the Nixon Presidency, Tom Hayden, an antiwar activist, used the word "paranoid" to describe how he and other antiwar demonstrators felt during the trials of the more violent leaders of that movement. The national leaders of the New Majority felt similarly paranoid, that they were being hunted down by anti-Nixon federal prosecutors. Their fears were reinforced not only because they saw Nixon officials being sent to jail, but also because of the string of trials that were taking place across the country.

The public saw the most prominent of the Democrats for Nixon, John Connally, tried in a circus-like atmosphere concerning the "milk scandal." During the witch-hunt, in which Connally was investigated for his role in raising campaign funds from milk producers, we talked about his trial. He said that he was sure he would be vindicated because the entire affair was a show trial similar to what Stalin had conducted to clear the party of everyone who could challenge his rule. Connally said that the whole affair was staged by the Justice Department to keep him from running as a Republican in the next presidential election.

He also said something that I dismissed at the time but today believe with all my heart. He said that when an administration, state or federal, wants to convict you of a crime, they will find a way to do it. He referred to Stalin's show trials saying that Stalin once said, "Show me the man and I'll show you the crime." Connally was acquitted.

Largely outside the national media spotlight, indictments were sought against dozens of labor union presidents of major locals who had been publicly supportive of both Nixon's plan to end the war and his reelection. Word among the labor unions was that the anti-Nixon bureaucrats in the Justice Department had declared open season on Nixon's labor supporters. As with Governor Connally's case, most of the indictments ended in expensive trials in which the defendants were ultimately acquitted.

Often after expensive legal preparation, the cases were thrown out of court. Such was the case of Pennsylvania union leader Fred Gualtieri, business manager for Local 154 of the Boilermakers, who was indicted on charges of violating a provision of the Landrum-Griffin Act. When it became clear that one of the key factors in his indictment stemmed from a $40 charge for his wife's hairdo being inadvertently charged to his hotel room during a union convention, a federal judge threw the case out of court.

Gualtieri took no comfort in learning about the investigations of other union leaders who were active in Nixon's reelection. "Pretty soon they will be investigating the people who *voted* for Nixon," he said. Many of us saw an element of truth in that comment.

Jesse Calhoon and his organization were also targeted. According to Calhoon, his support for Nixon cost the union a fortune in administrative and legal fees to deal not only with the various grand juries, but also with audits from the Federal Election Commission, the Labor and Justice departments, and the IRS. Calhoon said that the visits by auditors were so frequent each week that he provided the auditors with office space. Some of the auditors were there for years. To eliminate confusion among Marine Engineers' Beneficial Association (MEBA) personnel that these auditors might be employees, Calhoon required the investigators to wear badges labeled "VISITOR." Despite the fact that Calhoon told each investigator that in its hundred-year history no MEBA officer had ever been indicted, let alone convicted, the investigations went on. After hundreds of thousands of dollars in legal fees, no charges were ever made that the union had done anything illegal.

At the state level, Democratic Party officials targeted prominent members of the New Majority. Such was the case with Robert D'Anniballe, a prominent Democrat from Steubenville, Ohio, whose confrontation with the Washington press corps outside a restaurant where Nixon was celebrating his wife's birthday was carried on the morning network news. His spirited defense of Richard Nixon cost him a contract with the Ohio state government as a consultant on emergency medical services.

New Majority labor leaders were even more horrified when they learned of the partisan history of their prosecutors. The overwhelming majority of those who served on the staff of the special prosecutor were highly partisan Democrats. In Colson's book *Born Again*, he noted this fact, adding that the attorney who brought him before the grand jury had been an unsuccessful Democratic congressional candidate and state chairman for Bobby Kennedy's presidential campaign. After watching the convictions and jail terms given to senior White House officials, and juxtaposing this with the random indictments of Nixon's union supporters around the country, many of the apostles of the New Majority began to feel like it was Good Friday without the promise of resurrection.

I, too, was terrified about what I saw as attempts to get even with anyone who worked for Nixon. On this point, Tom Hayden and I shared a paranoia. While I was director of ACTION, I was summoned as a witness before one of the many grand juries investigating White House activities. When told by officials in the Nixon White House that I was "on my own," I sought the advice of my close friend of many years, Hubert Humphrey. After some research, he told me I was "a pawn in a much larger game" and that "the special prosecutor would love to knock off an agency director, just as they had indicted and convicted Bud Krogh." Bud was, at the time, Undersecretary of Transportation. Humphrey continued that the hatred and bitterness arising out of Nixon's victory had created "a witch-hunt atmosphere." Further, he cautioned me against retaining a Republican law firm. "This is no time for a Republican law firm . . . witness or no witness, you'd better protect yourself," he said. With that, he arranged for me to be represented by one of the most prominent Democratic law firms in Washington, Kampelman, Harris and Shriver.

I had met Max Kampelman several times at Jeane Kirkpatrick's house. When I met with him about my situation, he wanted to know if I had been involved in anything that was illegal or unethical. I told him I had no knowledge of the Watergate break-in or in the coverup that followed. He agreed to represent me when I went before the grand jury. He advised me not to talk with anyone on the White House staff about the case, especially anyone who had already appeared or was about to appear before the jury. He said he would get back to me in a few days.

When next we spoke, he told me he had met with the legal staff on the prosecutor's team. He said they were frustrated because Colson's entire staff obviously loved him and if anyone knew about his involvement they were not talking.

When the Washington papers carried stories that Nixon officials were being sent to prison and that I was appearing before a grand jury, my father couldn't believe it. "How is it that you got out of New Haven without having trouble with the law and you're now facing legal trouble because you worked in the White House?" The irony of that statement still haunts me today.

Despite Max's warning, one afternoon I went to the home of Chuck

Colson to share with him the stories of New Majority leaders who feared persecution. For the first time, I shared with him my terror at being summoned by the grand jury and told him of Humphrey's advice and help. I had already made one appearance before the grand jury. It was clear that I did not have what the prosecutor wanted. It was equally clear, I said, that I would be called again. Colson then told me that all of the investigations of his staff would soon be stopped; that he was taking steps to halt what was obvious harassment of his staff. Before I left the house that afternoon, he told me to tell my wife, "Don't worry about it; everything will be fine. Next week it will all go away."

Early the following week Colson pleaded guilty to non-Watergate-related charges. Colson had given the special prosecutor what he wanted, a plea. But his plea was conditional. And that condition was that the special prosecutor would stop harassing all of the people on Colson's former staff. After Colson's guilty plea, I was never again called before the grand jury.

Colson was successful in halting the unfair persecution of his staff. But his guilty plea did *nothing* to halt the persecution of ethnic labor leaders across the country that were guilty of nothing more than having supported Nixon. To this very day, these leaders still talk about the "witch-hunt." In short, the partisan nature of the Watergate investigations of the New Majority and its leaders contributed to their disillusionment.

It has been some forty-plus years since the Watergate explosion blew apart all the pieces of the Colson staff. On and off throughout the years, some of us have gotten together and talked privately about what we experienced. But, until the 1987 Hoftra University Symposium on the Nixon Presidency, none of us had ever spoken publicly about the roles we played. The "witch-hunt atmosphere" contributed much to our silence. At the risk of still sounding paranoid, like many of Nixon's supporters, even today, I continue to believe that a fair number of those who served as prosecutors used the cloak of the legal system to pursue a course of partisan revenge.

Shortly after Colson left the White House, he was pursued by publishers guaranteeing him a best seller if he would write a book detailing the story of the New Majority and the role he played in its construction. Each time I asked him about the publishers' offers, he responded that he had more important things to write. He certainly did. His first book, *Born Again*, detailed his conversion, his decision to plead guilty, his incarceration, and his heartfelt desire to bring hope to those serving time in federal prisons. After leaving prison he established a prison ministry to share his Christian faith with inmates. He wrote numerous books on Christianity which have been translated into many languages, but he neither wrote nor spoke about the role he played in creating a political strategy that broke the back of the Roosevelt coalition.

Richard Nixon was not the last president to consider the pursuit of the New Majority. In 1980, candidate Ronald Reagan attempted to reassemble Nixon's coalition.

CHAPTER 5

Reagan and the New Majority (1980-81)

The Reagan Campaign

During the late summer of 1980 I rented a house at Virginia Beach where I took my family for a summer vacation. While watching the news one evening, I saw clips of Reagan's campaign swing through states in the Deep South. The next day, Richard Nixon appeared on the morning network news saying that Reagan's campaign was not focusing on those areas where unemployment made Democrats most vulnerable: the industrial heartland.

About three days later, Gabrielle Hills, my secretary at the American Enterprise Institute (AEI), called to tell me that a Mr. Stanton Anderson was trying to reach me. *"Stan Anderson, hmmm,"* I thought to myself, *"I haven't seen him since I left the Nixon White House."*

When I reached him the next day, he said he and Bill Timmons were working on the Reagan campaign and that my name had come up at a senior staff meeting. Reagan's campaign manager Bill Casey, who had been chairman of the Securities and Exchange Commission under Nixon, told the senior staff that Reagan called Nixon to talk about the comments he had made on the morning news show. According to Stan, Nixon told Reagan that he was delivering the wrong message to the wrong target and potential supporters in the wrong states. Nixon recommended that Reagan track down two people who had worked on his 1972 campaign. The first was Ron Walker, whom Nixon described as "the best advance man in the business."

He also gave Reagan my name because I had worked with industrial unions, blue-collar workers, and ethnic groups. I knew all the leaders who were part of Nixon's New Majority coalition, and Walker could structure events to manage the outreach. The goal, Nixon told Reagan, should be to structure the right message for the right constituency in the right region of the country.

Anderson told me that the campaign had settled on a person to take the labor desk. He was the lobbyist for the Air Line Pilots Association (ALPA), Robert Bonatati. Stan was not asking me to take a position with the campaign. Stan asked if I would meet with Bonatati and introduce him to my labor groups.

When I returned to Washington, I spoke again with Anderson and Timmons and said that I was willing to help on ethnic and labor issues but only as an advisor to their labor desk. Stan gave me Bonatati's office number at ALPA and said that Bonatati had not yet moved into the Arlington, Virginia, campaign headquarters.

I reached Bonatati the next day. Bonatati told me that there was some mistake; he had never agreed to work at the campaign office. I asked if that meant he would work out of the ALPA office. No, he said, he didn't think he would be involved at all. He asked what my role would be, and I told him I was willing to help whoever took the labor desk, but that my involvement would be limited. I later reported to Anderson about my conversation with Bonatati, and added that I had a strange feeling about the call. I told Stan that Bonatati did not sound that enthusiastic about the possibility of working for Reagan.

Later Stan confirmed that Bonatati wanted to help, but that the pilots union would not let him. Strange, he did not indicate that to me. Stan asked whether I would consider taking the job. I told him I couldn't leave the projects I was heading at AEI.

A few weeks later there was an announcement by the campaign that a state senator from Ohio agreed to take the labor desk. That announcement was quickly withdrawn when Ohio labor unions told the national media that the state senator was not a friend of organized labor, and the appointment clearly signaled Reagan would be hostile to labor. The absence of a labor chairman was becoming a problem for the Reagan campaign.

A few days later I met with Bill Casey, who said that Ronald Reagan was going to initiate a major effort to reindustrialize America, an effort that would create millions of blue-collar construction and industrial-base jobs overnight. "We have to get this message out to Middle America," Casey said. "Nixon said you were his point man on this issue. Your help now would be crucial." I shared all of these conversations with my wife, who urged me to take the labor desk.

In 1977, Bill Baroody had left the Ford administration to join the American Enterprise Institute. I had joined AEI as a fellow and was working on a project entitled "To Empower People." I spoke with Baroody about the calls from the Reagan campaign and my reluctance to take the labor desk. He urged me to take the labor desk and assured me that I would be able to return to AEI after the election. With Baroody's assurances, I called Anderson and asked him to set up a meeting with Bill Casey.

Bill Casey was an imposing man. His physical demeanor projected an air of "I'm in charge." Both of us had been Nixon appointees heading up federal agencies. Casey was a giant, both in the state of New York as well as in the financial community throughout the country. I was not on a par with him, but he was not condescending. He was most cordial and genuinely interested in my history with the New Majority. I told him that my strategy would be to reconstitute the same ethnic and industrial union coalitions that formed the bedrock of the New Majority during the 1972 campaign. My strategy with the unions would be to develop a jobs message and to take it into those industrial states where I had worked in 1972. We then discussed field operations. The Reagan field operation was excellent. It was headed by Bill Timmons, who had selected three top directors: Paul Manafort, Charlie Black, and Roger Stone.

Casey was an old hand and knew that inserting a labor effort into the campaign would generate some competition in vying for the candidate's time, and he promised to help me. I was already well ahead in terms of obtaining his cooperation and was somewhat reluctant to tell him I had one final requirement – I needed to meet Ronald Reagan before I took the labor desk.

"Meet him," he said, rubbing his eyes under his glasses as though his eyes were tired. "Before you start?" he asked. "Reagan has not met with any of the other staff members before they started." Casey kept rubbing his face, then readjusted his glasses and wrote something on his pad. He said he would do what he could to at least get me to meet "the Governor," as they called him.

The following week I was told that the Governor would meet me in Washington, at the Sheraton Carlton Hotel at the conclusion of a meeting he was having with a constituent group. Following Reagan's meeting with the group, he met with me in an adjoining room. "You're Nixon's New Majority guy," Reagan said with that broad, warm smile. I reminded him that we had met at the 1972 Republican Convention, when we were the only two people on a bus passing demonstrators outside the convention hall. During that ride we talked about my being a high-ranking Democrat in the Nixon White House along with John Connally, Patrick Moynihan, and John Scali. Reagan told me that he, too, was a traditional Democrat and added, "I didn't leave the Democratic Party; the party left me."

As we talked, more men entered the small room adjacent to the hall where he had given a speech. I recognized Ed Meese from television appearances, but none of the others who, I assumed, were part of the advance team and campaign staff. We moved the chairs into a small semicircle. Reagan sat at my left. He smiled and nudged my left arm saying, "I understand that I am supposed to ask you to work for me. Is that right?" A feeling of embarrassment coursed through me when I realized that my request was pretty gutsy. I tried to marshal an appropriate response and remember saying, "Well, Governor, I need to be honest with grassroots leaders when I tell them I know you personally and that you really want a relationship with them." Reagan told me that he felt a special relationship with the labor movement because he had been president of the Screen Actors Guild, a very powerful labor union, and that he had led a successful strike against the movie industry. He added that he was a lifetime member of the AFL-CIO and was given a plaque by the Federation bestowing that honor upon him. We talked about the unemployment of blue-collar construction workers and the skilled craftsmen in the prime, subcontractor, and supplier base, and its impact on the defense industrial base. Reagan said that he was prepared to strengthen the nation's defense industry as well as the construction industry and repeated what Bill Casey had said about the central goal of reindustrializing America – bridges, roads, in fact, every part of our industrial base. He then shifted to exactly how he would work with all constituent groups.

"I'm going to run this government like a business. I'm not going to make wild promises. You bring the labor issues to me; I will give them to Ed Meese," he said pointing to Meese. "Ed will be the chief policy person in my administration. When Ed agrees that those policies are in line with our objectives to get this country moving again, Ed will give those policy objectives to Marty." He pivoted to Marty Anderson. "Marty will run the numbers and make sure we can afford to undertake any of the programs in line with those policy objectives. When that is done, we will sign a memorandum of agreement to assure those constituent groups that we mean business. Once we know exactly what we are promising, our word will be in the form of a written agreement."

I stood up and said, "Every campaign I have ever heard of made promises with a hand shake, which was usually enough. But if your administration will go to that length to assure unions by making written agreements, the unions will surely be persuaded that Ronald Reagan is a man of his word." I shook hands with him and Ed Meese. Marty Anderson nodded and left.

I didn't know it then, but one of those written agreements would later be alleged to be an illegal act that resulted in an almost certainly illegal act: the air traffic controllers strike that occurred eight months into the Reagan presidency.

Following that meeting, I went to the Arlington, Virginia, campaign office and met briefly with Bill Timmons, who told me that Elizabeth Dole was nominally in charge of coordinating all of the outreach groups but the person most accountable to Bill Casey was Max Hugel. Since Hugel would be dealing with grassroots outreach, Timmons cautioned me to stay close to him and in no way get on his wrong side.

I met with Max later that day. From my perspective, he already had a good start. He had divided his staff by voter bloc constituencies, and he was eager to share how he was pursuing those blocs. He also said he was working with maritime unions on issues important to them. He did not tell me who he was talking to, so I did not push him on his union contacts. It was clear that Hugel was on top of his portfolio. Later I would discover how effective he was in dealing with one of the most volatile labor issues in the 1980 campaign, the Jones Act.

Shortly after I carved out some office space in the building, Don Rodgers, with whom I served on Colson's staff in the Nixon White House, joined the campaign. At the campaign office, I quickly deferred to Don's experience with both labor unions and campaigns. We agreed to divide our activities along the lines that matched our expertise. With Don it was the giant New York building trades unions and the construction industry in the Northeast. With me it was the steel-workers, boilermakers, and industrial-base unions that dominated the upper and central Midwest: Ohio, Pennsylvania, West Virginia, Illinois, Indiana, Michigan, and Missouri. The other areas that we agreed I would handle were the ethnic and fraternal organizations: the Italians, Poles, Slavs, Greeks, and the Captive Nations fraternal orders that were decidedly Republican. This group was the heart of Nixon's New Majority.

While Don focused on the issue of completing the abandoned Westway Highway in New York, I went to the heart of the New Majority, Steubenville, Ohio, the gateway to the New Majority and Middle America. The residents were pro-union, Catholic, patriotic, gun-owning Americans that college professors and the intelligentsia love to hate.

I quickly reestablished my New Majority contacts in Pennsylvania, Ohio, West Virginia, Illinois, Indiana, and Michigan: Bob D'Anniballe in Ohio, Lefty Scumaci in Pittsburgh, and Jack Burgess, who had worked with Laszlo Pasztor and the Captive Nations heritage groups. All were eager to help the anti-communist Ronald Reagan and get the country back to work. In a few days, I had reactivated key players in the Democrats for Nixon groups.

Don Rodgers, too, was in high gear. He assembled a group of sea-soned colleagues who, knew how to communicate with unions. Don recommended that his colleagues design a pamphlet that would focus on the jobs issue. The goal was to tell the labor community that a Reagan administration would mean jobs. The group felt that they had to deal with union concerns that a Republican president or his staff might attack labor's sacred cows. Specifically, labor feared that conservatives would repeal the Davis-Bacon Act that helped to maintain the prevailing wage rate in the construction industry throughout the country. Labor also feared that Republicans would attempt to create a national right-to-work law that would outlaw the union shop. The jobs pamphlet addressed all of these issues. The first part of the pamphlet [28] focused on Reagan as a labor leader. It stated that Reagan was a union president who, as Governor, dealt with unions in the public and private sector. The heart of the pamphlet dealt with Reagan's promises not to touch the sacred cows of organized labor. It raised specific issues and answered each of them.

1. Would Governor Reagan seek the repeal of OSHA? NO.
2. Would Governor Reagan seek a national right-to-work law and would he seek repeal of Section 14(b) of the Taft-Hartley Act? NO.
3. Would Governor Reagan extend antitrust laws to labor unions? NO.
4. Would Governor Reagan seek the repeal of the Davis-Bacon Act? NO.

The pamphlet closed with a strong message to a country suffering from unemployment and a president who was seen as weak on defense. The final message of the pamphlet was powerful and meaningful to union leaders:

Elect a former Union
President, President.

Once the group of labor leaders agreed on the issues that would be highlighted in the pamphlet, the draft would be vetted by senior staff at the campaign. We knew conservative economists would be outraged at the thought that Ronald Reagan would support the continuation of the Davis-Bacon Act, and really outraged that a Reagan administration would not seek a national right-to-work law. Bill Casey, a savvy New Yorker, understood that the votes of union workers were vital to a Reagan victory and that they had to be offered some tangible evidence that Reagan was not going to strip them of protections they had enjoyed for decades. The pamphlet was a written promise to that effect.

A draft of the pamphlet was presented to Bill Casey, who gave it to Ed Meese, Marty Anderson, Bill Timmons, and Bob Gray, communications director of the campaign. Despite the reservations of the conservative economists, the pamphlet was approved as presented. The provisions of Davis-Bacon and right-to-work were left intact. I accompanied Ronald Reagan on a five-state swing through the industrial heartland, where we distributed the pamphlet to New Majority groups. Wherever Reagan appeared, the reporters who accompanied him had the pamphlet in their hand.

Carter's Secretary of Labor, Ray Marshall, said that the pamphlet was a deception and that no Republican would agree to its content. That gave our pamphlet national recognition and created requests for more pamphlets.

Reagan and the Maritime Unions

About two weeks after I set up shop in the campaign office, but before the labor pamphlet had been completed, I received a call from Jesse Calhoon, president of the Marine Engineers' Beneficial Association (MEBA), asking if I could meet with him in his office in Washington. Having heard stories about him from Colson, to me, Jesse was a legend.

Jesse opened that first meeting saying that, although we had not met during my time at the White House, he knew a great deal about me. He said that Chuck had told him that I would likely be his successor in the Office of Public Liaison in a second Nixon term. He admitted that he had lost track of me when I went to the American Enterprise Institute, but said he was pleased that I was taking the labor desk at the campaign.

I asked Jesse if he was considering endorsing Reagan. He rolled the ever-present cigar in his mouth and only removed it to say, "Not yet."

He said he had attended a meeting that maritime and ship operators had with Reagan at the Sheraton Carlton Hotel a few weeks earlier. Jesse said that at that meeting Reagan made very positive statements about reviving the maritime industry. He said he was not surprised that Reagan would support an industry that was so vital in wartime. In fact, there was an issue paper distributed at the meeting that clearly stated Reagan's intention to rebuild the maritime industry in the same way Nixon did. Calhoon then gave me that document. [29]

Jesse's concern was that Reagan was too close to extreme economic conservatives, who were free traders and globalists and who did not have Reagan's historical perspective of two world wars. I asked what he needed to hear from Reagan to consider an endorsement.

"Mike," he said in a soft voice. "There are three issues. The first is the Jones Act." The Jones Act required that any ship leaving an American port for another American port be built in a US shipyard, manned by an American crew, and repaired at an American shipyard. Given the subsidies paid to maritime companies in most industrialized countries, without the Jones Act there would have been no American maritime industry.

The second issue was Reagan's commitment to continue Nixon's ban on exporting Alaskan oil to anywhere but the lower forty-eight states, which was then guaranteed to be carried on American ships under the Jones Act. The ban Nixon had placed on Alaskan oil being exported internationally would have expired in September 1983[30] and, to protect the American tanker fleet, had to be renewed.

The third issue concerned using civilian merchant crews to man military cargo ships. All during the campaign, Reagan publicly stated his intention to build a 600-ship Navy. That goal would require dramatically increasing Navy personnel. As part of this buildup, Reagan stated his intention to man Navy cargo ships with licensed deck officers, marine engineers as well as unlicensed merchant marine crews and cargo handlers. Jesse said it would be similar to the old Army Transport Systems of World Wars I and II. The Army would simply lease the merchant cargo vessels, crew and all. Often the Navy put a captain and small crew of Navy personnel on the ships. For all practical purposes, the civilian crews were in the Navy.

Jesse said that he was comfortable with what Reagan was saying about rebuilding the civilian merchant fleet but again stated that Reagan would have to state clearly his position on the Jones Act as a first step for any endorsement.

Jesse then shifted topics to other unions that I should approach. He mentioned the Professional Air Traffic Controllers (PATCO) union and the Professional Air Systems Services (PASS), the technicians who worked the takeoff and landing of commercial aircraft at all the major airports. He said the leaders of these two unions had offices right in MEBA headquarters at 444 North Capitol Street. But he insisted that I not meet with them that day. He said he would suggest to Robert Poli, the president of PATCO, that he should call me. I was surprised that he did not want me to talk to these leaders while I was there in the building.

I later learned that both unions were affiliated with MEBA, but that the terms of the affiliation stated that MEBA could not act for PATCO and vice versa. Apparently, Calhoon wanted to maintain sufficient distance from PATCO to avoid the perception that he was speaking for PATCO.

I reported Jesse's comments on his approval of Reagan's overall support for the merchant marine industry as well as his concerns over the Jones Act to retired Rear Admiral Robert Garrick, who was on Ed Meese's staff. Garrick reported to both Meese and Casey and was my principal ally in the Arlington office.

Garrick said that Jesse was right about the opposition that Marty Anderson and other conservatives would have to the Jones Act, but said that he and Max Hugel were talking with someone who was working back channel and that Casey was on top of this issue. I later learned that Hugel, with Casey's approval, had agreed to get Reagan to support the Jones Act. Garrick then said it would be better for me to stay away from the maritime issues because he believed that Hugel had those issues covered. He said that the most important priority for me was to get the campaign pamphlet out to my New Majority constituencies. I also told Garrick that Jesse suggested that we meet with Bob Poli, the president of the air traffic controllers union. Garrick was eager to meet with Poli because he knew a great deal about the aviation industry from his years as an admiral; he wanted to be a part of any discussion I had with Poli.

Later that week I received a call from Robert Poli, who referenced my meeting with Jesse Calhoon and said he wanted to meet with me. I told him I would come to his office.

In terms of appearance, Calhoon and Poli were very different. Poli was about my age at the time and at least ten to fifteen years younger than Jesse. He was a good-looking man and quite masculine. He had bright blue-green eyes that looked like they belonged to a Siberian husky. Unlike Jesse, who sat perfectly still throughout our meetings, Poli was really Italian. He reminded me of me. He spoke very fast, punctuating his points with exuberant hand gestures. Having been around people like him in my youth, I was very comfortable with his style. He was passionate about his cause, and he spoke from his heart.

Poli said he knew of my work with Nixon and would feel comfortable meeting with me in the campaign office. He immediately announced that PATCO would not support President Carter. The question was could they support Reagan. Almost immediately Poli began to unload all of the grievances the union had concerning its federal employer, relating the history of its relationship with the Federal Aviation Administration (FAA). "It's the worst employer in the federal government. They treat their workforce like dirt," he said. He mentioned the 1970 sickout "strike" that resulted in the suspension of nearly 1,000 controllers and the firing of fifty-two. Later, at Nixon's insistence, the fifty-two were re-hired.

The major grievance Poli had with the rehiring of the controllers was that the issues and grievances that led to the walkout were never resolved. Poli was emphatic on this point. "The controllers were re-hired," he said, "but the grievances were never resolved." He described the controllers as intelligent, dedicated men and women, many of them former military who were disciplined and eager to work with management but who were shut off at every turn. He talked about the conditions and the environment in which controllers work. Controllers work in a dark room looking at a large round, lighted scope watching numbers cross a screen. These numbers represent aircraft moving across the sky at different altitudes and speeds. The controllers communicate with pilots in these aircraft and direct them in order to avoid collisions. When a flight reaches a certain point where an aircraft is moving out of the geographic range of a given center, the controller hands that flight over to the next center in accordance with the flight plan of that particular aircraft.

Poli insisted that to fully understand what air traffic controllers face, "You have to see this for yourself." I agreed to accompany him to a center. A few days later we visited the center in Leesburg, Virginia. I was guided into a dark room illuminated only by the large kettle-drum-shaped computer screens. I watched a controller talk with a pilot he identified by the flight number that slowly crossed the screen. All I could think of was without this voice coming from a black hole in Leesburg, the pilot would never be able to see any of the aircraft advancing toward him or know whether he was sharing the space with numerous other aircraft flying above or below him. Even I could feel the tension. These were not just numbers on a screen. They were thousands of passengers who might be having lunch or dinner on a flight, totally unaware of the controller who had their life in his or her hands.

Then Poli asked one of the controllers to describe a computer crash. "Computer crash?" I asked. "Oh yeah," Poli said, "these computers are almost two decades behind the state-of-the-art computers that are used by all European and Canadian counterparts." When a computer crashes, controllers must rely on their memory of where an aircraft was, its speed, altitude and direction, while the machine was quickly serviced. In such a case, the adjacent controller picked up that portion of the sky and guided the pilots.

"Why does the scope go black?" I asked. Poli again explained that the computers were sub-standard. "This computer," he said, pointing to the one in front of the controller, "is not even made anymore. It's so old it still uses vacuum tubes. In fact, the FAA is the only customer for the company that still manufactures vacuum tubes. Modern computers do not use vacuum tubes. The computer world went to transistors twenty years ago."

"Wow," I exclaimed. "Why don't we have modern computers? Is it a cost problem?" Poli responded that modernizing the computers was not a priority for the FAA. There were billions of dollars sitting in the Airway Trust Fund whose purpose was to modernize equipment and facilities.

"Every time you buy an airplane ticket you pay a tax that goes into that fund," Poli said. "There are billions of dollars in that fund, but the Carter administration will not spend them, because it is using the fund to balance the federal budget."

Poli then focused on the medical conditions common among controllers, including hypertension. Controllers were forcibly retired by FAA physicians all the time. "Once they are removed," he said, "they can't even go to another federal job because they are considered neurotics. They are tossed on the scrap heap." If a controller had a runny nose or a cold on a workday, they were not allowed to take any medication. "No Dristan, Contact, aspirin; nothing that could affect their mental acuity. They are sent home," he said. He then added, "All this increases the stress on the nervous system. That's why our people burn out."

He explained that controllers in Europe were required to work only thirty-six hours a week to guide fewer aircraft than fill the skies in any American city. "Some of our controllers are working sixty hours a week," Poli said.

During the next week Bob Garrick and I reviewed with Poli the issues that compelled him and his membership to turn to Governor Reagan for help. Poli never wavered from his list of grievances. The computers and air traffic control electronic equipment needed to be upgraded. Garrick understood that the computer crashes were totally unacceptable. The thought that the system was relying on vacuum-tube technology was almost impossible to comprehend. Besides, Reagan would surely expose how the Carter administration was balancing the federal budget by compromising the safety of the flying public.

Garrick agreed that the administration had to deal with the stress on the controllers emanating from compulsory overtime. In this instance all we had to go on was Poli's assertion that vacant positions were being filled not with new controllers but by depending on mandatory overtime by the existing workers. To solve this problem Poli sought an increase in the number of controllers. Again, Garrick believed that a Reagan administration, through careful due diligence, would assess the staffing workload and make adjustments in line with the safety of the flying public.

A key to all of this was Poli's belief that a new administration would carefully assess the problems and propose legislation where necessary to correct them. PATCO had excellent relations on the Hill and was no stranger to the legislative process. In light of that, Poli asked for access to the new administration's legislative policy staff, so that PATCO could make recommendations on both the draft policies and the strategy for using PATCO's congressional allies to pass needed reforms.

Garrick and I saw no problem with Poli's request. In fact, it could be an advantage for administration policymakers who might not have the background or experience dealing with the personalities on the relevant committees. Having a public employees union lobbying with the administration would make it easier to obtain support for policy initiatives. However, Poli's request for input carried with it a major concern. Pay scales for federal employees are set by law. They are not controlled by the administration. Poli assured us that their allies on Capitol Hill would side with pay increases. Poli was seeking parity with the postal workers who, because of their quasi-public status, had more flexibility than other federal workers.

Poli also insisted that the bureaucrats at the FAA would never stop throwing roadblocks at PATCO. They would work behind the scenes to confuse the issues so that a new and unsuspecting administration would not be in control. Poli was therefore requesting the right to strike "in certain circumstances." The only circumstances Garrick and I could envision that would cause the union to want to strike were if the controllers were forced to continue to work with inferior equipment or were forced to work so much overtime that they would endanger the flying public.

Garrick and I talked about the right to strike clause and reasoned that that situation would never arise. After all, PATCO would have the ability to consult with the administration at a variety of levels to correct any policy that might not be in harmony with the promises stated in a letter of understanding that we would subsequently draft.

In our view, PATCO would succeed because Ronald Reagan and his administration would stand behind promises we made.

Poli also raised the idea of privatizing the air traffic control (ATC) system. Poli pointed out that the ATC systems of Europe were not run by the government but were private sector companies. Poli said that there was considerable sympathy for this model on Capitol Hill. Garrick said that Ronald Reagan would look with favor on privatization and would bring that issue before Reagan's senior policy advisors. A few days later, Garrick said that the administration would be dealing with a variety of pressing issues and, while Reagan would support a private sector air traffic control model, he could not deal with that issue during the first year of his administration.

Poli offered another approach. He asked whether Reagan would support a bill to privatize the air traffic controllers, if PATCO were able to have it introduced and could get the votes to have it passed Garrick said, "Yes, if PATCO promoted the idea that led to the introduction of a bill, the administration would not oppose it." This was a major commitment that the administration later violated, and it was one of the elements that led to the air traffic controller strike of August 1981.

I advised both Poli and Garrick that there were a lot of issues being discussed, Garrick agreed and concluded that the privatization idea should not be included in any written promise, as it could generate opposition to other issues the administration needed to address, especially in the area of rebuilding our national defense. Having had the benefit of living in Washington longer than Garrick, I told him of a Nixon attempt to privatize the National Weather Service. Local news television stations had strongly opposed the idea, which quietly died.

Garrick and I agreed not to mention the privatization issue in a letter of understanding with PATCO. Poli also agreed.

The letter of understanding that later emerged from Reagan's policy staff contained most of the key provisions important to PATCO: the replacement of the current FAA administrator, with PATCO to be given reasonable opportunity to recommend a replacement along with the ability to reject a nominee; the replacement of outdated equipment in the centers; Reagan's commitment to reduce controller hours commensurate with safety of the flying public; and PATCO being given reasonable opportunity to advocate their positions to appropriate members of the Reagan administration on proposed legislation *prior* to the administration taking a position on such legislation. Finally, the letter of understanding included the most controversial position of all, it gave PATCO the "right to strike in certain circumstances." PATCO's attorney incorporated these provisions in a letter of understanding addressed to me, combined with a commitment to endorse Reagan if the campaign agreed to the provisions. The letter did not request a signature or request a written response by the candidate.

Garrick and I agreed that most of Poli's concerns named in the letter would be easily addressed, because all PATCO really asked for was its day in court. Following our meeting to clarify these issues Poli left, saying that he had to get the approval of his board for the plan. In the meantime Don Rodgers and I prepared to take our show on the road.

The Campaign Run

During September 1980 we did a great deal of work. Don Rodgers alerted New York construction unions that Reagan would complete the Westway Highway, a project that would put to work every union in the construction industry in New York as well as other surrounding states. I reached out to the steelworkers and boilermakers in Pennsylvania, Ohio, West Virginia, Indiana, Illinois, and Michigan. At the same time, I reconnected with the ethnic communities in those states: Italians, Greeks, Poles, Lithuanians and all who counted themselves members of the Captive Nations. Prominent among them was Polish National Alliance president, Al Mazewski, and members of the Captive Nations media. Members of the Captive Nations were strong anti-Communists who believed that the Carter administration was weak on national defense and had lost Iran by undermining the Shah and ensuring the creation in that country of a Muslim caliphate.

As we got ready to distribute the Reagan pamphlet, we began to target a number of strategic cities at the heart of the Democratic Party's blue-collar stronghold along the Atlantic seaboard and in the Midwest. Middle America had the lion's share of those constituencies that once were the bedrock of the Democratic Party. They were

Christians, usually Catholics. They were gun owners and target shoot-ers who cherished their Second Amendment right to bear arms. They were pro-life in accordance with their faith, pro-defense and decidedly anti-communist. These were the voters we pursued. We targeted the family that drove to church on Sunday in a pickup truck with a rifle rack on the back window.

Our strategy was to begin a series of campaign events at which Reagan would start a drumbeat that would echo throughout America's heartland. Our cry was jobs, jobs, jobs: construction jobs, defense jobs, aerospace jobs, jobs from building a 600-ship Navy. Rodgers and I saw "the run," as we called it, as a series of stops that would coincide with union endorsements just weeks before the election. It is important to note that, before starting the run, not one labor union had endorsed Ronald Reagan.

We began "the run" in New York City where Reagan announced his intention to complete the Westway Highway. From New York, Reagan made a strategic stop in New Haven, Connecticut, where Reagan vis-ited Wooster Street and the Santa Maria Maddalena Society of New Haven, an organization that was established by the Italian work-ing-class residents who came through Ellis Island in the late 1800s. Reagan addressed not only the Italian community from the portico of the building housing the Society, he also stopped at two neighborhood eateries, Pepe's, where he ate some pizza, and Libby's, where he had a lemon ice. Later, Ralph Marcarelli, one of the officials of the Society, brought a large tray of Libby's famous Italian cookies to the campaign airplane for the staff and press corps.

From New Haven, the campaign tour went to Pittsburgh, where the New Majority unions led by Fred Gualtieri and Lefty Scumaci gathered construction workers, boilermakers, and steelworkers to hear Reagan's promise to reindustrialize America. Marlene Beck, the Meals on Wheels assistant director for the Lutheran Social Services in Pittsburgh, coordinated the event.

We then went to Steubenville, Ohio, where Robert D'Anniballe assembled an enormous crowd to endorse Reagan's plan to revive the steel industry in Ohio, Pennsylvania, and West Virginia. D'Anniballe had been a strong supporter of Richard Nixon and had appeared on national news shows to defend President Nixon during the Watergate controversy. D'Anniballe had assembled a group of steelworker union presidents up and down the Ohio River into a coalition called "Save Our Steel."

Moving from Steubenville, we went to Youngstown to participate in a meeting with steelworkers from that community. Ron Walker did the advance work for the meeting, and met the limo wearing a hard hat. It was the first time I had seen Ron since the Nixon event at the Statue of Liberty. At the Youngstown meeting, Reagan focused on buying American products and once again committed his administration to re-industrializing America.

As we left the neighborhood, we saw a large flatbed trailer parked in a lot up the street with just two steelworkers carrying a large Jimmy Carter sign; two steelworkers on a platform that could have held sixty men. Lyn Nofziger leaned over to me and said, "It's over. If the steelworkers couldn't muster a crowd of protesters beyond two people, it's over."

Reagan jumped out of the limousine and quickly walked up to the two men telling them he wanted to save their jobs and reindustrialize America with American steel. The two men put the sign down and shook hands with Reagan. It was clear to me that at the rank-and-file level, Carter was finished. The question was, would we get any international unions to endorse Reagan beyond assurances from locals in Pennsylvania and Ohio? Our question was answered when we arrived in St. Louis where Reagan was to address the maritime unions.

In St. Louis, the last stop on "the run," we began to get major endorsements. Union leaders from the Missouri Carpenters Council, accompanied by leaders from the Pipefitters Union, one of the most prominent unions in the Midwest, started the ball rolling. Reagan was engaged in addressing a giant rally on the levee overlooking the Mississippi River. Here, Ron Walker allowed me all kinds of liberty. Unannounced and unplanned on the schedule, Ron agreed to let me lead a small group of union leaders through the crowd and climb the podium to hand Reagan a hard hat plastered with American flags, a symbolic gesture that said, "the carpenters are with you." Ron and I had come a long way from the tension that I caused his staff at the opening of the museum at Liberty Island.

The series of endorsements Reagan received from union locals as we moved through Pennsylvania, Ohio and Missouri was damaging to Carter. But the greatest damage occurred when the National Maritime Union reversed its endorsement of Jimmy Carter that had been made only one week earlier.

As previously stated, the maritime unions, especially Jesse Calhoon, were concerned with preservation of the Jones Act. Jesse made it clear that any endorsement of Reagan would first have to settle the issue of the Jones Act. In Ronald Reagan's position paper presented at his meeting with maritime industry and union leaders at the Sheraton Carlton Hotel on September 15, 1980, Reagan did not mention the Jones Act. There was no way that Marty Anderson, Reagan's chief policy advisor on economics, would have supported any statement that endorsed the Jones Act.

Nevertheless, and unknown to me, there was a back-channel strategy being worked to include an endorsement of the Jones Act in Reagan's speech to the National Maritime Union convention that would shock the campaign. Three men had conspired to keep the Jones Act out of any discussion at the Arlington, Virginia, campaign headquarters: Andrew E. Gibson, the head of the Maritime Administration under Nixon, Tom Schaaf, a maritime consultant, and Max Hugel, the head of Reagan's voter bloc groups and the closest campaign operative to Bill Casey.

Reagan's visit to St. Louis coincided with the national convention of the National Maritime Union (now part of the Seafarers International Union of North America). During the summer, President Carter had begun calling labor leaders, urging them to support him for another term. National Maritime Union president Shannon J. Wall assured President Carter that the union was solidly behind him. But Tom Schaaf and Max Hugel were dangling a commitment to support the Jones Act as part of Reagan's maritime strategy. Anderson was on the campaign flight to St. Louis, but had no clue about what Hugel, with Casey's blessing, was up to. Hugel decided not to go on the campaign flight. If he had, it would have raised a question about why he was there. Instead, Tom Schaaf gave Hugel his plane ticket, which it was possible to do in those days, so that Max could travel alone, get to St. Louis, and shepherd the Jones Act through the process to gain the National Maritime Union endorsement for Reagan and a reversal of their earlier endorsement of President Carter.

Reagan's copy of the speech on the campaign plane made no mention of the Jones Act, but Lyn Nofziger had a different draft of the speech prepared. In St. Louis, Reagan appeared before what was thought to be an unfriendly crowd and brought the house down with a ringing endorsement of the Jones Act:

> The principle that a nation's own ships should carry its coastal trade, presently embodied in the Jones Act, had been part of this country's maritime policy since the early days of the nation. I can assure you that a Reagan administration will not support legislation that would jeopardize this long standing policy or the jobs dependent upon it. [31]

In a tumultuous cry from the floor of the convention, Shannon Wall accepted the will of his members and agreed to reverse the endorsement of President Carter made only a week earlier and instead endorsed Ronald Reagan right then and there. Reagan went on to commit his administration to utilizing the merchant fleet by allowing merchant ships to carry military cargo as they did in World Wars I and II. Further, he criticized Carter for ignoring the advantage of using this vital asset to support the regular Navy:

> I know, and you know, that the maritime industry can assume many Navy support functions. It will save the Navy money, and it will release trained sailors to man the new ships my administration will build for the fleet. This kind of integration and cooperation will strengthen our defense, strengthen our maritime industry, and provide the American taxpayer with the most for his money. [32]

Carter had not had any contact with Jesse Calhoon or MEBA during his entire four-year term. Hence, when Carter called Jesse to talk about an endorsement, Calhoon told him he would be supporting Reagan.

Union Endorsements for Reagan

Reagan's support of the Jones Act was the down payment Calhoon was waiting for. Calhoon endorsed Reagan and also published a color booklet for MEBA port agents to distribute to union workers nationwide. The booklet, entitled "Reagan-Bush - A New Beginning for America's Maritime Industry," [33] featured a photo of Reagan and Bush linking arms and waving. The booklet contained all of the key points made in the October 8 St. Louis NMU address.

The next two endorsements were striking and shook the union world. Frank E. Fitzsimmons brought in the massive Teamsters Union, believing that Jimmy Carter had destroyed the country and our national security. Fitzsimmons endorsed Reagan without asking for anything in return. The two major endorsements for Reagan, the Teamsters and MEBA, were significant because of the message they sent to the rest of the labor movement.

In Jesse Calhoon's case, it was clear that Reagan's announced intention to preserve the Jones Act, as well as his support for civilian manning which would require the Navy to partner with the US merchant fleet, clearly meant the preservation of the US maritime industry. Reagan and Calhoon saw both of these policies as necessary to preserving US national security, especially in the face of an expanding Soviet Navy and commercial fleet. Calhoon could explain his endorsement of Reagan in terms of jobs for his members.

After the MEBA endorsement I fully expected that PATCO would also endorse Reagan. PATCO had by then drafted the letter of understanding [34] between PATCO and the campaign. We had already talked with the senior campaign staff about the issues of concern to the air traffic controllers, and no one seemed concerned about any of the issues. Poli delivered the letter to Bob Garrick and me, and Garrick passed it along to Casey and Meese.

The most controversial position in the letter of understanding was that it gave PATCO the "right to strike in certain circumstances." Again, both Garrick and I agreed that this was a provision that would only be used by the union if all negotiations with the FAA had failed over an issue that involved public safety. For example, what if the computers were not operating properly? What if the number of blackouts began to interfere with a controller's ability to handle the aircraft? What if the FAA refused to replace the antiquated computers currently in use, endangering public safety because they lacked the technical capability to make split-second decisions? In those situations the union might not have any recourse but to stop work, and appeal to the Reagan administration for help. No other reason for a strike, in our minds, could be justified. If the air traffic controllers approached the administration for help, surely Reagan appointees would assess the situation and fix the problem before a strike would be necessary. It was inconceivable that a strike would be called.

To assure himself of a close relationship with a Reagan administration, Poli agreed to endorse Reagan in front of one of the air traffic control centers in Florida. The day before Poli's endorsement, I called Bob Bonatati, the lobbyist for the Air Line Pilots Association, to see if the pilots might join PATCO and also endorse Reagan. I felt comfortable calling him because he had been slated to be the labor liaison for the Republican campaign. He expressed shock, saying that he would have to talk to ALPA's president. Shortly after I talked with Bonatati, J. J. O'Donnell, the president of ALPA, called Poli urging him not to endorse Reagan because it would split the unions in the airline industry. O'Donnell told Poli that ALPA was going to play it safe and not endorse either candidate. Poli responded that he had commitments from Reagan in writing to assure PATCO that he, Poli, was doing the right thing for his members.

That same night I flew down to Florida with Poli. When Poli told me about the call from O'Donnell, I asked, "Are you still okay?"

Poli replied in a very self-assured manner, "Yes. I told him I'm going to endorse." As Poli spoke, I reflected on the conversation I had had with Stan Anderson a few weeks earlier describing my phone call with Bonatati in which he declined to be the labor liaison for the Reagan campaign. Despite Poli's confidence, I found the implication of this series of conversations troubling.

On the day of the endorsement Poli and I traveled together in the limousine with Reagan. Reagan thanked Poli in advance of his endorsement and assured him that the controllers would have an open door to the White House on all of the issues important to PATCO. I also brought Poli a letter signed by Reagan affirming that commitment and recognizing the need to address the "deplorable state of our nation's air traffic control system."

I was unconcerned with the PATCO situation because everyone in the campaign who mattered had approved the letter of understanding. This was also true of the promises made by Reagan himself concerning the Jones Act and using the merchant marine seamen to serve on Navy ships under the control of the uniformed officers of the US Navy. In any event, the election was a few days away, and it was clear that Nixon's New Majority had been resurrected and coalesced behind Ronald Reagan. Later, political analysts referred to these voters as "Reagan Democrats." Yes, they were Democrats who voted for Reagan but, make no mistake about it, they were Nixon's New Majority.

Reagan's victory was resounding. After the election the campaign office was closed and a transition office was set up close to the White House. Ed Meese had spoken with me about my going back to the White House as labor liaison. However, I had no intention of going back into government.

The First Tremor of an Air Traffic Controllers Strike

In December 1980, soon after I returned to my desk at AEI, I received a call from a woman working on the Department of Transportation (DOT) transition team. She had been told to contact me concerning an upcoming strike by the air traffic controllers. I was half amused and half bewildered. "No. No." I said. "The air traffic controllers were supporters of the president. They endorsed the president and were on the team. There would be no problem with the controllers."

The caller sounded as bewildered as I was. She stated that she had been at a meeting with the DOT career employees who said they were already preparing the agency for a strike. I told her that what she was saying made no sense. But if anyone on the DOT transition team wanted to talk to me, I would be happy to assure them that the air traffic controllers would not be a problem. I also said that I thought the career bureaucrats under Carter might be trying to poison the relationship between the new administration and the air traffic controllers. I never gave that call any further thought. I should have met with her and talked more about what she had heard and from whom, but it just seemed too far-fetched to follow it up.

I was wrong. What I had heard within weeks of Reagan's victory was the first seismic tremor in the earthquake that was the PATCO strike. The FAA and Reagan's transition team had already taken steps to push PATCO into a strike.

About a week later I received a call from Jesse Calhoon who asked to see me. "Mike, there is a problem with one of the appointments that is being made at the White House. Apparently, Elizabeth Dole has hired someone to be the labor liaison at the White House. Do you know a man named Bob Bonatati?"

I told Calhoon I didn't know Bonatati but that I had talked to him on the phone during the campaign. Jesse said, "Mike, the pilots did not endorse Reagan. In fact, Bonatati tried to stop Bob Poli from endorsing Reagan." I told Jesse I knew that because Poli had told me the night before we flew to Florida. Jesse continued, "Mike, if he gets the job as labor liaison, none of the union leaders who endorsed Reagan will talk to Bonatati." He then said that the AFL-CIO was trying to identify all of those labor leaders who endorsed Reagan to punish them. Jesse asked me if I could talk to Ed Meese about this and assign Bonatati to a different job in the White House, anything except making him labor liaison.

I promised I would try. Later I explained the situation to Craig Fuller, the White House cabinet secretary, who said the only one who could stop the appointment was Reagan's Chief of Staff James Baker, but Craig did not think Baker would touch it. Nevertheless, I asked for and received an appointment with Baker. I explained the situation that occurs when the president of a union local decides to support a Republican for office over any Democrat endorsed by the AFL-CIO. Each of the labor leaders who defy the federation's Democratic candidate will be challenged in the next election and will lose. I told Baker

I had seen that happen too often to ignore the danger. I warned Baker that the labor leaders who had helped Reagan during the campaign would never trust Bonatati.

Jim listened then said that Elizabeth Dole held a high position in the campaign and knew what she wanted. "We cannot pick her team. It's a done deal."

When I explained this to Jesse, he expressed concern about how Poli was going to view all this. As I stated earlier, the pilots did not endorse Reagan and were at odds with the controllers. Their lobbyist now would hold a key desk in the White House. I then went through all of this with Poli. He could not believe that the White House would appoint as labor liaison Bonatati, who had refused to work the labor desk in the campaign. Moreover, despite their public neutrality, ALPA had quietly supported Carter. You could see the frustration in Poli's face. "This is not politically smart," he said. "The White House will cut itself off from all of the unions who supported Reagan." He could not believe that after endorsing Reagan he had to work with a White House labor liaison whose organization had supported Carter. "I'll be damned if I'm going to share my strategies with him on issues that affect my members. He's O'Donnell's guy. He's Kirkland's guy. [35] He'll be telling Kirkland everything. I don't believe it; the pilots are in and *I'm* out?"

I shared all this with Bob Garrick who now had a prime office on the second floor of the West Wing as deputy counsel. Bob understood the problem but felt that Poli had enough friends in the White House to go around Elizabeth Dole's office if that were needed. I shared all this with Calhoon, who listened quietly with a troubled look on his face, and said, "This is not a good sign, Mike."

Shortly after his appointment, Bonatati called Jesse Calhoon noting that since Calhoon endorsed Reagan, Bonatati's office would always be open to him. Then Bonatati asked for Jesse's help in identifying some of the local unions who were sympathetic to Reagan during the campaign. Jesse said that the only person who had that list was Balzano. Bonatati then contacted me for help in identifying those unions who supported Reagan. He invited me to the White House mess for lunch where he asked for the list of Reagan union supporters. I told him that I was not at liberty to share that list with anyone.

About a week later Jesse called asking to see me. "Mike," he said. "What are your plans? Do you think you want to work for the administration or stay at AEI?"

I responded that I was fairly certain that I would not return to government service because I had two young children and needed to think about college for them and at AEI, unlike government, I had the ability to consult with private entities outside the institute.

"Mike," said Jesse, "I'd like to put you on retainer as a consultant to MEBA. I need your help." He said that I knew all of the key officials now in the White House and the president and vice president on a personal level. He noted that they came to government to help the country, and they sought to develop a relationship with organized labor. "They made promises to work with those unions who endorsed them; all newly elected administrations say that. Then the administration begins to bring in people who have their own agenda."

I had to agree with Jesse. As he talked, I recalled all of those in the Nixon White House who were totally opposed to Nixon's goal of bringing ethnics and blue-collar labor unions into his administration.

Calhoon told me that I did not see how much opposition there was to Reagan supporting to the Jones Act. He said that Reagan gave his commitment to support the act because Bill Casey knew that without the Jones Act he could not have carried the maritime unions.

Jesse said that Casey was acting as Reagan's chief of staff during the campaign and that all of Reagan's conservative campaign advisors couldn't overrule Casey. He explained that with Casey at the CIA, Reagan would be at the mercy of a cadre of appointees who would be recommended for those jobs by industrial interests with their own agendas. Calhoon believed that these appointees would be most likely opposed to all the labor issues Reagan supported. Jesse said that they would be be anti-union if not anti-labor; they would be free traders who have a global agenda. Finally, he said that they would oppose implementing the promises Reagan made during the campaign.

Jesse took a long drag on his cigar, and said resolutely, "Within a year the unions that supported the president for patriotic as well as economic reasons will have no voice in this White House. Look at what's happening already. The White House labor liaison is a person who represents the pilots who did not endorse Reagan and will be Kirkland's eyes and ears on policy issues."

As I look back over this period, it is clear to me that the air traffic controller strike that occurred months later was inevitable. It began the day that Robert Bonatati became the labor liaison for the Reagan White House.

"Here is what I want," Jesse said. "I want you to go across the hall to the Joint Maritime Congress (JMC)." Jesse explained that the JMC was a trade association for ship owners. It was funded by the shipping industry but relied on the unions in the companies to lobby with them on issues of mutual concern. "Let me put you over there," Jesse said. "I'll give you a title that will cover government relations and give you the authority to work on Capitol Hill as well as in the White House."

I accepted Jesse's offer, left AEI, and became the Director of Government Affairs for the Joint Maritime Congress. It was clear that my role would be very specific: I was to be the liaison with the newly elected Reagan administration and monitor the fulfillment of the promises that Reagan made to the maritime unions during the campaign.

This was to be another life-changing experience and a fantastic adventure.

CHAPTER 6
Reagan and Calhoon – A New Adventure (1981-85)

Jesse Calhoon – Labor Capitalist

Jesse Calhoon was a national icon. He was respected on Wall Street where he was deemed a financial wizard. In the nation's capital he was known and recognized by successive presidents from both parties and in the halls of Congress. He was seen as a major power by presidents of unions in the AFL-CIO. But most of all, Jesse was loved by the engineers and mates who sailed the world's oceans and who knew him as a seaman. As I entered his world, I knew I was about to receive my greatest education. At the same time, Calhoon, like Charles Colson, was in many respects an enigma. Calhoon gave no interviews to the media either print or televised. Except for testifying before Congress and attending charitable events in which his wife was involved, he seldom appeared in public.

When I met Jesse in 1980, the union pension fund was in excess of $1.5 billion, a prize that every major investment house on Wall Street sought to manage. However, Jesse managed the pension fund himself. Jesse was facing a declining number of merchant seamen because the merchant fleet was shrinking. During World War II, the United States carried 61 percent of the world's tonnage, but by 1980 this had fallen to well below five percent. (In 2009 only 0.6 percent was carried by US flag vessels. By 2013 this had barely increased to one percent.)[36]

In addition to the membership decline, Calhoon explained that the commercial viability of the ships subsidized under the US Maritime

Administration (MARAD) was being negatively impacted by the Navy. Before MARAD would grant subsidies for the construction of any ship, they would send the blueprints over to the Navy for unofficial approval. It was common knowledge that the Navy, which wanted merchant ships that could be useful in wartime, was making decisions that limited the commercial viability of those ships in peacetime., because their operating costs and limited cargo capacity undermined their profitability.

Calhoon saw new markets that required innovations in the merchant fleet. His investments were designed to make money. But he also wanted to create jobs for his union engineers who would be sailing those ships. He was a visionary with big ideas about the future. This was the Jesse Calhoon who now wanted me to work for him. It was an exciting prospect.

Punched Out at the White House

Before signing on with MEBA, I talked with Chuck Colson who was delighted with my decision. Chuck said, "Jesse Calhoon is the most unusual man you will ever know. His name is loyalty. He will never betray a friend or break a promise." Colson continued, "Jesse is a sophisticated man, but deep inside he is a seaman capable of volatile behavior. He is like an ancient volcano covered with snow but on occasion he is capable of violent explosions." I witnessed these two extremes of behavior within the first few weeks that I worked with Jesse.

On the first occasion, which was my first day on the job, Jesse strolled into my office and told me that he wanted me to accompany him to a White House reception that night. The reception was held in the Benjamin Ogle Tayloe House, located across the street from the White House. The new administration sponsored a meeting there with the AFL-CIO, which included Federation President Lane Kirkland. Kirkland had pulled out the stops to defeat Reagan but failed because rank and file union members bolted and supported Reagan.

One by one, administration officials paraded into the large room. President Reagan, Vice President George Bush, and OPL Director Elizabeth Dole all promised the AFL-CIO an open door to the White

House. As administration officials left and the crowd thinned, I headed for a large bowl of strawberries on the side of the room away from the crowd. I became aware that the conversation among union leaders was becoming loud. In fact, it had become hostile. The same union leaders whom Mrs. Dole had invited to the reception to demonstrate that the administration would have an open door to the AFL-CIO were now demonstrating their hostility to the only labor leader in the room who had endorsed Reagan: Jesse Calhoon.

I wandered over to a small circle of men where the volume was the loudest. The circle was around Jesse. I recognized two of the men. One was Robert Georgine, president of the Building and Construction Trades Department of the AFL-CIO. The other was Angelo Fosco, president of the Laborers International Union of North America. As the group besieged Jesse, the tone of the conversation became reminiscent of my childhood, when such insults were the prelude to punches being thrown.

"*No,*" I thought to myself. "*These are grown men at a White House reception. They are not boys in a schoolyard or on a street corner.*"

One of the most serious insults you can make to anyone in the labor, ethnic or traditional community is to laugh at them. It challenges the manhood of anyone in these communities.

I saw the expression on Jesse's face change. Then it happened. Fosco was still laughing at Jesse about something. I watched it all happen in slow motion. Jesse threw his drink in Fosco's face. For some reason I became fixated on how the ice cubes rolled down Fosco's tie and bounced off the tie bar he was wearing. He was stunned. Everyone was aghast.

As Fosco blinked from the double scotch that had been splashed in his eyes, Jesse let him have a roundhouse and knocked Fosco across the room and onto the table where Jack Burgess and I had been eating strawberries. Fosco, still in shock, pushed himself to his feet and began taking off his suit coat. Big mistake. Jesse let him have another roundhouse, knocking Fosco back onto the table.

Bob Georgine, who had been an amateur boxer, began yelling at Jesse who responded, "You want some of this?"

"Are you crazy?" Georgine said. "You're an old man. I'll break you in half," he said, taking off his jacket.

I was trying to push Jesse back when Georgine threw a straight right at Jesse that I intercepted with my left shoulder. I noticed all the white-gloved military aides, standing aghast, and the waiters who were in shock at what began to look like a John Wayne western featuring drinks, strawberries, chocolate, and Fosco still on the floor.

"Get into this," I yelled at the military aides. "We've got to break this up!"

The White House military aides pushed their way in between the combatants, and I shoved Jesse out the door past the White House police rushing the room. Jesse was exhilarated.

"Jesse," I said. "You just punched out the head of the Laborers Union. There are going to be reprisals."

"No," Jesse said, as he took out a fresh cigar from his pocket. "This is all in the family. I'm a seaman. I've seen people killed in barroom fights and on ships. I saw a man killed right next to me in a bar with a hammer. Call your wife. Let's go to dinner."

I repeated to Jesse that I was frightened that the Laborers Union might have criminal ties and that his life might be in danger.

"Don't think about that anymore, Mike," he said. "It's okay."

Don't think about it? This was my first day on the job. What would the future hold in store for me?

Calhoon the Financier

About three weeks after that White House reception, Jesse called me to say that we were going to a White House meeting the next day. Jesse said that he had received a call from someone on the president's Council of Economic Advisors who was assembling labor and business leaders to discuss ways of jump-starting the economy. The caller said that Professor Murray Weidenbaum would be conducting the meeting. Was I facing a situation where Jesse could lay out Weidenbaum the way he laid out Fosco?

With all of these thoughts in mind, I accompanied Jesse into a fairly large meeting room in the Old Executive Office Building. Murray Weidenbaum and I had been colleagues at AEI. He was an erudite professor-type who was generally impressed by academic credentials.

After presenting statistical charts showing economic trends before and during the Carter administration and flooding the room with problems emanating from a prime interest rate of over twenty percent, a decline in the GNP, and an inflation rate that gave rise to the term "stagflation," Murray gratuitously asked the gathering if anyone had an idea of how to improve the nation's economy.

Jesse Calhoon raised his hand in the room filled with economists and business leaders and announced himself as the president of MEBA, adding that MEBA was a union. Jesse said that he thought Reagan should keep one of the promises he made during the campaign to privatize Social Security.

Murray smiled, saying that he never thought he would ever hear a labor leader advocate privatizing Social Security.

"Well," Calhoon responded, "that's because you don't know how to explain it. If you explain it properly, you can sell it to the country."

Murray took the bait. "Well, Mr. Union President, how would you sell the idea?"

Jesse responded by computing the Social Security taxes that a marine engineer from his school would have to pay as a seaman over the next fifty years. He then computed the earning that the seaman would realize in the stock market over the same period, demonstrating that the seaman would realize a multi-million-dollar portfolio rather than receiving an $800-a-month check from the Social Security fund.

Calhoon reminded the group that Social Security was going into the hole each year and that, when Baby Boomers began to retire, the system would be nearly insolvent because people were living longer. Jesse somberly said that, at some point in the near future, a US president would have to deal with the reality that, between Social Security and Medicare, the country would face a mounting debt crisis. The room was dead silent. All Weidenbaum could say was, "Interesting."

Working for Calhoon

When we returned from the Old EOB, Jesse said, "I want you to go to all of the Republicans in the Senate, especially those that were elected in the Reagan landslide." He told me to introduce myself as the director of government affairs for the Joint Maritime Congress. "In my experience," he concluded, "when they see that our union is essential to maintaining America's industrial base in terms of energy and national security, the members will vote to preserve an American fleet."

One of the first Senators I contacted was Dan Quayle of Indiana, whom I had met several months earlier. At a luncheon I arranged between Jesse Calhoon and Quayle, Jesse told Quayle that he supported Birch Bayh, Quayle's opponent in 1980, because Bayh had always supported the maritime industry due to its importance for national security. Jesse also told Quayle, "We do not expect members of Congress to vote against their constituencies, but we would like them to be open on issues important to America's industrial base. All I would ask of you is that you give us the chance to present our case." He continued, "As of this hour I will assign Mike to be your labor advisor."

For the next three years, I worked closely with Tom Duesterberg, Quayle's chief of staff, and I became Quayle's unofficial labor advisor. Quayle and I became close friends, and because of my relationship with MEBA, I made many trips to Indiana to meet with the unions in the Indiana AFL-CIO state federation. Five years later, the Indiana unions declared neutrality and Quayle carried the unions by such a majority in his successful reelection bid that later Vice President George H. W. Bush began to look at Quayle as a possible running mate.

Most of the people I introduced to Jesse were senior White House staff like Vice President Bush, Ed Meese, Michael Deaver, Lyn Nofziger, and occasionally the president himself, who Jesse had not met during the presidential campaign. I also introduced him to Craig Fuller. Craig was an extremely talented young man who had been an intern in Governor Reagan's office and had worked in the public relations firm, Deaver and Hannaford. Following Reagan's victory, Fuller had become cabinet secretary and was one of the first people I met in the Reagan White House. I introduced him to Jesse and the two became friends.

The PATCO Strike

As I have previously indicated, my assignments with MEBA focused on working with the White House and the Republican leadership in the House and Senate. I was to ensure that the Republican leadership was familiar with the promises made by Reagan to MEBA during the campaign and to eliminate any roadblocks to their implementation. For Calhoon, the most important issues were preservation of the Jones Act, the renewal of the Export Administration Act preventing the export of Alaskan oil, and fleet support, the civilian manning of Navy cargo ships. Jesse also wanted to help PATCO resolve concerns that were stated in the letters exchanged between Reagan and the union. Unfortunately, PATCO's aims placed Jesse's targeted goals in jeopardy.

The first tremor signaling a problem between PATCO and the FAA had come while I was still at AEI. The second tremor came after I joined MEBA. Late one afternoon I received a call from Craig Fuller. After exchanging pleasantries, he said, "Mike, do you know anything about a letter of understanding [37] between President Reagan and PATCO?"

"Yes," I responded, "there were actually two letters: one from PATCO which had been coordinated with Bill Casey and a letter to PATCO from Reagan himself." [38]

"Mike," Craig said, "would you mind speaking with Drew Lewis [Secretary of Transportation] about this?"

"No," I responded.

"Well, I have him on the other line," Craig said.

Suddenly I was on a conference call. Craig asked Drew to talk about a meeting he just had with Bob Poli, the president of PATCO.

Drew said that he met with Poli that afternoon and that Poli said that he had a letter of understanding with Ronald Reagan concerning issues related to PATCO.

I acknowledged that Drew was correct. "In fact, the letters were exchanged days before PATCO endorsed the president."

"Letters," Lewis repeated.

"Yes," I told him. "I transmitted them before Poli went to an FAA Center in Florida to personally make the endorsement."

"Really," Lewis replied. "Do you have a copy of those letters?"

"No," I responded. "I can't believe *you* don't."

"Well, who has them?" Craig asked, avowing that he had never heard of such letters.

I repeated what Reagan had said to me concerning the business relationship that he wanted with any union that I brought to the campaign; that once an agreement had been made between a union and the president there would be a formal letter of understanding.

The phone line was dead quiet. "Are you still there?" I asked.

"Yes, we're both here," they responded.

"Who has the letters?" Craig asked.

"I have no idea," I responded. "But I cannot imagine why neither of you has a copy."

Craig asked, "Who at the campaign staff saw these letters?"

"Well," I said, "I know Admiral Garrick and Ed Gray saw them. But there's no way anything got past Bill Casey without his knowing about its content. He was part of the sign-off process." (Ed Gray, a deputy assistant to President Reagan, had been press secretary to the campaign in 1980.)

Lewis said, "Yes, well, we'll have to get a copy of them." He then got off the phone and Craig said he couldn't believe that something that important would not be available to everyone involved in the negotiations. I advised Craig that Lewis ought to call Poli and ask him for copies.

I later told Craig that in meetings Poli and I had with Garrick, all of the issues that affected public safety were discussed and stated in the PATCO letter to candidate Reagan. Fuller, a pilot himself, understood the concerns of the union: obsolete equipment, forced overtime for controllers well beyond requirements of international standards, and controller burnout. All these issues definitely would affect the flying public. I spoke with Jesse the next day. "This is not a good sign," he said.

Suddenly, the Washington newspapers were filled with a possible air traffic control strike. On the day the strike was announced, as I entered the MEBA building, there were signs directing PATCO board members to rooms where meetings were already underway. For a brief moment, Poli poked his head out of his office door, and I grabbed him. "Bob," I said, "what's going on?"

"We're going. We're going out," he said, disappearing back into the crowded room.

Jesse had not come in yet. I went back to my office. About a half hour later Jesse buzzed me. "What's going on?" he asked. I told him of my conversation with Bob.

Jesse responded, "Mike, go in there and get him to come into my office."

Moments later the three of us were sitting in Jesse's office. "Bob," Jesse asked, "what are you doing?" Poli repeated that they were going out. "Bob," cautioned Jesse, "this is a president with massive public support. Why are you challenging him?"

"Jesse," Bob responded, "I've got an agreement with him, and I'm dealing with everybody at the FAA and DOT, but I'm not talking to Ronald Reagan. I need to get his attention."

He continued, "Jesse, the strike will be over in hours. The FAA cannot run the system without us; it's impossible. The skies will be silent. They will have to settle."

"Bob," Jesse said, "you are a public employee union. You can't strike. You will bring the business community out in force; they will join all of the anti-union forces both in and out of government. They will hang all of you on crosses down Pennsylvania Avenue like in that movie *Spartacus*. Don't give them the chance."

Poli assured Jesse that the strike would be over in days if not hours. He told Jesse that the skies would not be safe. Pilots would not fly and the air traffic control centers would not open.

"Bob," Jesse said in a lower voice before Poli left the room. "Obey the law, Bob, obey the law, and you will win."

I turned to Jesse and asked if I should call Craig Fuller. "No," he said resolutely. "Bob is being pushed over the edge by a militant membership. If he resists them, he will be run over."

"Well, I said. "I'll go to the White House and see if I can get this situation reversed."

"Mike," Jesse replied, "sit down. I brought you into this organization to work MEBA issues. If you become identified with this strike, it's going to cause MEBA to lose a chit we may need later."

The strike did not end as Poli predicted. First, the FAA brought in military controllers. Second, ALPA President J.J. O'Donnell immediately went on the air and announced that the skies were safe. The FAA increased the distances between flights, which created delays, but the system stayed in operation. Where was Reagan, the candidate that PATCO endorsed? He was in the White House. But Bob Poli could not get to him; to do so, he would have had to go to the White House labor liaison in Elizabeth Dole's office. Given the history of Bob Bonatati's position with ALPA, Poli felt, with every justification, that Bonatati was probably using his position to have ALPA be seen as helpful to the administration. Again, the irony of it all is that ALPA did not endorse Reagan and now the president of ALPA was working with the administration to assure the public that the skies were safe! All the White House doors were closed to PATCO.

Later, Jesse unveiled a strategy that he believed could end the strike and save the employees. He proposed that Poli and the entire PATCO board would stand in front of the White House and apologize to the president and to the nation for their illegal strike. They would all resign and turn the union over to a Joint White House/Congressional Committee that Jesse had persuaded Senator Paul Laxalt and Congressman Guy Vander Jagt to chair. They would address the air traffic issues presented by the controllers.

Lyn Nofziger, longtime trusted aide to Reagan, agreed to carry this proposal to the president. Nofziger would go around Elizabeth Dole and Bonatati, the labor liaison, and go through Meese to the president himself. None of this would take place in the public eye. While Drew Lewis and the federal mediation services appeared to be working to solve the crisis, a back-channel plan was put into place to link a congressional offer to the White House to engage in a joint effort to reform the FAA's personnel relations. The plan would deal with staffing problems, mandatory overtime, substandard equipment, and a confrontative history of labor relations between the FAA and its workforce. What was needed was the president's acceptance of an apology by PATCO's leadership and an announcement by the Republican-controlled Senate that the Congress and the White House would work together once the "militant leaders" of the strike were duly punished. The leaders of this coalition were Senator Paul Laxalt of Nevada and Congressman Guy Vander Jagt of Michigan. Other conservative Republicans led by Dan Quayle would add their weight to the effort. Vander Jagt was ready to deliver House conservatives as well.

The entire plan rested on a Republican conservative Congress reacting to the president's acceptance of PATCO's surrender and admission of guilt, and everyone showing mercy to those public employees who had broken the law.

Nofziger headed off to the White House one afternoon after a meeting with Jesse, Laxalt, Vander Jagt, and me and returned later with terrible news. He could not see the president. Instead, he was forced to deal with political operatives on the national security staff whom he would not name. He said that the strike now had national security implications.

"National security?" we all repeated.

"Yes," Nofziger said. "The White House wants to send a message to the Soviet Union: 'If this is what we'll do to our friends, imagine what we'll do to our enemies.'" Nofziger continued, "The president is telling the Russians that when he makes a decision, it's final."

"Oh boy," Vander Jagt remarked. Laxalt said nothing. Jesse noted that the president had invited Lech Walesa to the White House to celebrate the Polish leader's strike against a Soviet-controlled shipyard and, at the same time, considered sending the PATCO leadership to the jailhouse! PATCO was completely isolated.

When we returned to the office, Jesse told me to stop all back-channel communications with my allies in the administration. "Bob bet the company and lost," he said. "I cannot risk any of the relationship we have in the White House or the Congress on this strike. We cannot justify it; we can only lose credibility. We will look like we support behavior that the public simply won't condone."

He continued, "The administration is in the early days of what will probably be eight years. We have oil and fleet support issues ahead of us. We must not be embroiled in this issue."

To put the strike in perspective, one must carefully read both the letter of understanding that preceded PATCO's endorsement and Reagan's acceptance of that endorsement in his letter of response on the day they held their joint press conference in front of the air traffic control center in Florida.

PATCO's letter begins by stating the reason that PATCO was endorsing Reagan was because PATCO "believes that the Governor

(Reagan) more than any other candidate has a better understanding of the needs of the flying public and the air traffic controllers who provide service to that public."

How did the governor come to an "understanding of those needs?" Reagan had never talked to Poli about the antiquated computers that were subject to blackouts. He had never heard Poli talk about the stress of 60-hour workweeks where, for public safety purposes, other countries limit the number of hours a controller can work. Poli had never told the governor about the skill required to handle the lives of thousands of people per minute.

So where did Reagan obtain this "understanding" of the plight of the controllers? He apparently got it from his staff, who analyzed the conditions Poli described in meetings with them. Garrick, who was no stranger to the aircraft industry, passed the main issues to Bill Casey—again, not a lightweight—who agreed that Ronald Reagan would listen to PATCO and correct the problems presented to him in the letter from PATCO.

The first item on PATCO's list of expectations was "The present Administrator of the FAA will be replaced by a competent Administrator." That was easy; as a presidential appointee, he would leave with the outgoing administration. The letter went on to say that PATCO would be given "a reasonable opportunity to recommend nominees." But the individual who was to be the administrator of the FAA, J. Lynn Helms, had a history of difficulty dealing with unions and was hostile to them. Helms stated that controllers were already overpaid. Hence, from the first days of his appointment, it was clear that a hostile FAA administrator violated the major promises of the letter of understanding as soon as he took command.

Why didn't Poli go to the White House and tell the president that the spirit of the letter of understanding had been violated? He had the opportunity on two occasions following the Inauguration. The first occasion was a small breakfast with the president. The second opportunity arose when the president met with the unions that had endorsed him. Why didn't Poli at least express his concerns? He said he did not want to create a problem for his members so early in Reagan's administration, so he let the opportunities pass.

The spark that triggered the explosion between PATCO and the administration occurred that summer of 1981 when PATCO proposed legislation to the Congress concerning improving their situation within the federal system.

The letter of understanding clearly stated that PATCO was to have the opportunity to put its case before the Congress. This issue was addressed in point number 6 of the letter: [39]

> The Reagan Administration will give PATCO a reasonable opportunity to advocate PATCO's position to appropriate members of the Reagan Administration with respect to any proposed legislation directly affecting air traffic controllers, prior to the Reagan Administration taking a position on that legislation.

In the meetings held during the campaign period between Garrick, Poli and me, Poli expressed the view that PATCO had allies on the Hill who were willing to offer legislation to address controller concerns. Senior campaign officials did not want to commit a new president on specific pieces of legislation but said they would allow PATCO to work with the Congress on issues they felt were important to their members. These included increased pay for controllers in light of the technical competence required to manage the high-tech systems that ensure the public safety. This was reasonable. Instead, following the Inauguration, the Office of Management and Budget went to Capitol Hill to block PATCO's attempt at legislative reform. In doing so the administration clearly violated the spirit and the letter of point number 6 quoted above. OMB's action was viewed as a declaration of war on the controllers.

The PATCO letter of understanding contained the most controversial position of all. In point number 6, section c, it gave PATCO the "right to strike in certain circumstances." Again, both Bob Poli and I had agreed that this was a provision that would only be used by the union if the FAA failed to reach reasonable accommodation over an issue that involved public safety. For example, what if the FAA refused to replace the antiquated computers? Or if they refused to hire the requisite number of controllers needed to operate the system but instead forced tired, overworked controllers to work fifty or sixty hours? What about public safety then? Clearly, public safety would be jeopardized.

From the vantage point of one who helped negotiate the letter of understanding with PATCO, the right to strike and the circumstances in which it might occur were clearly understood by the senior staff at the campaign. However, Poli was no longer dealing with Reagan's staff and instead was dealing with a hostile FAA bureaucracy that would never have supported a Republican president and was in a position to punish the controllers who did. Poli's lack of access to the White House staff is why the PATCO membership and Board eventually turned on him for endorsing Reagan for president.

Poli told Jesse Calhoon that he did not believe that the strike would last more than a day or two because it would not be safe to fly. Poli told Jesse that the pilots would come to his aide because they would be playing Russian roulette with potential midair collisions that could occur. But with the lobbyist for ALPA holding the labor chair in the Reagan White House, it is not hard to see how ALPA president J. J. O'Donnell, could not resist the temptation to get ALPA in the administration's good graces.

O'Donnell told the public that the skies were perfectly safe to fly, which the air traffic controllers and many ALPA members knew was false. O'Donnell's statements convinced many that the FAA could run the system without the fired controllers. In his 1990 master's thesis, [40] John J. Seddon, a former controller, states that President O'Donnell assured the public that the skies were safe to fly, ignoring contrary statements from his own safety council:

> Significantly, the absence of PATCO support by the Airline Pilots Association proved most damaging when its President J.J. O'Donnell went on national television and stated that the aviation system was safe and that the public had nothing to be concerned about.

Most importantly, Seddon also points to the later appointment of J. J. O'Donnell as undersecretary of labor as a reward for silencing those ALPA members who were truly concerned with the public safety.

Poli's experience in dealing with a White House was based on his experience with the Nixon administration. During a two-day interview I had with Poli in January 2013, he stated, "Nixon was a man of his word. If he made a promise to you, that was it. It was done."

If Poli had listened to Calhoon on the day he left Jesse's office and followed Jesse's advice to "obey the law," Poli would have won on every issue highlighted in his letter. But he did not listen. And Jesse may have been talking in code anyway. He was trying to protect MEBA. When I asked Jesse to explain what he meant by "obey the law," I thought he meant that public employees can't strike. That is not what he meant. Jesse was referring to the federal law that limits the maximum number of takeoffs and landings that are permitted for each airport. If Poli had "worked to rule," there would have been an air traffic jam at Chicago, Los Angeles, or any major airport worldwide, since all these airports were exceeding the maximum. It would have created a public demand to look into the problems that led to the slowdown. Congress would have to have been involved and all of the problems aired. Instead, by striking, Poli forced the president to fire the strikers. Nobody won.

During my 2013 interview with Poli, I asked him a hypothetical question: If Ed Meese had called him into the White House and said, "Bob, look, I know things have gotten off track; let's take time to see how we can fix it, but for God's sake don't take the controllers out," what would you have done? Poli responded that he would have left the White House, called his board together, and said, "I have been to the White House. I have talked with the powers that be. We will not go out."

Alaskan Oil

In the chapter of this book dealing with the birth of the New Majority, I discussed Nixon's secret agreement to open Alaskan oil fields and require that the oil be shipped on US tankers crewed by American merchant seamen for ten years, or until 1983. With Reagan's election in 1980 came the question of a renewal of the ban on the export of Alaskan oil outside the United States.

I was concerned about Marty Anderson, one of Reagan's most conservative economic advisors, who had lost the fight during the campaign about the Jones Act. Anderson was not on the Council of Economic Advisors, but he was a free trade proponent who had great influence in the White House. I had been talking to Craig Fuller from the earliest days of the administration about the collision that was going to occur between the free traders who wanted to repeal the ban on exporting Alaskan oil and those who were concerned with the national security implications of doing so.

During the first and second years of the Reagan administration, I arranged meetings in which Jesse Calhoon met with UN Ambassador Jeane Kirkpatrick, Lindley Clark of the *Wall Street Journal*, and Don Hodel, Secretary of the Interior, among others. Although all of these meetings were in social gatherings, Calhoon was able to educate them about the importance of Alaskan oil to our economic and national security. After talking with Craig about the conflict that Jesse Calhoon knew was coming, Craig agreed to set up a private meeting with Marty Anderson to get each side to see the other's point of view.

Calhoon's understanding of the issues was profound. He had a grasp of the economic, military, and strategic issues that spanned nearly four decades. When Marty agreed to a meeting with Jesse, he had no idea who Jesse Calhoon was. He did not understand that he would be dealing with an intellectual and industrial financial giant. He thought he would be talking with a union leader who would probably focus on jobs, and bread-and-butter issues that affect local unions. Anderson greatly underestimated Calhoon.

At the meeting, Calhoon raised one issue after another. First was Reagan's commitment to the Jones Act; second was the need to protect America from another Arab embargo started by oil rich nations who could starve our economy. Third, Calhoon raised the national security issue. Anderson could only repeat his argument in favor of free trade. Craig later told me, "You know I had heard the stories about Jesse being the labor capitalist, but I had no idea that Jesse knew more about the international implications of moving that oil than any of us at the White House."

I picked up Jesse shortly after the meeting concluded and he told me that Craig Fuller understood the national security and the geopolitical issues more than anyone in the administration. "I told them to remember that World War II started over oil shipments to Japan," Calhoon said. "I also reminded them that one of the reasons we beat the Germans in Europe and in North Africa was because they ran out of gas and couldn't refuel their tanks." Calhoon concluded that he could see Craig's face as he realized that Marty was losing the argument. When he finished giving me his thoughts, I enthusiastically said, "We won. It's over."

Jesse responded, "We won this battle, but the war goes on." Jesse said that Marty had talked not only about the right to sell Alaskan oil to Japan, but also about allowing oil to be imported from Mexico to replace oil sold to Japan. "I could see where he was going," Jesse said. "This fight is not over."

Once again Jesse's instinct was right. I received a call from Craig Fuller a few days later in which he said, "I think we have a problem. Marty has arranged for the Alaskan oil issue to be reviewed at a Cabinet council meeting. It will not be the main issue, but it will come up."

With little time to waste, I went to Jeane Kirkpatrick and told her about the possibility of an oil swap in which America would sell Alaskan oil to Japan, and would import an equal amount of oil from Mexico. Both Kirkpatrick and her principal deputy on this issue, Jose Sorzano, said, "No way." Sorzano, who was Jeane's key advisor on Latin America, said the idea of relying on the Mexicans was ridiculous. Sorzano noted that there were no free enterprise oil companies in Mexico. "PEMEX is controlled by the Mexican government; tomorrow they could have an election in Mexico and bring in another Cesar Chavez and suddenly what happens to the deal that we made?"

At a White House meeting held shortly after Jesse's meeting with Marty Anderson, the subject was raised about the possibility of an oil swap with Mexico. Craig later told me that the president clearly focused on the national security implications of this discussion. It was stated that we could get away from Middle Eastern oil and the domination of OPEC by working closely with our allies in Mexico and Venezuela. Jeane Kirkpatrick then entered the discussion, saying, "If we're talking about allies here, I can tell you that the Mexican government does not vote with us at the U.N. As a matter of fact, they are constantly voting against us. So what would lead anyone to believe that the Mexicans would side with us on any issue? When it comes to our national security, I would not bet on the Mexicans or the Venezuelans. I would say no to any swap."

It made no sense to Jeane that we should exchange oil from a Mexican supplier for American oil in Alaska. Don Hodel agreed with Kirkpatrick. Reagan then concluded that he would not favor a swap or a change in the export ban because it went counter to the promise that he had made to preserve those maritime jobs that were protected by the Jones Act. In this situation Reagan kept his promise to the maritime unions.

Jesse then notified his members through his newsletter that he had had a White House meeting over this issue, obviously referring to the meeting with Craig Fuller. He then told his members of the action that the Cabinet Council took. Contrary to the situation in which Poli was unable to even approach the White House during his time of crisis, Jesse demonstrated that he could talk to key White House staff, key cabinet members, and that the president stood behind MEBA.

I said, "Jesse, we won in the White House."

He pointed his cigar at me and said, "That's the executive branch. Now we have to deal with the free traders in the legislative branch." He went on to say, "Mike, I want you to create a massive coalition for a legislative battle that will now begin."

The battle began in the House when a bipartisan group of members led by Republican Stewart McKinney of Connecticut and Democrat Howard Wolpe of Michigan introduced H.R. 1197, a bipartisan bill to renew the Export Administration Act, which continued the ban on exporting Alaskan oil. Calhoon sent a letter to every member of Congress arguing that the ban was "vital to our nation's goal of achieving energy independence" and that it was also of primary importance to MEBA members. The major points in his letter [41] concerned consumer protection, energy independence, and national security.

H.R. 1197 began to roll through the House on a bipartisan basis. The House generated 237 co-sponsors, and there were 45 co-sponsors in the Senate to retain the export ban. Senators Scoop Jackson and Ted Kennedy worked the Democratic side while Quayle and Laxalt worked the Republicans. Quayle looked at me when he signed as a co-sponsor and said, "I don't know, Balzano, look at what you've got me doing—voting against free trade; voting against my Senate colleagues who are pleading with me to vote with them." Dan Quayle's name on the co-sponsorship gave many free trade Republicans comfort when they joined to co-sponsor as well as the 45 Senators who co-signed the bill. Prominent among them were Republican Senators Mark Andrews of North Dakota and David Durenberger of Minnesota. The final vote was seventy in favor versus twenty against lifting the ban. [42]

The legislative battle over ending the export ban of Alaskan oil began in 1983 and went on for two years. It finally ended in 1985, when Senator John Heinz, a Republican, introduced S.883 that became law and preserved the ban. [43]

It is important to note that Ronald Reagan stood by his campaign promise to support the oil export ban and the Jones Act, stating that it was "the most significant since the original shipping act of 1916." Unlike the PATCO case, the issue came to the president's attention by Cabinet officers, especially Jeane Kirkpatrick, who raised the importance of this issue to the nation's energy and national security. Concurrently, Republican senators who had helped MEBA told me they didn't want another PATCO situation. Reagan did the right thing by keeping his word. The Republican senators also did the right thing by supporting the spirit of what the president had promised. They did so even though they had to mobilize votes against their friends in the Senate.

When it was clear that we had won a major victory for MEBA, Jesse and I went downstairs to the restaurant on the first floor of the MEBA building. He sat there with his double Chivas Regal, lifted his glass, and said, "Now do you see why I wanted you to work for MEBA after the campaign?" He said that we would never have won without my friendship with Craig Fuller, Jeane Kirkpatrick, Dan Quayle, and Paul Laxalt. He concluded that we would do the same thing to secure civilian manning.

I told Jesse I thought that would be easy given Reagan's understanding of the issue and his personal commitment to fleet support.

He took a large sip of scotch and said, "We'll see."

During Reagan's first term, the White House constantly asked

Calhoon to support the administration on public policy issues. On one occasion Jesse told me that the White House had called him asking if he could help in planning an event at a major port facility in Los Angeles. Apparently, the president was going to announce a free trade initiative and needed to draw a large crowd.

At 6:00 a.m. on the day of the event, I stood at the door of the union hall, passing out tickets to the engineers as they departed for the event. It must be kept in mind that MEBA has a seagoing membership. If you are not at sea, you are waiting for a sailing. In the line of engineers filing past me was a young, red-bearded man whose son was riding atop his shoulders waving an American flag. As I looked at this beautiful little boy, I said to him, "Hey, are you going to be a marine engineer like your dad when you grow up?" His father quickly responded, "I hope not. His dad hasn't had a sailing in more than a year."

Following the event, we flew back to Washington in the first-class cabin enjoying lunch. As I drank my glass of white wine, I couldn't help thinking about the red-bearded man and his little boy. At one point Jesse remarked on what a good day we had. "Mike, every CEO at that event knows that MEBA has clout with Reagan. It will help us when we negotiate contracts." It became clear to me that Jesse was now seen as a quasi-spokesman for the administration.

I told Jesse I was feeling guilty. Here we were sitting and having lunch, flying first class, while that poor engineer did not have a job. Jesse grabbed my wrist and squeezed it very tight. "Now you better understand your job," he said. "Look around this cabin. Three of the corporate officials who attended that event are flying up here with us. How the hell would it look if we were riding in the back of the plane? They have to see us in first class. Your job is to influence and lobby for jobs. You will never influence anyone if you look like a beggar. Stand tall and exhibit confidence. If you behave second class, the companies will treat you second class. If the companies see us as living from hand to mouth, they will treat us that way. Everyone has a job on this ship. Your job is to create jobs. If you fail, that red-bearded engineer will never have a job."

This same attitude carried over into MEBA's contribution to House and Senate candidates. One morning I attended a relatively small breakfast in San Diego with Mayor Pete Wilson, who was then running for the Senate. As the participants introduced themselves, they announced their affiliation and told the mayor they were making a specific dollar contribution to his campaign. The highest contribution made that morning was $1,500. When it was my turn, I introduced myself as a representative of the marine engineers and had two checks, each for $5,000, one for the primary and one for the general election. As the next person began to speak, Pete Wilson interrupted, "Wait, wait, wait. Ten thousand dollars! Who are you and what do you want?"

I explained again who I was and that I represented the marine engineers. He repeated his question: What did I want? I responded that our major concern was our ability to carry the nation's oil from Alaska to the lower forty-eight states and at least to be able to present our views to him and his staff during the legislative cycle. If he became senator, MEBA's goal was to have the opportunity to educate him on the desperate situation that was facing the US merchant fleet.

After he was elected to represent California in the Senate, we briefed Wilson and his defense staff on the role the merchant marine played in carrying supplies and troops in both World Wars. A former Marine, Pete Wilson became one of MEBA's strongest supporters. He understood that the maritime industry is an essential part of the nation's defense industrial base.

Reagan and Civilian Manning

Calhoon's victory in preserving the ban on exporting Alaskan oil could not have been won without Republican allies in the Senate. The victory meant that the fleet of Alaskan oil tankers would continue to provide maritime jobs for licensed and unlicensed US crews flying the American flag. But the Reagan promise to have civilian mariners move military cargo, i.e., fleet support, had not happened by the end of Reagan's first term.

In Reagan's speech before the National Maritime Union during the campaign, his commitment to the Jones Act clearly indicated that he supported a commercial maritime industry. He did so because of its importance to America's economic security and national security. A veteran of World War II who understood the need to move millions of tons of equipment and personnel to war zones, Reagan appreciated the availability of merchant ships as well as the seamen who spent their lives in transit from one battle zone to another. Most importantly, he understood the role of those men who remained in the engine rooms of ships under attack by aircraft or submarines.

Of all the statements Ronald Reagan made during the campaign concerning the goals he set for his presidency, none was clearer than his intention to revive the US maritime industry. The white paper he presented at his September 1980 meeting with maritime leaders entitled, *A Program for the Development of an Effective Maritime Strategy,*[44] clearly states Reagan's intent to revive the fledging industry. It should be noted that the revival of the maritime industry is even more crucial today, because the maritime industry is weaker now than it was thirty-five years ago when Reagan offered his plan.

In the white paper Reagan noted that America had lost prestige and power because of the "decline of both our naval forces and our maritime industry . . . at a time when the United States is more dependent upon the use of the seas for our political, economic, and military well-being than ever before in our history." He pointed to the United States' status as the world's greatest trading nation and its dependence on ships to carry both raw materials and our manufactured goods. Noting that US shipyards were also in decline, Reagan pledged to rebuild them. Most important, he noted that the US merchant fleet once "carried 42% of the US trade" and "currently carries less than 5% of our own commerce, while 95% of US trade is carried by ships of other countries, whose availability in time of crisis is problematical at best."

Pointing out that our naval fleet had shrunk below 500 ships, Reagan noted that the Russian fleet had increased to 2,500 ships and that they were using their foreign commerce merchant ships as part of their military fleet, much the same as the Chinese are now militarizing *their* merchant fleet.

Reagan then set out a seven-point plan to reverse the decline of the US merchant fleet. Point 3 dealt with Reagan's goal of increasing commercial participation for auxiliary functions. The pursuit of this agenda would not only have reversed the decline of the US maritime industry but it would also have boosted America's industrial base. It would have called for an increased investment in America's steel and machine tool industries and all of the ancillary industries that required skilled workers and master craftsmen. The one advantage that the Reagan plan offered was to immediately reverse the decline in employment of skilled seamen by using them to move military cargo.

When Reagan addressed the National Maritime Union (NMU) convention on October 9, 1980, he focused on two issues that would be addressed in his presidency: the Jones Act and civilian manning of military cargo ships.[45] Reagan stood by his word on the Jones Act with respect to the Alaskan fleet of oil tankers. In his NMU speech, it was clear that he understood the concept of civilian manning and its practical value of stopping the constant erosion of skilled mariner jobs. Reagan criticized President Carter, a naval officer who also was committed to civilian manning, but who had failed to implement a responsive plan during his term:

> Our merchant marine is a vital auxiliary to the US Navy. At a time when the Navy's support capability is open to serious question, we should be increasing the merchant marine's role—and we are not. . . . I know, and you know, that the maritime industry can assume many Navy support functions.

How would a civilian manning program work? In 1980 the Navy moved cargo using what is called the Military Sealift Command (MSC). Here, the Navy owns the ships, which are crewed by civilian mariners and operate under the control of a Navy captain or other naval officers in charge of the vessel, its cargo, and its destination. These ships accompany a Navy fleet at sea, replenishing fuel, ammunition, food, and other crew necessities. The MSC also makes major deliveries of cargo to prepositioned forces and large ports.

The Navy also retains a group of ships called the Ready Reserve Fleet. In the early 1980s there were fewer than a hundred of these ships. They were World War II break-bulker cargo ships and Liberty ships, a mothballed fleet without crews. The Navy would periodically call a drill. Seamen who lived in the general vicinity were required to muster to their ship and start its engines. All World War II steam engines required warm-up before the ship had the power to move. The Navy was apparently content with this system. Theoretically the Navy had a fleet it could call upon in a national crisis, but the fleet was in fact a floating junkyard of antiquated ships that had been mothballed for nearly forty years. Calhoon maintained that the fleet was useless. Leon Shapiro, secretary-treasurer of MEBA, shared with me the story of an inexperienced crew that, during an exercise, burned out an engine on one of the ships. The ship had to be towed back to port. Shapiro added that there were no parts available to repair a breakdown and no engineers on-board to make the needed repairs.

Reagan's major point was that he was going to build a 600-ship Navy. There would be no time to find enough personnel to man a 600-ship Navy, let alone move cargo. Reagan's plan was to transfer all Navy personnel moving cargo to combat ships and move cargo using merchant seamen.

Civilian merchant marine officers are professionals who love their work and enjoy being at sea. They are seamen. During wartime they can expect to be fired upon by enemy aircraft and torpedoed by enemy submarines. That is part of the job. The 1943 film *Action in the North Atlantic* vividly depicts the life of merchant seamen during wartime. Although I had seen this film as a young boy, Jesse asked me to watch it again because, in his experience, it was the most accurate representation of life on board a merchant ship during World War II. The film demonstrated life and death on the high seas during that time, as Jesse well knew. His oil tanker had been torpedoed, resulting in his crew being set adrift in a lifeboat. Jesse told me that the German submarine that sank his ship surfaced and the captain asked if the crew was all right. Jesse said the men were cold, their life jackets soaked in oil, but they were alive. They were grateful that the German captain did not order the lifeboats strafed by machine guns. The German U-boat submerged, leaving the lifeboats to make their way back to shore. In short, throughout our history, civilian-manned commercial ships carried military cargo to our war fighters and to our allies, and provided a quick solution to skilled manpower shortages to win every war we have fought.

The other way that a civilian manning program would operate was for the Navy to simply move cargo using the commercial merchant fleet, which they did from time to time anyway. The merchant fleet was engaged during the Korean and Vietnam wars. There were no complaints. During World Wars I and II, the booking agent for merchant ships was the Army Transport Service. Merchant ships were scheduled in the same way commercial companies booked cargo for destinations. The civilian crews would be literally in the Navy. They would be under the control of a Navy captain and subject to all Navy rules and regulations.

Early in the administration the newspapers were filled with Reagan's desire to rebuild the long-neglected combat capabilities of the Navy. There was coverage of the need for new submarines, aircraft carriers, and the recommissioning of World War II battleships. But there was no coverage of the need to build cargo ships or revive the nation's sealift capability. Knowing that the Navy would resist any attempt to lose control over their cargo fleet, Jesse told me that the Navy would first agree wholeheartedly to study it for at least four years, as they did under Carter's first term. Then, if pushed, the Navy would run a cost comparison between a civilian-crewed ship versus a uniformed Navy crew. By the time that analysis ended, a new president would be elected and the Navy would repeat the process.

Jesse concluded that the Navy would not be supportive of civilian manning and that there would be no promotion of the advantages of that concept from the think tanks, i.e., Brookings, AEI, or other public policy research organizations. Hence, Jesse, through the Joint Maritime Congress, funded a study by Booz Allen Hamilton, a management consulting company. Jesse chose Booz Allen because it had conducted studies for the Navy.

In December 1981, Booz Allen released a three-volume study [46] entitled, *Civilian Contract Manning of Government Ships – Military Sealift Command Nucleus Fleet.* The study concluded that commercial manning could relieve serious Navy manpower shortages that would result from operating a 600-ship Navy. President Reagan's stated goals for civilian manning were right. Now came the question of how fast could we begin the process.

Jesse said that his goal was to get Booz Allen to shorten the time frame of the deliberative process. Months went by and Calhoon saw a repeat of events that occurred under President Carter: "Once you get into the third year (of an administration), the first term is over. That's what happened with Carter," he said. President Carter was committed to civilian manning and in four years got nowhere.

I was ordered to get White House officials to deal with this issue. Lyn Nofziger told me he had been banging his head on this issue for almost a year. Craig Fuller said, "I've tried every door and I get the same man returning my call. I call Lawrence Korb at the Office of Manpower and Readiness, and I get a return call from George Sawyer (Assistant Secretary of the Navy for shipbuilding and logistics.) I call Admiral Harold E. Shear (administrator of the <u>US Maritime Administration</u>) and I get Sawyer again.

When Fuller reported to Jesse and me that he simply could get nowhere on the issue, Jesse and I went again to our strongest supporter in the Republican Party, Senator Paul Laxalt. Laxalt went to the White House and spoke directly to the president, reminding him that Jesse Calhoon was always there supporting him and other Republicans on economic issues; that he served on Reagan's trade commission, and engaged in a variety of activities as a result of this service. He also reminded the president that he had criticized Carter for failing to implement civilian manning and that he, Reagan, had pledged to do so. Fuller said that Laxalt broke the deadlock.

Ed Harper, assistant to the president for policy development, convened a meeting April 7, 1982, at the White House that included Sawyer and Admiral Shear and announced that he was appointed to follow the president's initiative himself and asked that a timeline be established to monitor progress, or lack thereof, on civilian manning. Shortly thereafter, the Navy announced a test of the civilian manning concept. Jesse's prediction concerning the Navy's tactics now entered phase two: a test of the concept.

Also in April of 1982, Jesse met in the White House to expedite President Reagan's promise to transfer some cargo operations to the private sector. Jesse brought the Booz Allen study to the meeting that was attended by Vice President Bush and other senior officials, including Craig Fuller. Calhoon made a brief presentation covering the study and said that it was undertaken to provide data that would demonstrate the wisdom of the president's plan.

On May 28, 1982, as a result of direct orders from the White House, the Navy issued a Request For Proposal (RFP) inviting private sector merchant marine operators to bid on carrying oil on three T-1 tankers in the South China Sea. While the Navy was conducting the survey, union crews on the ships being bid reported that the Navy was rigging the outcome of the analysis so that the private sector companies would appear noncompetitive. Calhoon knew exactly what was happening. I asked Jesse, "Should I go to Ed Harper or Fuller with this?"

"No," Jesse said, rubbing his forehead, "we know they are cheating. Let's see if they really intend to engage in criminal bid rigging before we do anything."

In September 1982, the Navy declared itself the winner in the competition, stating that the test of the cost effectiveness of civilian manning revealed that the Navy was the least expensive way to man the three tankers. A group of us sat in Jesse's office as he read the letters that were sent to the private companies, most of them Joint Maritime Congress member companies.

"Okay, I'll call Fuller to set up a meeting with Ed Harper," I said.

"No," Jesse responded, "Let's not get Fuller into this. It's going to get dirty, and I don't want to involve him. We know the Navy cheated. I don't know if they understand that bid rigging is illegal."

On July 14, 1983, Calhoon filed suit in federal district court alleging illegal bid rigging of a federal contract. [47] The Navy went berserk and immediately told the White House the allegations were not true. The White House insisted that the appropriate office of the inspector general in the Department of Defense conduct an investigation, not the Navy inspector general. The Navy was horrified.

Jeff Gerth, a reporter who covered defense issues, wrote in a November 1983 *New York Times* article: [48]

> The Justice Department has opened a preliminary investigation into allegations raised in a civil lawsuit that the Navy rigged bidding procedures last year to

favor the Navy over civilian contractors in the manning of Government vessels.

The Inspector General's eight-page report [49] contained the usual government legalese and stated, "We found no evidence of a contrived effort within the Navy to retain the operation of the three T-1 tankers in-house." The report then cited all of the information that the Navy withheld from the bidders resulting in the Navy winning the competition. It then listed those specific critical elements in terms of information that was denied to the bidders.

Barton Gellman, who reported on defense issues for the *Washington Post,* focused on the Navy decision repeatedly to ignore a major presidential directive to implement the civilian manning program.[50] Gellman noted that the years of delay resulted in the Joint Maritime Congress appealing to the White House for help. Gellman's article exposed the flawed cost comparison that resulted in the Navy winning the contract (it argued its cost would be $28.5 million versus the private sector's cost of $44.9 million). Gellman then spelled out how the Navy stacked the analysis against the commercial bidders.

After the Inspector General's report, Jesse felt that the civilian manning program was dead. If the Navy engaged in bid rigging following a White House meeting where they were ordered to implement the president's program, it was hopeless. Jesse said it was clear to him that the Navy would not yield to the direct orders of two US presidents to utilize civilian manning.

"Mike," he said, "the next time this country goes to war we will not be able to resupply our war fighters. We have no sealift and years from now it will be worse than it is today. Ronald Reagan was absolutely right on civilian manning but there is no Charles Colson in this White House to make it happen. The president is alone." Faced with insurmountable opposition, Jesse decided to abandon his effort to obtain civilian manning.

Why did the Navy take such drastic steps to stop civilian manning? It is universally known that the Navy does not like change of any kind. Perhaps the best description of this is in Richard E. Neustadt's classic work, *Presidential Power.* Neustadt quotes Franklin

D. Roosevelt, who had been assistant secretary of the Navy before he became president. In 1940 Roosevelt discussed with Marriner S. Eccles his experience with making changes in the Navy. "The admirals are really something to cope with—and I should know. To change anything in the NA-A-VY is like punching a featherbed. You punch it with your right and you punch it with your left until you are finally exhausted and then you find the damn bed just as it was before you started punching."[51]

As we approached the presidential election of 1984, Jesse ordered me to help with the reelection of Ronald Reagan. At that time, we had already renewed the ban on exporting Alaskan oil and we were fairly sure that the Jones Act would remain intact. Jesse was grateful to Ronald Reagan for having kept his promises on those two issues. The situation with PATCO was behind us. But we were still struggling with the Navy to get it to implement the civilian manning program.

After Reagan had won his second term, I assumed I would be working on Capitol Hill to get our Republican friends, who been so helpful on other issues, to continue supporting us on the civilian manning issue. But that is not what Jesse had in mind.

As we approached the Christmas holiday of 1984, Jesse took me downstairs to the restaurant that we frequented in the MEBA building for a Christmas lunch. As we talked about a variety of things, Jesse casually said to me, "I would like your resignation by close of business today." He followed that statement with a question about what my plans were for the Christmas holiday. I was stunned. I asked Jesse what I had done wrong. "Nothing. I just need your resignation by tonight," he said.

I did my best to smile through the rest of the luncheon, but I felt like I was at a wake and the wake was for me. I went upstairs, called my wife, and told her about my conversation with Jesse. She said Jesse was the best friend we ever had and he must have a reason for asking you to leave. Deborah Prochaska, my assistant, was in tears as she typed he letter. I brought the letter over to Jesse's secretary who said he had already left for the day. That night my wife and I joined friends singing Christmas carols through the neighborhood. It was a freezing cold night and my eyes were filled with tears, only some of which were from the cold. All I could think of was that I had just lost the best job in Washington.

I went to work the next morning as though nothing had happened. Jesse called me to come in and see him. And then, as though he had won the Academy award, he said he was shocked by my resignation and he refused to accept it. At that point I simply asked Jesse, "What the hell is going on?"

He then said, "I will only accept this resignation if you agree to give MEBA forty percent of your time for the next year, and you can go and consult for other companies. Keep the office, keep the car, and keep your salary." I was dizzy with confusion.

He then said that Leo Wright from Westinghouse wanted to talk with me, as did Interior Secretary Don Hodel, and Secretary of Defense Caspar Weinberger. "You need to meet with them right after January 1." He wished me Merry Christmas and Happy New Year, shook my hand, and then left.

The following week the newspapers carried the story that Jesse Calhoon, president of MEBA, the labor capitalist, had resigned. Early in January, his successor took over and fired everyone close to Jesse. He couldn't fire me because I had a signed contract for the next year.

Per Jesse's instructions, I met with Wright, Hodel, and Weinberger. Within days I was representing the nuclear power industry, a trade association engaged in doing site testing for nuclear waste burial, and the Strategic Defense Initiative for the Defense Department. Jesse had pushed me off the cliff, while at the same time ensuring the tripling of my income in less than a week. As I look back on it now, Jesse was trying to help me establish my own company, and take me away from a major legal controversy that developed at MEBA. I escaped all of it.

For the next twenty-five years, I designed specialized communications programs for the aerospace, defense, energy, transportation, telecommunications, and the shipbuilding industries. I assisted corporate clients in predicting, preventing, and stopping strikes. I also worked with unions on performance improvements that helped reduce cost and schedules for major defense programs. John Connally was right. My talents were better appreciated by American corporations that wanted to improve communications with their employees rather than by political candidates who wanted to become president.

Following the presidency of Ronald Reagan, still another Republican presidential candidate sought to capture the presidency by reassembling that broad base of the American electorate that catapulted both Nixon and Reagan into the White House: George H. W. Bush.

CHAPTER 7

George H. W. Bush and the New Majority (1988)

In the third year of Reagan's second term, Vice President George Bush began structuring his campaign for the presidency. Craig Fuller, who had been cabinet secretary for Reagan, was now Bush's chief of staff. Fuller was most familiar with the concept of the New Majority. We had spoken about it many times when he was cabinet secretary. Moreover, he was most familiar with the different workforce coalitions that I was now building for private industry. Craig asked if I would be willing to build those same coalitions for George Bush. I told him that I thought it would be easy, having already worked with Bush on labor, ethnic, and nationalities constituencies in the Nixon and Reagan years.

I told Craig that I could arrange meetings with unions from the different workforce coalitions that I had created. I also told him that I would alert him to defense and energy issues that were important to these unions so that he could develop relationships with unions on policy issues.

The first such target emerged over the sale of F-15 fighters to Saudi Arabia. The Democratic presidential candidate in 1988 was Michael Dukakis. Dukakis, like most Democrats at the time, was not strong on issues of national defense. All of the union leaders in my coalition were Democrats, but they were also aware that Republican administrations support a strong defense industry that creates jobs and employs union members.

In July of 1988, Vice President Bush, who had already locked up the GOP nomination for president, was in St. Louis, Missouri, for an event at which he would administer the oath of allegiance to a group of immigrants who had completed the requirements for becoming American citizens. St. Louis was also the headquarters of McDonnell Douglas, which manufactured the F-15 Eagle fighter aircraft. The Bush visit to St. Louis coincided with the annual Veiled Prophet Fair, an event that draws millions of people to the large grassy area under the famous Gateway Arch.

I asked the president of the International Association of Machinists representing the workers at McDonnell Douglas, Cassell Williams, if he would like an opportunity to meet with the vice president. I reminded Cass that if George Bush became president, he would have before him a decision on the sale of F-15 fighters to Saudi Arabia and it would be important for Bush to understand the relationship between that sale and jobs.

Cass Williams, who has since passed away, was a conservative black trade unionist who was a strong supporter of America's national security and always fought for the jobs of his members. I told Cass I could arrange a private meeting for him with Vice President Bush. Cass agreed to the meeting but insisted on including his entire bargaining team. He also insisted that, for their sake, the meeting would have to be off the record. If his team were seen with a Republican candidate, they would face severe reprisals from their International.

This presented a real challenge. Imagine, if you will, finding an inconspicuous location for a meeting with the vice president of the United States, who would be accompanied by a large delegation of Secret Service men and women, an advance team, and a motorcycle escort, in the middle of an event where at least one half million people would be gathered. After much deliberation, we chose the main dining room of the *Becky Thatcher*, a Mississippi paddle-wheel boat moored on the river adjacent to the Gateway Arch. Prior to the meeting, Cass and I agreed that we would provide as much privacy as possible to protect the members of the bargaining committee from being seen. Craig agreed that after the labor meeting, George Bush would view the air show from the open deck of the boat.

It was a boiling hot day when George Bush, accompanied by Mrs. Bush, boarded the vessel. Both he and Mrs. Bush greeted each labor delegate with a warm, vigorous handshake. The Bushes were well received. Vice President Bush began talking to the group about job issues and the difference between the two political parties on the defense budget. He concluded by saying, "You have a choice. You can go with Mike Dukakis and you will get favorable treatment when it comes to labor issues because Democrats are usually good with labor issues. But they are not good on jobs; especially defense jobs." He continued, "So, you want to know where I stand? I want America's defense to be second to none. I will sell F-15 jets to Saudi Arabia because they are our ally. So here's your choice. You vote for me, you get a job. You vote for Dukakis, you get a pink slip. You choose." The room erupted with applause.

After the meeting, Bush told the group that he was going up to the top deck to watch the air show and added, "I understand that most of you will leave by the back door so you won't be seen meeting with a Republican." Cass interrupted saying, "I don't know about any of you," referring to the shop stewards, "but I'm going to watch the show with the vice president." The entire bargaining team went up top with Vice President Bush and was visible on the evening news, drinking lemonade and watching the show. The group remained on the top deck for over an hour and the event ended with everyone pledging their support for George Bush in the upcoming election. What started as a clandestine meeting made the St. Louis papers as well as television coverage on the evening news. The union was committed.

A few days later, I received a note from Craig Fuller, which said that George Bush was ecstatic with the meeting and to set up more of them. The note was followed by a call from Fuller who said he would like to come to my lake house and take a boat ride. He asked if he could stay overnight. He arrived the next morning with a small briefcase stuffed with large loose-leaf binders. As we sat on my deck overlooking the beach, Fuller said that the vice president was now considering a running mate to put on the ticket. There were two major factors in the selection. First, he had to be conservative to satisfy Republican voters who viewed Bush as a liberal. Second, despite being conservative, he had to demonstrate that he could draw Democratic votes. Again, Craig and I were looking at a Nixon-Reagan situation where conservative

Democrats would vote for a Republican. We began going through the book and I was asked to comment on several potential running mates.

As we went through each potential candidate, Fuller would ask, "How does he fare with your aerospace and defense workers?" As we exhausted the list of potential candidates, the only person who met all the qualifications that Fuller demanded was Dan Quayle. I told Fuller that Quayle had a better relationship in the aerospace and defense unions than any of the other candidates. Moreover he had one of the most conservative voting records in the Senate.

Days later, Fuller called and asked if there was a small union delegation that would be willing to offer testimony before a Republican Party platform committee in New Orleans. I suggested that we select union leaders from four regions of the country, all of whom were all part of my national workforce coalition. I chose leaders from the states of Washington, California, Maryland, and New Jersey. These included Leonard Ricks, Executive Director of the Southern California Professional Engineering Association representing aerospace engineers at McDonnell Douglas (Ricks also chaired the Council of Engineers & Scientists Organizations); Darrell Matthews, president of the Seattle Professional Engineering Employees Association representing workers at Boeing; Harold Ammond, executive director of the Association of Scientists and Professional Engineering Personnel representing workers at Lockheed in New Jersey; and Gary Eder, executive director of the Salaried Employees Association representing workers at the Westinghouse Electronics facility in Baltimore. Len Ricks, a brilliant engineer who had led numerous labor delegations in testifying before congressional committees, was well known to the White House and members of Congress on key defense committees. These union leaders attended the convention in New Orleans, testified before the platform committee, and had a private meeting and photo op with Vice President George Bush.

The week before the Republican convention in New Orleans, Dan Quayle brought his family to my lake house. I asked him if he had any notion that he might be selected as a vice presidential running mate for George Bush. He waved me off and said, "Are you kidding? That will never happen."

I said, "Dan, I think you have an eight out of ten chance of being nominated. Are you not aware of that?"

He replied, "Aw, people talk all the time."

I responded that two weeks earlier the vice president's chief of staff was sitting on this very porch going through potential candidates and that I thought it was inconceivable that Bush would select anyone other than Dan Quayle.

Before Dan and his family moved into the vice president's house, Liz Prestridge and I went to Dan's house in McLean, Virginia, and gave him and Marilyn a comprehensive briefing on Nixon's Office of Public Liaison. We explained how Colson built the grassroots army of labor unions and ethnic organizations that constituted the New Majority. I discussed the relationship that Colson had with Nixon that was central to accomplish all of our objectives. If Dan wanted to capture the New Majority for the president and later for himself, he had to stay close to Middle America.

He understood what we were telling him. He said there were already plans to set up an Office of Public Liaison, but it would be part of the president's staff, not the vice president's. I told him it didn't matter. The important thing was establishing the outreach to the unions. I could help Dan do this without having a formal structure.

After George Bush won the election, he selected former New Hampshire governor John Sununu to be his chief of staff. Vice President Quayle was asked to form a National Space Council to advise the president on civil and military space policy. In this capacity he met with all of the unions he had worked with during the Reagan years as well as with unions that I had brought into his office when he was senator. Quayle was strong on defense, strong on the civilian space program, and strong on shipbuilding and other components of America's industrial base. Quayle enjoyed working with all of the labor unions as vice president as much as he had as senator. During those first two years, Bush also stayed close to the unions as did his Secretary of Defense, Richard Cheney.

Later, Mark Albrecht, a close friend who had served on Pete Wilson's Senate staff, became executive director of the National Space Council, and Liz Prestridge became the council's director of communications.

Both of these people knew the drill, especially Liz, a former student who worked with me in the Nixon White House, at ACTION, and at the American Enterprise Institute (AEI), and was on the *Becky Thatcher* during the Bush visit in St. Louis. Through the National Space Council, both President Bush and Vice President Quayle remained on a first-name basis with aerospace and defense union leaders who also worked closely with NASA Administrator Dan Goldin and Defense Secretary Cheney. Thus, the workforce leaders were able to obtain public policy input as unions did in the Nixon White House.

In addition to the aerospace and defense workforce, a major opportunity arose to expand the president's relationship with unions in the airline industry. In March of 1989, the mechanics at Eastern Airlines struck the company and pushed the airline near bankruptcy. Pilots generally do not have a good relationship with their maintenance crews, and in this instance did not support the strike. The pilots at the Air Line Pilots Association (ALPA), seeking to save Eastern, approached me. They wanted President Bush to declare a Taft-Hartley injunction to provide a cooling-off period to give the pilots time to reason with the mechanics.

I asked for a meeting with Quayle. His secretary, Cynthia Ferneau, had worked with me when Dan was in the Senate. I could always show up at Dan's Senate office in the Hart Building. But as vice president, everything had changed. Cynthia had to know a subject matter before scheduling a meeting. I told her it concerned the strike at Eastern Airlines and the need to invoke Taft-Hartley to get a cooling-off period.

As I walked into Quayle's West Wing office, he was clearly nervous. I opened with the comment that I had talked with members of the pilots' union, who felt that they were victims of the International Association of Machinists maintenance crews and did not want this strike. The pilots believed they could work out a settlement if they had time. I suggested that Quayle advise Bush to invoke Taft Hartley to provide the sixty or ninety-day cooling-off period needed to settle the strike.

Dan responded Bush had DOT, FAA and OMB all involved and that he could not cut into that debate. Suddenly he was heading for the door. I stopped him before he opened the door and said, "Dan, I'm trying to stop a strike that could kill Eastern Airlines."

He repeated, "I can't cut into the process. That's not my area of responsibility."

Ultimately, in the face of an insurmountable conflict, Eastern went out of business. The Eastern pilots blamed Bush for not trying to save the company and its employees. ALPA's leadership believed that if George Bush had invoked Taft-Hartley, Eastern could have been saved.

There were yet other opportunities for President Bush to establish a positive relationship with ALPA. During this time, I got to know the organization's first vice president, Captain Duane Woerth, who would later become ALPA's president. My relationship with Duane, coupled with my personal friendship with Andrew Card, then-deputy chief of staff at the White House, led me to believe I could be helpful in improving relations between ALPA and the White House.

My friendship with Andy Card began before he went into government; he and his family had visited our family at our lake house just outside Washington, D.C. I invited Card and Woerth to spend the day at the lake. Andy listened to Duane as he explained the concerns of ALPA over the sale of routes by airline companies to improve their cash flow. ALPA also feared the potential sale of another US airline that would result in a devastating loss for ALPA pilots. Card responded that he saw no problem because no airline would be able to sell its routes without government approval. "It would not be a back-room deal," he said, as the pilots feared. Andy's assurance was made more definite when, in February 1992, he became Secretary of Transportation, which had oversight over the FAA. Shortly after his appointment, Woerth met with Andy in Boston, and both men reassured each other that the sale of airline routes would not be permitted. As far as I was concerned, the problem was resolved.

On August 2, 1990, Saddam Hussein invaded Kuwait and started the first Gulf War. I received a call from Chief of Staff John Sununu, who asked if I could bring a delegation of unions to meet with George Bush to talk with him about the implications of the invasion. He said that it looked like we were going to go to war in Kuwait, and Bush knew that the Democrats on the Hill would oppose the war. This situation was too serious to become a political issue. As the U.S. began moving men and equipment in position to strike Saddam's forces, the code name that was used for the exercise was Operation Desert Shield. Sununu said that Bush wanted me to get labor unions to urge Democrats on the Hill to support the president in the upcoming war, just as unions had supported President Nixon's efforts in Vietnam.

Sununu arranged for labor leaders to meet with the president in the Roosevelt Room of the White House on October 11, 1990. The president had already previously met most of these labor leaders, so we knew he would be comfortable talking with them.

Prior to the president entering the room, Secretary of Defense Cheney briefed the unions on the Kuwait situation. He said that the president was committed to pushing Saddam Hussein out of Kuwait. He said Saddam had invaded Kuwait in August, and noted that it would not be easy to get him out because of the amount of arms that Saddam had amassed in Kuwait. Saddam had the largest standing army in the Middle East, equipped with modern Soviet weapons.

During Cheney's presentation, Cass Williams spoke up, "Why are we waiting to attack Saddam? We have the best fighter aircraft in the world. What are we waiting for?"

Secretary Cheney looked at me, smiled, and said that the Navy did not have enough cargo ships.

"Oh, my gosh," I said. "I wish Jesse Calhoon could be in this room today."

Williams said, "What do you mean we don't have the ships? I thought the troops were already there."

Cheney responded that the troops were flown into the area by military and commercial aircraft that were part of the Civil Air Reserve fleet, which, like the National Guard, are called upon when needed. He continued that there was a need for a massive resupply of equipment: drinking water, food, toilet paper, ammunition, oil, among other things. All had to be brought in every day by ship.

I couldn't help but ask, "The Ready Reserve Fleet can't do that?"

Cheney conceded that the Ready Reserve Fleet was unable to meet the need. He noted that the ships were too old and that Bush was working with our allies to borrow tonnage all over the world. I thought to myself that Jesse Calhoon had made the argument for four years that the Ready Reserve Fleet was so old it would be useless in any major war. During the Gulf War, I learned how right Jesse was.

In preparing this book I interviewed Captain Lee Kincaid, then-president of the American Maritime Congress.[52] In 1990, Kincaid was assigned to help activate the Ready Reserve Fleet from the Port of Beaumont, Texas. He was one of the port captains for Apex Marine at Lake Success, New York. The Ready Reserve Fleet at Beaumont, like those in other ports, was comprised of World War II Liberty ships. It took six weeks to get one ship out of mothballs.

From the start of reactivating those old ships, getting able-bodied seamen—whether officers, engineers, or deck hands—was a problem. Most of the personnel to be called were in their late seventies and eighties. Some of them were unable to stand for long periods of time. Kincaid said, "I felt sorry for one pilot who couldn't stand behind the wheel. We made a high seat so that he could stand his tour at the helm."

Many of the seamen who were called had not seen ships as old as those in the reserve fleet, every one a steamship. Few of the seamen called had experience with a steam plant. Inexperienced crews damaged some of the Beaumont ships. Since there were no spare parts available for these old ships, they had to be towed back to port. The entire exercise was a wake-up call for the Navy. The first Gulf War was extremely short. In a protracted war, the Ready Reserve Fleet would have been less than useless.

The unions met with Cheney for about an hour prior to the president's arrival. When President Bush came into the room he laid out much of what Cheney had already told us, but focused on the need for these labor leaders to impress upon members of Congress that the war in Kuwait was necessary. The president indicated that we would go to war soon, but he did not give us a date. At the end of the meeting, I assured President Bush that whenever he launched the war, unions from at least thirty states would flood the Hill with letters, telegrams, and phone calls supporting his decision. I told him that a national industrial base workforce coalition would be with him.

On January 17, 1991, Desert Shield became Desert Storm. As

promised, labor leaders from around the country sent telegrams and letters of support to their members of Congress, as well as to the White House. John Sununu called me and said, "The president is grateful for everything that you're doing." Shortly thereafter I received a brief handwritten note from the president thanking the unions for their support: "I'm proud you'll be with me 'throughout the storm.' Thanks so very much. George Bush." [53]

It then became important for President Bush to nurture the relationship with the unions and stay close to them when the war ended. Unfortunately, from this point on, the relationship with the unions that supported his administration began a downhill slide.

On February 28, 1991, President Bush announced that Kuwait had been liberated. He began hosting receptions at the White House to honor all those who participated in Saddam's defeat. Not only was I unsuccessful in getting the president's staff to invite some of the workforce leaders to watch the victory parade in front of the White House when Army General Norman Schwarzkopf and his staff were honored as they returned in triumph, but I was also equally unsuccessful in getting White House staff to invite the labor unions to the receptions held throughout that victory week. No one on Bush's staff would take my message to the president. As a result, no labor union supporters were invited to participate in these celebrations, all of which would have sealed the bond between the president and the unions. The White House staff simply did not understand why being friendly to unions was important to the president.

At a White House Christmas party in December 1991, my wife and I were in the receiving line waiting for our annual Christmas photo-op with the president. When we approached the president, he grabbed the labels on my suit jacket with both hands and pulled me close saying loud enough for the man in line behind me to hear, "Mike, I'm going to need your help this year."

I responded, "Workforce coalition reporting for duty, sir," and saluted.

"No. Listen," the president said. "I mean it! I'm going to need your unions this year."

I repeated, "We're ready to help." I resisted the temptation in that receiving line to say to him that I had been trying to get through to him. Instead I thought that I finally had what I needed, a personal request from the president himself.

John Sununu left the administration after the Gulf War. Samuel Skinner subsequently became chief of staff to the president. Following up on the president's request at Christmastime that I revive his relationship with union supporters, in January 1992, I wrote to Skinner, urging him to set up a meeting of the labor unions with the president. I attached a white paper that highlighted the layoffs that would result from the delay or cancellation of a number of defense programs.[54]

Knowing that Skinner had no knowledge the workforce coalition I represented, I went to Dan Quayle, who had a good relationship with Skinner, and asked him to endorse my request. Quayle read the materials I sent to Skinner and understood the importance of Skinner getting on board with the labor unions. He also knew that Skinner most likely did not realize how close George Bush had been to these unions. Quayle sent Skinner his copy of the package, along with a handwritten note: "Sam, he's the best labor outreach person on our side that I know. Plug him in. (signed) DQ." [55]

I also gave Craig Fuller a copy of the Skinner package, which he sent to Skinner along with a personal note which read: "Sam Skinner: This is an important paper. I've worked with Mike for several years on workforce issues and to develop support for the president. Please take a look. Thanks, Craig." Despite the endorsement of both Quayle and Fuller, Skinner never acknowledged receiving the package and never contacted me.

Early in 1992, I began receiving calls from workforce coalition members expressing their concern that they had not seen or talked to George Bush or anyone on his staff since the October 1990 meeting in the White House. I began calling Dick Cheney's office to see if I could get him to meet with the unions, especially since the president himself had asked for my help in gathering the unions together.

In July 1992, the word leaked out that the Senate Armed Services Committee was planning a fifty percent cut in the C-17 transport aircraft program. The program was important to unions in California,

Texas, Missouri, Illinois, Ohio, and Connecticut. Knowing that it was important to defend the C-17, I told Cheney that Quayle was most sympathetic to demonstrating to the unions that we were fighting for their jobs. The Democrats were cutting defense programs. This was an opportunity for Bush to speak up for the union defense jobs in those key states.

Unable to get through to the White House on the C-17 issue, which was important to California, in desperation I called Governor Pete Wilson who said that the president had conceded California to Clinton. "The defense workers can carry this state," he said. "We must not lose them."

On July 22, 1992, I sent a memo to Secretary of Defense Cheney,[56] which had as an attachment a memo I had sent to Craig Fuller expressing the hope that someone could tell the president of the need to stop the erosion of the only labor constituency we might still be able to keep. I told Cheney that to do so we had to take advantage of the fact that the Democrats were now shredding the president's defense budget. I also noted that the AFL-CIO sent several buses to Cass Williams' IAM local in St. Louis to transport aerospace workers to a large Clinton rally and that Cass would be meeting with Clinton privately.

"Dick," I wrote, "There must be something we can do before the Clinton bus tour reaches California. We have a good story to tell and a hell of a case to present. This is <u>our</u> constituency. My God, we can't let Clinton take it away from us. Please let me know how I can help."

I suggested a union meeting at the White House where Bush would personally thank the unions for the support they provided during Desert Storm. I said that it must be kept in mind that following George Bush's meeting with the workforce leaders on the *Becky Thatcher*, unions had begun writing to the president, the vice president and other members of his administration concerning the defense budget. In my memo I indicated that a trail of letters beginning in 1988 from Cass Williams and others attempted to alert the administration to the consequences for labor of defense budget cuts. Letters had been written to Secretary Cheney, Vice President Quayle, the White House chief of staff and President Bush himself. I told everyone that the president had personally asked me to revive his relationship with the unions before the election of 1992.

It is important to note that Bush's approval rating had reached a high of 89 percent in February 1991, according to the Roper Center. By July of 1992 his approval rating had dropped to a low of 29 percent, and his disapproval rating was 60 percent.

Throughout the early part of the summer of 1992 I pleaded for Bush to return to St. Louis for the Veiled Prophet Fair and again take credit for the F-15 program that he previously approved. I urged him to promise that he would continue to back the program in his next administration by approving another F-15 sale to the Saudis. He could take credit for having kept his previous promise to the workers.

On August 5, 1992, I wrote to Fuller urging him to contact Bush on the need to set up a union meeting with the president who was losing his relationship with the unions. [57] The memo concluded:

> If Republicans are guilty of anything, it is in not being sensitive to the fears and the deteriorating economic conditions of the wage earner. The real crime here is that George Bush is probably more sensitive to people than most Republicans. Our problem is he has left to others to make that case, others who cannot make it as well as he can.

Late in August 1992, Bush did return to St. Louis to announce the F-15 sale, but by that time it was a moot point with the unions. During the trip to St. Louis, Bush spoke with Cass Williams, who urged him to meet with the unions again in the White House. But Clinton, who was already campaigning in St. Louis, promised that he would support an F-15 sale, rendering Bush's promise irrelevant. Clinton had already convinced the unions that he would do it. Jobs for St. Louis aircraft workers were no longer an issue. [58]

As I was busy trying to get the aerospace and defense workers back in to see the president, another issue emerged in August involving the Northwest Airlines pilots. Duane Woerth, who had by then become president of ALPA, called to share with me his concern about a rumor that

Northwest was having financial problems; to boost cash flow it was considering the sale of its exclusive routes to Asia. Duane said that he had tried to call Andy Card, who by then had become secretary of Transportation with oversight of the FAA, but could not get a call returned.

"I have to get to him on the sale of the routes, and I can't get through," Duane said. I responded by suggesting that he write a letter to Andy citing earlier conversations they had had and ALPA's concern about the administration's position on the commercial airlines and the routes.

Duane addressed his concerns in a letter which he sent to Secretary Card at the Department of Transportation. Weeks later he got a letter from a staff member at Bush campaign headquarters extolling Bush's virtues as a pilot who was shot down in World War II and rescued at sea. The letter made no mention of the issue raised to Andy Card at the Department of Transportation. It was more than a mild brush off. Duane described it as an insult: "I write a letter to the Secretary of Transportation, and I get a response from the Bush campaign? Come on!"

I told Duane that I would call Andy Card immediately. The problem was that I could not reach Andy either. Nobody could, because he was in Florida dealing with the damage from Hurricane Andrew. Unfortunately, Card's inaccessibility had become a political problem for the administration. There was no one on Card's staff in Washington who understood the routes issue. Moreover, there was no one who was sympathetic enough to the union to initiate an inquiry. The pilots then went to Clinton who was only too happy to promise that in a Clinton presidency no airline company would ever be allowed to sell trade routes. ALPA broke with the coalition and endorsed Clinton.

When Andy Card returned to Washington from Florida in September, he called me, saying, "Hey, we're going to need a lot of these coalition guys. Where is Duane?"

I responded, "Andy, they're gone."

"Gone?" he said.

"Gone," I replied, and told him the story of Duane's letter and the response from the Bush campaign. Andy was furious. "Why didn't Duane call me?" he said.

I responded, "He did call you. I called you and was told you weren't there and no one on your staff listened to my plea that it was important for me to talk to you."

Andy said he never saw Duane's letter. I responded, "It's over, Andy, they've endorsed Clinton."

The loss of ALPA support for the president coincided with the beginning of the end of the workforce coalition's support for Bush, because he would not meet with them. At the same time, the Democrat-controlled Senate Armed Services Committee was raiding the defense budget and Bush was not complaining.

I began getting calls from leaders in the coalition stating that Clinton was now making inroads in their locals and that without *some* overt signal from the White House that the president still valued their support, the leadership of these unions would have to abandon Bush and support Clinton. I believed that if I could talk to Bush, he would listen to me. I decided to approach Craig Fuller again. He knew Bush better than anyone on the White House staff.

Craig told me that he could not open the Bush door. He said, "You have a reputation of going through doorways, windows, and skylights when all avenues are closed to you. You have a reputation of smashing through the walls. It's time you go talk to Quayle. He's going to be having lunch with the president either Wednesday or Thursday." We had two days to spare.

I didn't want to go through the switchboard or through Quayle's staff for fear that, once again, he might shy away from the subject matter. For me to succeed I would have to surprise him. Once again, I went on automatic pilot. About 8:30 pm I got into my car and drove over to the vice president's residence. I drove up to the front gate and an officer came out asking if I was lost. I said, "No I'm not lost. I know Dan Quayle very well, and I want to go in and talk to him."

The officer said, "Fine. Just pull your car up inside the gate here."

Suddenly there were four officers surrounding my car ordering me to get out of the car. Oh, *boy*, I thought to myself, *they probably think I'm a lunatic.* I said, "Look. I know you guys think I'm a crackpot. Let me just reach into my pocket, give you my driver's license, and you can go over to the phone and call the White House switchboard."

I asked if I could call the White House switchboard myself, stating that even a prisoner gets one phone call. They looked at each other and again I said, "Just give me one phone call." I called White House communications and got one of the staff people on the phone who knew me. "Can you put me through to the residence?" I asked. Two minutes later Dan Quayle was on the line.

"Dan," I said. "It's Mike Balzano."

"Mike Balzano," he responded. "It's 8:45! Why are you calling this late?"

I said, "Dan. I need to talk to you."

He replied, "Why can't we do this at the office?"

I said, "Dan, I have an emergency and I need to talk to you."

He gave a long groan and said, "Call me back in thirty minutes because I'm tutoring the kids; Marilyn's in New York."

"Dan, you need to look out the window," I said. "There's a white Corsica parked inside the gate and the police are about to arrest me and take me to St. Elizabeth's Hospital. Would you please tell them you know me?"

Dan got on the phone with the agent, while I watched them looking at each other. Then the agent responded to Quayle, "Okay, absolutely, sir." An officer then motioned for me to pull over next to the house. At 9:00 pm I walked up to the mansion. Dan opened the door and led me to the couch in front of the fireplace.

"What is so important that you have to come to my house at night?" Dan asked.

"I want you to read some memos," I replied.

"You're kidding," he said.

I said, "No."

Dan responded, "You're going to sit here while I read memos?"

"Yes," I answered. "There aren't that many, only seven. Just read the memos for me," I pleaded.

So Dan started reading and began moaning. "Ooh, ow, oh boy. Has anyone in the White House seen these?" he asked.

I responded, "I don't know; that's my problem."

When he finally got through the memos, he raised his arms behind his head, sat way back on the couch and said, "What do you want me to do?"

I said, "Dan, I want you to give these memos to the president. He asked me in December 1991 to help him put together a workforce coalition. We are now weeks from the election and I'm losing all my unions to Clinton on issues where Clinton is never going to keep any of his promises."

Quayle replied, "I can't do that."

I said, "Dan, you're having lunch with the president on Wednesday."

"How do you know that?" Quayle asked.

I said, "I know."

"All right," he said. "So I'm having lunch with the president."

I said, "Dan, you need to give him these memos, and tell him: You asked Mike Balzano to do something for you; he's done it. You asked him to come in for Desert Storm; he did it. You then said to him that you're going to need his help. He's been trying to build a coalition to help you, but he can't get in the door to talk to you. These people have been trying to meet with you for a year."

Dan began shaking his head and said, "I'm not going to do that."

I replied, "Dan, you've got to do that. You're the only door he's got."

"You want me to tell this to the President of the United States?" he said. "I can't."

"You won't," I said.

"No," he said. "I can't." He explained that there was a standing order that any piece of paper given to the president must be reviewed by his staff. "I might be able to say something, but I can't give him the memos," he said.

I told him the memos were self-explanatory and then said, "Dan, if the president chokes on a chicken bone tomorrow, you are the President of the United States."

He stared at me and repeated, "I can't do it, Mike."

I sat back on the couch and said, "Dan, have you thought about what you are going to be doing next year—practice law?"

He gave me a half smile and said, "You think we're going to lose."

I said, "No, Dan, I *know* you're going to lose and you're going to lose big time."

He replied, "Mike, I don't believe that."

I said, "Okay. I hope I'm wrong and you're right."

Unable to meet with Bush, each union in the coalition, one by one, endorsed Clinton.

The day before Clinton's inauguration, the Quayles hosted a farewell party in their home. All the administration officials and all the party bigwigs were there. Toward the end of the evening when only the four of us remained, Dan dragged me back into the room in front of the fireplace where we had sat that September evening. He said, "You remember that night when you were sitting in that chair? You called it."

I said, "Yeah, I did."

"You were right," he said. "I should have done what you asked."

I said, "Dan, I don't know if it would have done any good by that time. It was awfully late." Quayle was a team player who supported the president. He followed the White House rules because he did not want to circumvent the system that the president had put in place.

Unquestionably the most important relationship that Bush forged with the unions was with the National Industrial Base Workforce Coalition. Under the leadership of Leonard Ricks, the coalition had testified before the House and Senate on defense programs and NASA issues. Ricks also directed the coalition in testifying before a variety of prestigious presidential and congressional commissions, investigations and platform committees of both political parties.

Unfortunately, the last meeting that President Bush had with any members of the workforce coalition was in 1990. The 1992 Bush campaign had little interest in unions. The only reasonable explanation could be that White House officials did not give President Bush information about how unions were trying to meet with him.

One of the recurrent themes in this book is the tendency for Republican presidents not to maintain relationships with those workforce representatives to whom they appealed and whose votes they won. I do not suggest that the president himself constantly communicate with that network of supporters, although both Vice President George H. W. Bush and Vice President Dan Quayle did just that early on. However, in Bush's last year as president, chief of staff John Sununu had left the administration. Sununu was known and respected by the majority of the unions who voted for Bush. As a nuclear engineer committed to building the nuclear power plant at Seabrook, New Hampshire, Governor Sununu had an excellent working relationship with the building and metal trades unions. As chief of staff, he still relied on the unions to support the administration on Desert Storm and other public policy issues. When John Sununu left the Bush administration, there was no one who talked to the unions.

George H. W. Bush was the last Republican president who enlisted the labor coalition in a presidential campaign.

Opportunities Lost: the 2008 Presidential Campaign

Unlike Nixon, Reagan, George H. W. Bush, and George W. Bush, all of whom reached out to the workforce, John McCain and Mitt Romney made no attempt to court unions. During the George W. Bush years, Don Rumsfeld had a good relationship with the unions because he made an effort to talk to them, especially unions in a national industrial-base workforce coalition.

Having known John McCain since his return to the United States after Nixon obtained the release of the Vietnam POWs in 1973, I was willing to help him in his bid for the presidency. Developing a relationship between organized labor and John McCain should have been easy. In his first term in the House of Representatives, beginning in 1983, McCain was friendly to the unions.

During his run for reelection to the House in 1984, I went to Arizona to campaign for him. I organized a series of labor meetings with the building trades unions. The state AFL-CIO affiliate had been running a food bank in which postal workers collected food at mail stops along their routes. Without warning, the regional postal authority issued a policy stopping the drivers from collecting the food. I arranged a series of meetings with the union leaders who ran the food bank. McCain contacted postal authorities in Washington and was able to maintain the collections. During these discussions, I occasionally told McCain in good humor that it was the labor unions who maintained the pressure on Democrats to reject any peace talks until we got all of our prisoners back. In a sense, I told McCain, "The labor unions got you out of prison in Hanoi."

During my tenure at MEBA I visited with McCain on a variety of labor issues and always found him friendly on these issues. Since he had supported MEBA's position on the Alaskan oil issue, the maritime union became a solid base for McCain in the labor movement. In 1985, when I left MEBA to launch my own company, John McCain joined Jeane Kirkpatrick, Senators Bob Dole, Paul Laxalt, Dan Quayle, and Pete Wilson at our opening reception held in the Senate Caucus Room. Because of my long-term relationship with McCain, I believed I had a good chance of linking the labor unions in the defense sector to John's campaign for president in 2008.

As I began canvassing labor unions in the defense sector, I found unions generally sympathetic to the possibility of a president who was a Vietnam veteran and war prisoner. But the industrial unions were also aware that the leadership of the AFL-CIO had become more progressive. Given that the unions were more comfortable providing testimony before both platform committees, their view was that if the Democratic candidate refused to consider the union testimony, as occurred in the Dukakis campaign, at least they could tell their members they offered testimony to both parties. As usual, the Democrats would not accept union testimony. But, then, neither did McCain.

I went to the McCain campaign headquarters in Crystal City, Virginia, and tried to talk with the campaign strategist. I spoke with a few of McCain's lower-level campaign aides about my relationship with McCain over the years and the role the unions played during the Vietnam War in helping Nixon bring the POWs home. But I could see that dealing with McCain's staff, many of whom were not even born when he was released in 1973, would be unproductive.

It soon became apparent that it would require a major effort to meet with McCain in person. I would have to deal with all of the young gatekeepers whose answer would invariably be negative. Maybe it was because after over thirty years of having to fight Republicans on the benefits of reaching out to labor, I was tired; maybe it was because my business and family commitments were consuming all of my time. Whatever the reason, I decided not to pursue McCain or his campaign.

I then received a call from Pat Malvaso, a retired colonel who was well connected within the Defense Department, with whom I had worked on some sensitive personnel issues. Pat said that he had spoken about me with a young man who was deputy campaign manager for McCain and the man wanted to talk with me about unions. I accompanied Pat to McCain's campaign headquarters and met with Christian Ferry, a bright young man who had worked in McCain's Senate office. I gave Ferry a brief history of my dealings with Nixon, Reagan, and George H.W. Bush on labor issues. He was comfortable with my background and said that McCain would appreciate the potential of working with defense industry unions. I then offered the strategy of building a campaign around reindustrializing America, the issue that Reagan had campaigned on, and then abandoned. Ferry stated that McCain would not want to embrace such a broad effort but said that McCain was committed to reviving the nuclear power issue. Here, I felt we could assemble enough union leaders to put together a reasonable outreach to major unions.

Unfortunately, days later, Ferry became a casualty of the campaign life cycle. That is, there is a first campaign team that usually consists of staff members who know the candidate as Ferry did. Then there is a second wave of campaign leadership that usually appears before the convention. Finally, there is a third campaign team consisting of old, reliable individuals who are considered "seasoned political veterans." Each wave of newcomers displaces those who were personally close to the candidate. Ferry was caught in the changing of the guard and was unable to implement any of the ideas we discussed.

Before Ferry left, I mentioned the idea of allowing the unions to testify before the platform committee on issues important to the industrial base. He told me that the person in charge of that subject would be Christopher Koch, former chief of staff to Senator Slade Gorton from the state of Washington and later to John McCain. I had worked as a labor advisor on the Slade Gorton campaign in 1986. Gorton ran an excellent campaign against Brock Adams But nonetheless, lost. In that election I learned that in some states no matter how much of an ally a Republican is to the unions, in a solidly Democratic state a Republican cannot win.

Koch, being a friend and eager to help McCain, told me that he was willing to have pro-jobs testimony from the unions, but said that there would be no platform hearings as such. The RNC decided to have all testimony submitted online. [59] But labor leaders attempting an outreach to a Republican candidate wanted face-to-face contact with committee members. Having been denied this access, the unions declined to participate. They abandoned all efforts to reach out to McCain.

Fast forward to 2010. During Obama's first term, I had been working with industrial clients to predict, prevent, and if necessary, stop strikes. I also worked with defense industry clients who sought cooperation from their workforce in order to significantly reduce costs. During this time, the defense industrial-base workforce faced many cuts beginning with a $500 billion dollar defense cut over ten years followed by sequestration that cut another $500 billion. Obama's Secretary of Defense, Leon Panetta, vigorously fought these cuts, stressing that the impact on the defense budget was intolerable and would weaken the nation's national security. NASA's budget did not fare any better. The Constellation program that was to replace the shuttle was canceled, along with the jobs of thousands of NASA's high-tech workers and contractors. The aerospace and defense workforce was decimated. Unions that had been part of the Kennedy space program and were involved in the Constellation program were abandoned.

In 2012, unions that were involved in workforce activity to protect NASA programs contacted me. They were aware that the Democratic leadership of the congressional oversight committees was clearly uninterested in the negative impact that defense and space cancelations would have on the industrial-base workforce. They were not even interested in talking with union leaders involved in these programs. The few that did listen did their best to offer sympathy, but not help. And why not? The AFL-CIO would support Democratic candidates anyway, so why worry about local unions losing their jobs?

Ironically, the AFL-CIO would use PAC funds collected from these very locals to support Democratic candidates. There was no window of opportunity for these local unions to participate in candidate selection in the Democratic Party. The question was, would there be a window to the Republican Party?

In Mississippi, where Republicans faithfully vote for shipbuilding interests, the Republican congressional delegation had no relationship with the unions. Those same shipbuilding unions in 2010 helped ensure the defeat of the incumbent Democrat, Gene Taylor, the chairman of the House Seapower and Expeditionary Forces Subcommittee. Taylor ignored the unions and would not allow them to testify at a crucial hearing on Navy shipbuilding. Further, the unions were not allowed to submit testimony for the record. For the first time, the shipbuilder unions in the Gulf understood that the Democratic Party was only interested in the AFL-CIO PAC contributions. In that year, Republicans won both the Mississippi US House and Senate seats.

Labor and the Romney Campaign (2012)

Almost all of the unions in the aerospace and defense sector knew of my relationship with presidents from Nixon through George W. Bush, and that I had assisted the unions in dealing with policy makers to maintain jobs. A small group of union presidents asked if I could set up a meeting with candidate Mitt Romney to address the issue of shipbuilding. I called John Sununu, with whom I had worked on nuclear power issues when he was governor of New Hampshire. I had also worked with him on a variety of issues when he was chief of staff to George H. W. Bush. Sununu had joined the Romney campaign as an advisor.

I told John of my conversations with the unions and asked if he could facilitate an outreach for them to Romney. Since we were still three months away from the election, I told him I would be willing to brief the person who occupied the labor desk for the Romney campaign. He said he would set up a meeting. He called the next day to report that there was no labor desk but would I agree to assume that position for Romney? I told him that my workload made that impossible but I would help find someone for that position. In my opinion the best candidate to work with unions who might be available was Cynthia Cole.

Cole is a engineer who served as the president of the Society of Professional Engineering Employees in Aerospace (SPEEA), which represents some 25,000 engineers and technical employees who work for Boeing. Not only did she have the right credentials to deal with the large engineering workforce in Massachusetts and other unions in the aerospace and defense industry, she was also a respected Republican who served as the Washington state labor coalition chair for the Bush/Cheney 2004 campaign. Through her efforts, Cole delivered a percentage of the labor vote for Bush that was three percent higher than the national average. Cynthia would have been an excellent person to chair the labor desk for Romney.

Unfortunately, Cole's family commitments made a move to Boston impossible. There would be no labor desk in the Romney campaign.

I still agreed to help Sununu, who suggested we meet with Ron Kaufman at Kaufman's home in Washington. At the meeting, Sununu noted that it would be almost impossible to get Romney to meet with these labor leaders, but Sununu offered to meet with the unions.

I brought the offer to key labor leaders who accepted Sununu as a substitute for Romney because they had worked with him when he was chief of staff to George H. W. Bush. While we planned the meeting with the labor leaders, a controversy arose over Romney's comment that many people would be voting for Obama because they paid no taxes. This offhand remark caused the unions to withdraw from any meeting we might have set up.

Sununu asked what I thought we could do. I told him that, lacking a labor person on Romney's staff, the only industrial-base expert on the Romney team we could rely on was former secretary of the Navy John Lehman. The unions would remember him from the Reagan defense buildup and most importantly his commitment to the 600-ship Navy. I told Sununu that Romney himself had to state, during the presidential debates, that if he were elected he would be committed to a 350-ship Navy. Sununu delivered.

During the debate Romney stated his support for a 350-ship Navy, enough to ensure employment in the major yards for at least ten years. Unfortunately, lacking any sustained direct outreach to the industrial-base workforce, the targeted remark was not sufficient to cause a

Reaganesque mobilization of workers. Moreover, as with the McCain campaign, there were no labor professionals associated with the Romney campaign to amplify his comment.

In both the McCain and Romney campaigns, we clearly see similarities in the problems that Republicans face in reaching out to the workforce in general and the labor unions in particular. Unlike Nixon, Reagan, and George H.W. Bush, who were comfortable meeting with workforce leaders, most Republican candidates seem fearful of rejection and simply ignore these important constituencies. This fear is picked up by their campaign staff who are either too inexperienced to see the value of that outreach, or are strongly attached to the business community and avoid contact with the unions.

Worse yet is the belief that unions are insignificant because their membership does not have the power it once had. True, but as I tell anyone seeking my help in an election bid: "If you expect to win in a landside you don't need my help. But when the margin for victory is narrow, you ignore the workforce at your own peril." Republicans seem destined to throw away opportunity after opportunity after opportunity. They do so because they do not see the benefit of making an outreach to this potential Republican constituency and the basis of the long-sought New Majority. In McCain's case, he was too far removed from the unions to see the opportunity. Romney had no prior relationship with national unions outside of Massachusetts. Moreover, the absence of a workforce outreach made the class war campaign against him more credible.

Mike Balzano (3rd from right, in white shirt) and
friends in Wooster Square, New Haven, CT.
(personal photo)

Sitting on back steps with favorite alley cat.
(personal photo)

Optician Michael Balzano in front of Harvey &
Lewis Optical Co., New Haven, CT (1960)
(personal photo)

First meeting with President Nixon in the Oval Office on July 9, 1972. Provided by the Nixon Presidential Library & Museum.

Meeting of Colson staff members with the leadership of the Committee to Re-elect the President in Colson's office. (May 8, 1972). Provided by the Nixon Presidential Library & Museum.

President Nixon is surrounded by shipyard workers during his January 4, 1972, visit to National Steel & Shipbuilding Co. in San Diego, CA. Provided by the Nixon Presidential Library & Museum.

Following the Hard Hat March in New York City, President Nixon
invited the building trades leadership, who organized the march, to
come to the White House on May 26, 1972. They presented the President
with their hard hats and left them on the table in the Roosevelt
Room. Provided by the Nixon Presidential Library & Museum.

Following Nixon's victory in 1972, Balzano met with Mayor Richard J. Daley
(center) and Alderman Vito Marzullo (left) in Chicago. On the right is Myron
B. Kuropas, Region V Director for the ACTION Agency. (personal photo)

At a July 1, 1972, meeting Marine Engineers President Jesse Calhoon presents a model of the first of sixteen tankers to be used in the Alaskan oil trade to the President as Maryland Representative Helen Delich Bentley looks on. Provided by the Nixon Presidential Library & Museum.

President Nixon was the keynote speaker at the dedication of the American Museum of Immigration on Liberty Island on September 26, 1972. He and Mrs. Nixon were greeted by children in native dress during the opening ceremonies. Provided by the Nixon Presidential Library & Museum.

Governor and Mrs. Reagan made a campaign stop in New Haven's Italian community and visited Libby's Pastry Shop on Wooster Street to taste lemon ice (October 6, 1980). Printed by permission of the Reagan Foundation.

President Reagan meets at the White House with labor leaders from the Midwest (October 25, 1984). Provided by the Reagan Presidential Library & Museum.

President Reagan signed a trade bill at Sea-Land terminal in Los Angeles, CA. To his right, Jesse Calhoon, President of the Marine Engineers' Beneficial Association, looks on. Provided by the Reagan Presidential Library & Museum.

On July 4, 1988, Vice President and Mrs. George H. W. Bush met with labor leaders aboard the paddlewheel boat *Becky Thatcher* while attending the Veiled Prophet Fair in St. Louis, MO. This was his first meeting with an entire bargaining committee of a union. Provided by the George Bush Library and Museum.

Following the July 4th meeting, Vice President and Mrs. Bush viewed the Independence Day Air Show with union leaders on the upper deck of the *Becky Thatcher*. Seated next to the Vice President is Cassell Williams, president of District 837, International Association of Machinists and Aerospace Workers.

A multi-state coalition of labor leaders met with President George H. W. Bush and Vice President Richard Cheney (foreground) on October 11, 1990, to express their support for Desert Storm. Chief of Staff John Sununu is at the far end of the table. Provided by the George Bush Library and Museum.

President George W. Bush met with labor leaders following the signing
of the 2004 Defense Authorization Bill. Present were Defense Secretary
Rumsfeld, Charles Bofferding, Executive Director of SPEEA, Jennifer MacKay,
President of SPEEA, Mark Glyptis, President, United Steelworkers Local
2911, Joseph Grabowski, Executive Director of ASPEP. (personal photo)

At an April 6, 1992, meeting with President Nixon, Michael Balzano
promised the former President that he would write the history
of Nixon's efforts to create the New Majority, the key to Nixon's
overwhelming victory in 1972. Printed by permission of Maura Valis.

PART II

CHAPTER 8

Promises Kept and Broken

During presidential campaigns, candidates appeal to voters by making statements that indicate how they will administer the government. They project a determination to embrace all of those policies that will improve the lives of people. Candidates make promises to improve the economy, create jobs, and defend the nation from enemies foreign and domestic as well as a host of other implied promises.

Candidates seeking the support of labor unions undergo far more scrutiny than they do from the general public because unions try to assess the candidate's intent about programs and projects that the candidate might initiate if elected. If victorious, will the candidate build nuclear power plants and defense systems like ships, aircraft and missiles? What is the candidate's commitment to space exploration? Such programs and policies will affect the American workforce, especially the union members employed in the design and manufacture of defense systems.

In addition, with the unions there are other concerns. Unions are directly affected by a candidate's intentions with respect to laws that protect wage scales and bargaining rights. During the presidencies of Nixon and Reagan, promises were personally made by both candidates that constituted the foundation of the relationship between their administrations and American workers.

Having examined the promises of three Republican presidents who sought to create or to resurrect a New Majority, we can assess their success or failure in achieving their goals.

The specific promises that Nixon made to the unions fell into six categories.

First, he promised to reinstate the air traffic controllers dismissed during the sickout of 1970. He kept his promise.

Second, for the unions in the industrial base, Nixon secretly promised Jesse Calhoon that he would create a fleet of modern oil tankers to carry Alaskan oil. He kept his promise. But he went further; he declared the Alaskan oil Jones Act trade, preventing it from being sold to foreign countries. He locked in that trade for ten years with an export ban.

Third, he promised I. W. Abel he would create a federal program to protect employees from losing their pensions if their employers filed for bankruptcy. This was a major commitment that would benefit workers for generations. Nixon kept his promise to promote the concept. He accomplished this completely back channel because Colson did not want to involve the Domestic Policy Council on this decision.

Fourth, he promised hunters, sportsmen, target shooters, and collectors that he would not sign a Saturday Night Special handgun bill. He kept his promise. To the embarrassment of his own Domestic Council that promoted the bill, Nixon reversed his position, abandoning the bill which later died.

Fifth, Nixon promised that he would appoint New Majority candidates to government positions within his administration. He took steps to keep that promise but Watergate interrupted the process.

Sixth, Nixon told the unions that he would not end the Vietnam War while one prisoner of war was still in Hanoi. The POW issue was extremely important to those union leaders who had served in World War II. Nixon kept his promise. I recall sitting in White House Cabinet meetings where Nixon pointed out again and again that the release of the US prisoners was nonnegotiable. At the same time, during campaign events, George McGovern repeated that for prisoners to be released, the war had to be over first. Nixon constantly reminded everyone that when the French ended their war in Vietnam in defeat in 1954, French prisoners of war were never returned. They rotted to death in bamboo cages and were never accounted for. Nixon said that not one American soldier would be left behind. In fact, during the height of the Vietnam War in 1972, before he left on his trip to China to meet with Chairman Mao, Nixon intensified bombing in Hanoi and mined Haiphong Harbor. Arriving in China, Nixon met Mao with a big smile on his face as though they were close friends.

After the Paris Peace Accords were signed in 1973 and the Vietnam prisoners of war got off the plane back on American soil, many of them kissed the ground, but all of them thanked Richard Nixon for not abandoning them. Nixon's promise to the POWs became more meaningful to me when I met and befriended Everett Alvarez, Jr., the longest held prisoner of the Vietnam War. I asked Alvarez what he and his fellow captives were saying when Nixon intensified the bombing in Hanoi. In an interview, Alvarez confirmed what he had told me upon his release from Hanoi: [60]

> After there had been no bombing for almost four years after the peace talks started in Paris in 1968 to May of 1972. . .one bright spring day in May of 1972 the sirens came on: we hadn't heard those for a long time. Then we heard the bombing and triple-A fire off in the distance. The bombing continued through the night and the next day so we knew the bombing had resumed.
>
> The 1972 bombings at Christmas time were horrific—the 52s kept coming and coming. It got so bad the Vietnamese wouldn't even man the prison towers because of the pounding. The day after Christmas we knew this was it, and a couple weeks later they rearranged us in groups and began to be nice to us. They read us the terms of cessation of hostilities and told us we were going to be going home. If McGovern had won . . . we'd had been there forever.

The bombing of Hanoi was noted by the unions, who respected Nixon because he projected an image of a strong, resolute man. The union support for Nixon's position on the American POW issue solidified his relationship with the American labor movement. In those days the unions were patriotic and decidedly anti-Communist. Those

Democratic members of Congress who might have been willing to ally with McGovern would not dare to reject the position of the union locals or AFL-CIO president, George Meany, who supported Nixon on the war. Republicans never fully understood their debt to the unions.

Chairman Mao respected Nixon because he had backbone. Both the Russians and the Chinese respected Nixon because of his knowledge and understanding of history. Even before Nixon served as Eisenhower's vice president, the Soviets and the Chinese viewed Nixon as a dedicated anti-Communist. They saw him side with Whitaker Chambers, the former Soviet agent who exposed a ring of Soviet spies in the US government. They knew Nixon chaired the congressional hearing in which Hiss committed perjury, a crime that later sent him to jail.

During the intense rivalry between the Chinese and the Soviets, Nixon declared that if the Russians engaged in war with China, the United States would enter the war on the side of China. Nixon made this statement in the middle of the Watergate hearings. The Chinese-Russian controversy subsided but still the Soviets respected Nixon. Following Nixon's resignation *Pravda*, the official organ of the Soviet Union, declared that he had been driven from the White House by a hysterical press. Similarly, Jeane Kirkpatrick shared with me a report from her Parisian friends that when the Nixons entered the dining room of a Paris restaurant several years after his resignation, everyone in the restaurant gave them a standing ovation until they were seated.

The relationship between the POWs and the Republicans has always been strong. During the 1986 Senate campaign of Jeremiah Denton I tried to persuade his campaign manager, who had written off Alabama's labor vote, that Denton owed an enormous debt to the American labor movement. [61] In my memo to the campaign manager, in which I tried to persuade him to make an outreach to the unions, I wrote:

> Democratic legislators sympathetic to ending the war
> by surrender, had their feet held to the fire by the delega-
> tions of union leaders who walked the halls of Congress.
> . . Denied a majority in Congress, the anti-war activ-
> ists took to the streets. Again, they found the unions.

The unions waged a three-front war: they fought the anti-war lobbyists in the Congress, the professors and students in the streets, and the McGovernites in the voting booths. In the end, they held off the proponents of surrender long enough for Nixon to end the war and bring home the John McCains, the Everett Alvarezes, and yes, the Jeremiah Dentons.

In addition to the specific promises, Nixon also championed the nuclear power industry, which would create tens of thousands of jobs in the steel, machine tool, and construction industries. He supported the coal miners, arguing constantly that the United States had two-thirds of the world's known supply of coal and that we should move to gasify that coal or export it to other nations.

Nixon was also pro-science, supporting the advancement of aerospace programs that would preserve America's global leadership in aircraft design and production. Nixon fought a losing battle against a Democratic Congress on supporting the development of a supersonic transport (SST), arguing that America had been the creator of the aircraft industry and that if we did not keep pace with developing technology we would lose global market share of future aircraft.

It should be stated here that during the discussion of the supersonic transport there were economists who made the case that a supersonic trip across the Atlantic would only save two hours from the 5-1/2 hr flight currently available. Time savings would not be worth the price of a ticket that would exceed by many times the current cost of a regular commercial jet. The economists were absolutely correct. Once the regularly scheduled Concorde flight from Europe to the U.S. began, it was clear that from an economic perspective the SST would not be profitable. That was not the point Nixon was making. Nixon wanted to put American aircraft manufacturers on the cutting edge of future avionics. However, the SST did have a major consequence for American aircraft builders.

Nixon's unheeded warnings were profound. The Europeans built the SST by a consortium of three nations: Britain, France and Germany (Germany eventually bowed out of the consortium). Later Britain and

France subsidized the same consortium to build the Airbus. Boeing's dominance of the world's commercial aircraft industry ended, which very likely would not have happened had America initiated an SST program earlier. The building of the SST by the Europeans gave them the knowledge necessary to develop a competitive passenger airplane industry.

Nixon was not seen as an enemy of labor, but was universally respected as a friend of the workforce, both union and non-union. Labor unions were never fearful that Nixon would attempt to repeal the Davis-Bacon Act, the McNamara-O'Hara Service Contract Act,[62] or ever seek a national right-to-work law. Nixon allowed market forces to operate both in the business world and the labor markets.

The New Majority and Gerald Ford

President Ford had no real opportunity to make campaign promises. However, he did honor Nixon's commitment to I. W. Abel and signed a bill on September 2, 1974, creating the Pension Benefit Guaranty Corporation (PBGC) aimed at protecting the pensions of millions of blue-collar workers. [63]

Reagan and the New Majority

As stated earlier, in 1980 Reagan was committed to resurrecting Nixon's New Majority. Reagan shared the core values that were held by the vast majority of Americans. Point for point on the issues, Reagan was in harmony with the presidents of local unions. No labor leader could come into the presence of Ronald Reagan and not like him. Like Nixon before him, Reagan respected the labor unions and sincerely liked all those union leaders who viewed him as someone who understood their problems. Because of their natural affinity for Reagan there was no question that he would be a man of his word. Moreover, Reagan was well known to Middle America.

Reagan's televised broadcasts focused on the country's western exploration. His movies and love for horses gave him a John Wayne aura that enhanced his cowboy reputation. Further, his battles as governor with the California universities over student unrest gave him a no-nonsense reputation as a person who would side with Middle America on social issues. More importantly, his strong anti-communism gave comfort to union leaders of that day who understood that in communist countries independent unions were nonexistent. Progressive Democrats and Hollywood elites abhorred Reagan's testimony before the House Committee on Un-American Activities warning of communist inroads into Hollywood.

To my knowledge, Ronald Reagan made eight promises during the 1980 campaign regarding unions, Three dealt with the maritime industry, three dealt with the building and construction trades, one dealt with the air traffic control workers, and one dealt with the major unions in the industrial base.

With respect to the maritime industry, Reagan pledged to:

- Renew the Jones Act;
- Continue the ban on the export of Alaskan oil;
- Require the Navy to use civilian manning to move military cargo.

With the building and construction trades, Reagan promised to:

- Complete the Westway Highway in New York, abandoned by the Carter Administration;
- Make no attempt to repeal or diminish the Davis-Bacon Act;
- Make no attempt to create a national right-to-work law.

With the air traffic controllers, Reagan promised to:

- Repair the system in response to a memorandum of understanding of specific items negotiated by his campaign manager and his senior staff.

With the industrial base, Reagan promised to:

- Re-industrialize America.

With respect to the promises, the record was mixed. On the Jones Act, President Reagan kept his promise made at the National Maritime Union Convention of 1980 and went against the wishes of his economic advisers who sought its repeal. [64] This one commitment saved the U.S maritime fleet, whose very existence requires Jones Act protection.

Second, on the renewal of Nixon's ban on selling Alaskan oil to markets outside the United States, Reagan kept his word. Here the leadership of the Republican House and Senate made sure that the White House knew that the Congress would stand behind Reagan's promise to the maritime unions.

Third, on Reagan's promise to utilize the US Merchant Marine to move Navy cargo, he completely failed. Like Jimmy Carter before him, Reagan was unable to get the Navy to obey his direct orders.

Fourth, on the Westway Highway, Reagan kept his promise to the unions by presenting an $85 million check for the purchase of the right of way for the highway. However, the project was never completed due to anti-development forces and environmentalist objections based on the perceived harm to the spawning grounds of striped bass that would have been affected by landfill to be pumped into the river during construction. In August 1985, US Judge Thomas Griesa ruled in favor of the environmentalists and the project was abandoned and not pursued by Democratic Governor Mario Cuomo and Democratic Mayor Edward Koch. [65]

Fifth, during the campaign of 1980, one of the most difficult promises that Reagan made to the labor unions was that his administration would not attempt to weaken or repeal the Davis-Bacon Act. Reagan did not break his promise, but officials in his administration did work against Davis-Bacon. The promise was stated in writing in the Reagan labor pamphlet. Democrats always support the Davis-Bacon Act whereas Republicans have a history of opposing it based on the argument that it raises the cost of federal construction projects. In fact, both Davis and Bacon were Republican members of Congress who introduced the act to protect construction workers in their states during the Depression when jobs were scarce and unemployment was catastrophic. To win contracts, contractors would structure their bids on very low wage rates. They would set up tent cities and bring in workers from other poorer areas and pay them at a rate well below the prevailing wage. The workers would then send their paychecks home to other states, leaving the host state without jobs for their local workers. The goal of the Davis-Bacon Act was to ensure that the wages paid with federal money were in harmony with the prevailing wages of the local economy. When Reagan pledged not to weaken or repeal Davis-Bacon, it sealed a bond with the building trades unions. As an issue, Davis-Bacon was never mentioned during Reagan's first term.

After Reagan won his second term in 1984, former Tennessee Senator William Brock became secretary of labor. Brock then issued a letter to members of the House and Senate informing them that the Department of Labor was now going to try to reform the Davis-Bacon Act. But labor unrest following the PATCO strike and the filing for Chapter 11 bankruptcy by Eastern Air Lines created the impression that Brock was moving on Davis-Bacon to dismantle the act, not adjust it. Brock's action began to look like a Republican plot to break up the unions. Brock's letter [66] of August 7, 1986, stated:

> I am writing to request your support in obtaining necessary reforms to the Davis-Bacon and Service Contract Acts, the statutes which govern wages in Federal construction and service projects. These reforms are currently contained in the FY 1987 Defense Department Authorization bill, S. 2638.
>
> Since 1935, the Davis-Bacon Act has required that prevailing wages as determined by the Secretary of Labor, be paid on contracts for federally funded or assisted construction projects of $2,000 or more.

Following receipt of the letter from Secretary Brock, Senator Pete Wilson called me and asked, "Didn't we make a promise to leave Davis-Bacon alone?" I responded by recounting the history of OMB's role in the PATCO strike and told Wilson that I believed the president knew nothing about OMB's action. I told Wilson that Brock's inclusion of the Service Contract Act would negatively affect low wage minority workers. The Service Contract Act is used on military bases and in military hospitals to hire minimum wage workers.

I then went to Paul Laxalt and Dan Quayle. Finally, I went to Secretary Brock himself whom I had known since the Nixon years. I showed Brock a copy of his letter and asked what was going on. Brock responded that the act had been in place for a long time and that the Labor Department had to make an adjustment to it. I explained that the president had promised not to touch Davis-Bacon. Brock replied that it was an old promise and that the president had not renewed that promise in the 1984 campaign. I said there was no constituency for the repeal and that it would never pass in a Republican Senate. I cautioned him that Reagan's promise to the unions on Davis-Bacon had as its goal bringing labor unions into the Republican Party. Brock would not back down.

I then went to Senator H. John Heinz III, chairman of the National Republican Senatorial Committee. Heinz informed OMB and Secretary Brock that there was no way that even a Republican-controlled Senate could muster the votes needed to repeal Davis-Bacon. Heinz then told the administration that he would lead the fight against it. As a senator from Pennsylvania, Heinz was very close to his state's building and construction trades as well as the steelworkers. He told the adminis-tration that Brock's move on Davis-Bacon could cause the loss of the Republican Senate majority. Heinz kept most Republicans from voting for the repeal, but it was too late; the damage was done. Even though Davis-Bacon was not repealed, or even amended, Democrats made it clear that a Reagan administration was determined to repeal the Act if not in this session, certainly in the next congressional session following the 1986 election. I firmly believe that Ronald Reagan was not informed and that OMB and the Labor Department were tearing up one of his promises. If he had known, I believe he would have put a stop to their actions immediately.

The sixth promise Reagan kept was to make no attempt to create a national right-to-work law.

Seventh, with respect to PATCO, Reagan did not keep at least two specific promises. The administration promised to take steps to ease the tension between the controllers and the FAA by appointing administrators who would work harmoniously with the unions. In that regard, the appointment of J. Lynn Helms as FAA administrator was the worst choice to head the FAA. In addition, when PATCO was trying to work its agenda through the Congress, OMB went to the Congress to oppose PATCO's legislation, which violated Reagan's pledge not to interfere with PATCO's right to seek improvement of their situation through the legislative process. It could be argued that OMB should not be held responsible for breaking an agreement with PATCO that it did not know existed. Nonetheless, PATCO felt betrayed.

Reagan's eighth promise was to reindustrialize America. That promise was never set in writing but Reagan repeated it at every campaign event where unions were present. The promise was applauded by the steel workers. Reindustrializing American would have been a bonanza that would have required our steel mills to be upgraded and modernized to produce the steel girders and pipes needed to replace the antiquated infrastructure that carries water underground beneath major US cities such as New York and Chicago. The day Reagan made his final campaign speech in 1980 he never uttered the words "reindustrializing America" again. No one in the Reagan White House was assigned to pursue this issue.

The commitment to reindustrialize America is as important today as it was in 1980 and should be a commitment of the Republican Party not an individual candidate or a president who only serves for a limited term. Rebuilding America and its industrial base must be seen by Republicans as a serious commitment, just as Democrats see their commitment to protecting entitlement programs.

I believe that Reagan failed to deliver on some of his promises because he did not know that his appointees were ignoring his orders. With respect to the promises on civilian manning and PATCO, no one had been appointed to the White House staff responsible for conveying the president's wishes and for implementing the president's policies. If Secretary of Defense Caspar Weinberger, a personal friend of the president, had been called to the Oval Office before assuming command of the Department of Defense and told by Reagan, "Cap, there is one thing I want you to do for me. I want you to report to Ed Meese, Craig Fuller—someone in the White House—on the plan to implement my civilian manning program. This is very important to me. I really want to get this implemented." Does anyone believe that Cap Weinberger would have failed? Cap was the consummate loyalist. He would have saluted, and the president's order would have been carried out.

Similarly, if Drew Lewis had been called to the White House before starting at the Department of Transportation and given a copy of the PATCO agreement and told to come back with a plan to do everything he could to help reform the air traffic control system, does anyone believe Lewis would have ignored the president's orders? That does not mean that Bob Poli would have gotten everything or even most of what he wanted. But if Ed Meese had called Poli into the White House, the outcome would surely have been very different. There were only two people in the White House chain of command who were allowed to talk to Poli: White House labor liaison Bob Bonatati, the former ALPA lobbyist whose union did not endorse Reagan and whose president urged Poli not to endorse Reagan; and Elizabeth Dole, who oversaw the labor function in the Office of Public Liaison. But Dole had given Bonatati the sole authority to be the contact with labor unions. There was no way that Poli would deal with Bonatati and there was no way to get around Dole.

There was no Charles Colson in the Reagan White House. The lesson here is that future Republican candidates must understand and embrace what they promise and, if elected, they must appoint trusted individuals intimately familiar with every promise made and the authority to see that they are kept.

Ronald Reagan was a great president. I wish he were still president. The New Majority coalesced behind him. Most historians refer to them as "Reagan Democrats," but in reality they were Nixon's New Majority reassembled to elect Reagan.

Reagan focused on defeating the Soviets and stabilizing the US economy. But unlike Nixon, Reagan did not make building the Republican Party a priority. If he had, he would have nurtured the constituencies that made up the New Majority and embraced his candidacy. In turn, they would have found a new home in the Republican Party. Reagan's commitment to the aerospace and defense workers, his stated commitment to restart the nuclear industry, and his intention to reindustrialize America would have solidified his relationship with every union in the AFL-CIO: scientists, engineers, industrial unions, and the building and construction trades. Reagan would have created jobs for half a century. Solidifying a permanent relationship with any of these unions was simply not part of Reagan's agenda.

There were only two people in the Reagan White House who saw the opportunity and could have been ombudsmen to the New Majority: Craig Fuller and Lyn Nofziger. Nofziger had worked for Reagan when he was governor of California. But he was shut out of policy issues important to the unions, namely the PATCO strike and the civilian manning issues.

When Nofziger left the White House, he wrote a letter to his replacement concerning the civilian manning program that was still in chaos, arguing that Reagan had made a promise to the maritime unions to implement the plan and the administration owed it to the unions to keep its word. Somehow the letter was given to the Justice Department, which charged Nofziger with violation of a federal law that prohibits any former administration official from contacting anyone in an office they held prior to leaving the administration for one year. Because I worked for Calhoon that year, still another special prosecutor questioned me about my knowledge of the letter, of which I had none. Nofziger was indicted by a grand jury and spent several hundred thousand dollars to clear his name, as did others who were called before the grand jury. In the end, a federal judge, who found the law vague and most likely unconstitutional, dismissed the case.

Preserving a Permanent Majority

It is one thing to capture a majority of voters during an election. Preserving and growing that majority is a function of keeping the promises made to the electorate, both voters in general and the constituencies that deliver an electoral victory.

Once elected, candidates who make written promises during the campaign should immediately hold briefings with incoming cabinet and agency officials to clearly convey all agreements made by the candidate with a particular constituency. There must also be a high-ranking White House official close to the president who is assigned to see to it that the agencies and departments follow the president's instruction on these promises to the letter. I would call this the "Colson function." Charles Colson saw to it that Nixon was apprised of any attempt to undermine his promises.

Had any of these actions been taken in the Reagan administration, and a person appointed to monitor the promises he made, there would not have been an air traffic controllers strike, and Reagan's commitment to civilian manning would have been carried out. For many labor unions, Reagan's legacy is marred because members of his own administration ignored his promises.

Keeping promises is part of a larger goal: A president should set the momentum for other party candidates to follow. This is what I would call the legacy of trust. Trust goes to the heart of all relationships. Of all of the presidents I served, Nixon kept his word on commitments to the letter.

In the Reagan White House there was no Colson. During the campaign, Bill Casey signed off on every promise that was made to the labor unions. There was no question that he was in charge. Had Casey gone to into the White House instead of to the CIA, promises made would have been kept. Poli could have gone to him. The same was true on the fleet support issue. Casey knew that fleet support was a high priority for Reagan. It is essential for any president to have someone in the White House who knows and understands the promises made during the campaign and will fight for them.

The real tragedy of the Reagan presidency was that he lost the opportunity to restructure the Republican Party and bring into it the reassembled New Majority constituency.

The New Majority and George Herbert Walker Bush

In an attempt to coalesce the New Majority behind his candidacy, George H. W. Bush had one major advantage: He was more familiar with the history of the New Majority than Reagan was, because he was in the Nixon Administration when the concept was formulated. Bush was familiar with the nationalities groups because he worked with their national leaders when he was Republican National Committee chairman. He understood the importance of the labor leaders who were close to Nixon. He knew Jesse Calhoon and was familiar with the major issues of the maritime industry and the unions that operated the merchant fleet. Moreover, he knew about the civilian manning issue and the promise that Reagan had made to implement it.

Bush had another advantage: While he was vice president, he assigned Craig Fuller, his chief of staff, to structure an outreach to the labor unions he had worked with prior to the 1988 campaign. Fuller was a seasoned veteran in the Reagan White House. He was knowledgeable and sensitive to the issues that were important to powerful constituencies. Calhoon and I believed that he had the chance to be another Colson. He was the best ally George H. W. Bush had going into the 1988 election.

It is notable that when Bush was faced with his first foreign policy challenge that required military action, Operation Desert Shield/ Desert Storm, he, like Nixon, turned to union leaders for help. Nixon relied on the labor unions to prevent the Democrats from cutting and running in Vietnam, leaving the American prisoners in Hanoi. Bush went to the unions because he knew they would help him fight his battle with Democrats in Congress and support the invasion of Kuwait. Bush followed Nixon's example in obtaining union support for his public policy agenda.

The next move should have been to solidify that union support to help his reelection in 1992. Union locals across the country would have welcomed him in their regions. Bush had won the Gulf War, and the union support had been crucial to his victory. Shortly after the victory in Kuwait, Bush chose to ignore the relationships he had built with union leaders. What is more, his staff chose to cut off contact with these leaders. Whatever inroads Bush made to bring New Majority unions into the Republican Party during the first two years of his presidency evaporated during his last year in office.

George H. W. Bush never made any specific campaign promises to the unions, except the commitment to grant Saudi Arabia's request to purchase F-15s. However, Bush did convey the impression that the aerospace and industrial base unions would have access to him on issues that were covered in their platform testimony. The closest thing to a promise that Bush made was his Space Exploration Initiative. That initiative would have required a restart of the Kennedy space program. Such an effort would have produced a quantum jump in technology advances required to create a base on the Moon from which travel to Mars would be possible. These new technologies would have dwarfed those of the original lunar program. It would have sparked an investment in education and manufacturing that would have touched every aspect of the American workforce. Unfortunately, Bush abandoned his effort in the face of Democratic opposition.

In any case, there was no attempt to maintain the inroads that Bush had made with the unions in his first two years in office, let alone to expand the Republican Party. After the Gulf War, it appeared that the president had no interest in any relationship with the unions. What also disappeared was the term "New Majority," and with it any attempt to broaden the base of the Republican Party.

George W. Bush (2001 – 2008) Opportunities Lost

Prior to George W. Bush's campaign, I met him at a reception and had a brief conversation with him concerning my role as labor advisor to Nixon, Reagan, and his father. He said he would like to follow up on our conversation because he wanted to reach out to labor unions. I did not work in his campaign and, as far as I know, there was no specific outreach to unions or other members of the New Majority as part of his campaign. However, shortly after his election I was able to reconnect some members of the workforce coalition with the Bush administration through Defense Secretary Donald Rumsfeld, whom I had gotten to know during the Ford administration.

In December 2000, at a Christmas party hosted by Senator and Mrs. Paul Laxalt, I encountered newly appointed Secretary of Defense Donald Rumsfeld, whom I not seen since he was chief of staff to President Gerald Ford. When he didn't recognize me at the party, I joked with him about what I would have looked like twenty years earlier when I still had a crew cut and was forty pounds lighter. "Balzano!" Rumsfeld said. "I'm going to need your help." He said major changes would be undertaken at the Defense Department and he wanted me to work with Jerry Jones, his personal advisor during the transition.

Jones had worked with Rumsfeld and Dick Cheney in the Ford White House and had remained a close friend of mine since he recruited me for the Nixon White House. He had talked to Vice President Cheney, who agreed to meet with the leadership of the workforce coalition on the day before the 2001 Inauguration. At the meeting the unions presented Cheney with the workforce testimony they had delivered to the Republican National Committee. During the photo op, Cheney told the unions that they would enjoy a close working relationship with the new administration. While we were still in the meeting, Andy Card, the president's chief of staff, entered the room. He promised there would be an open door and a resumption of a working relationship that the unions had enjoyed with Nixon and Reagan. I was encouraged by the attitude of both Cheney and Card and was eager to open a dialogue with George W. Bush to get him involved in pursuing the New Majority.

I ran into Karl Rove at a Washington cocktail party about six months after Bush won the presidency. Rove knew of my reputation from the Nixon years. He was a fan of Charles Colson and was very familiar with how Colson had run the Office of Public Liaison. He asked if I would call Lezlee Westine, the new director of OPL, and talk to her about how Nixon interacted with the OPL. I went to her office and briefed her and two staff people. The real heavyweight on her staff was Ken Mehlman who was out of town at the time. I gave her a copy of the chapter that I had written for the Hofstra University symposium on Nixon that described Colson's operation. I also gave her a briefing on how the OPL functioned during the Nixon years. Westine smiled and said, "That's exactly how we're going to run the office." I offered my help if needed and agreed to answer any future questions they might have.

Since I never heard anything further from OPL, I decided to turn my attention to working with Don Rumsfeld, Jerry Jones and David Patterson at the Department of Defense, since they were amenable to reaching out to the unions. Patterson and I had worked for McDonnell Douglas and Boeing on labor union issues. With Patterson and Jones in the Defense Department encouraging Rumsfeld to make an outreach to labor leaders, Don began to host meetings with international presidents of the AFL-CIO. More importantly, Jones and Patterson held meetings with local union presidents. Patterson included union testimony he gathered from labor unions throughout the country to construct a review of DoD's acquisition process. The 2005 DoD Defense Acquisition Performance Assessment Project was the only assessment of the acquisition process that ever allowed the unions to participate in the process.

One year before the 2004 election, Rumsfeld invited a small group of workforce coalition leaders to attend the signing of the Fiscal Year 2004 Defense Authorization Bill at a Pentagon ceremony. The unions were seated in the audience when Rumsfeld unexpectedly dispatched an aide to bring them backstage to meet President George W. Bush. As we lined up for the photo, the president insisted that we delay taking photos until he had the chance to talk with the union leaders one-on-one. After the photo, Bush asked why this was the first time I was taking labor union leaders to meet with him. I said something to the effect that the unions were working closely with Rumsfeld and were satisfied with the attention they received from the Secretary of Defense. A wave of guilt spread over me. Perhaps I should have been more persistent in approaching Lezlee Westine, Karl Rove, Vice President Cheney, or to anyone who could bridge the gap between the administration and industrial-base workers.

A few weeks later I learned that Karl Rove was holding briefing sessions for Washington insiders in the Old Executive Office Building. *Here is an opportunity,* I thought. Let me at least try to open a door for labor. I went to the EOB to argue that the unions should be invited to some of these briefings. As I entered the Old Executive Office Building, I walked past a long line of K Street lobbyists. When I got into the office, I found that neither the political director nor the deputy director were there. But there was a very nice young man in the office who apologized that no one was there to meet the executive director of a national workforce coalition. Without trying to embarrass him, I asked the young man how old he was. "I'm twenty-five," he said cautiously, "Why?"

I told him that I, too, was a young White House aide twenty years earlier and had great sympathy for the position that he was in. I told him that I knew that the entire political West Wing of the White House was busy setting up briefings for Washington business leaders. I also told him that I knew quite a few of the K Street lobbyists who were lined up outside the EOB for that day's briefing and that I had passed all of them to get to see the political director. I then said to him, "All of those people have money, but very few have votes. The unions who would have come to a White House briefing have votes but no money." Ignoring the unions is a major weakness of the Republican leadership at the national level: They welcome Washington lobbyists who represent clients but ignore the unions who represent a constituency.

As it turned out, Bush won reelection in 2004 anyway but any chance of creating a relationship with the unions beyond the one they enjoyed with Rumsfeld was gone. Bush's victory in 2004 did not have a coattail effect for John McCain's race that followed in 2008. Sadly, it did not have "legs," that is, it did not help anyone else get elected nor did it create anything to build on that would reach out to the New Majority.

In conclusion, three presidents reached out to the New Majority: Nixon, Reagan, and George H.W. Bush. Of these, only Richard Nixon understood the promises he made to the unions and kept every promise. He did so because he shared the same value system as those to whom he made the promises. Further, he had a promise-keeper, Charles Colson, as a watchdog to make sure that the promises would be kept. Additionally, Nixon was laying the foundation of a new Republican Party, one that would include the groups that were the bedrock of the Roosevelt Democratic Party.

Reagan kept the promises that he made when faced with a policy decision concerning those promises. At the same time, he was deceived by some in his administration at critical decision points because there was no trusted promise-keeper to warn the president of their activities.

CHAPTER 9

Republicans Are Not Political

Aside from not taking advantage of the political opportunities to reach out to labor unions and other New Majority voters at a time when they would be most receptive, there is another reason why Republicans are reluctant to reach out beyond their comfort zone: *Republicans are not political.*

In 1974, following the resignation of Richard Nixon, I spent considerable time with former Texas Governor John Connally, who served as Secretary of the Treasury in the Nixon administration. Immediately following Jerry Ford's defeat by Jimmy Carter in 1976, Connally helped me set up meetings with corporate leaders to market the concept of corporate social responsibility. Before the 1980 Republican presidential primaries, I agreed to reassemble the New Majority coalition to support Connally's candidacy for president.

On one occasion, speaking about the Republican Party, the governor said, "Republicans are not political." Keeping in mind that I was talking with a former Democratic governor of Texas who was taught by Lyndon Johnson, one of the most astute Democrats of the 20th century, I cautiously asked him why he said that. He responded, "Lyndon and I talk about this all the time. They (Republicans) don't understand politics; to them it's a gentlemen's game. Nixon understood it; he had been brutalized enough to really understand it."

Republicans do not appear to know when it is in their interest to work with New Majority voters, in particular union leaders, on issues on which they agree. John Connally once told me that it was time that corporate executives understand that labor and management are eating off the same plate; they have the same enemies. I better understand the meaning of these words today, more than when I first heard them.

I generally make Republicans angry when I say that Republicans are not political, and my Democratic friends laugh at me. I admit that, at face value, my statement seems absurd. Of course Republicans are political. Republicans have political differences with Democrats on economic, social, industrial, and national security issues.

By "political" I mean something quite different. I'm referring to the tendency for Republicans not only to engage in battle on an issue that they cannot win, but also to fight a battle that will ultimately cost them in the long run. This nonpolitical nature of Republicans goes beyond their dealings with labor unions. There is a tendency for Republicans to choose the wrong issue on which to make a stand. I'll give an example from when I headed ACTION between 1973 and 1977. ACTION was the federal agency that housed all of the volunteer programs funded by the federal government.[67] These programs included the Peace Corps, its most recognized international program, as well as Volunteers in Service to America (VISTA), its most recognized domestic anti-poverty volunteer program; and the Retired Senior Volunteer Program, the less exotic but largest program in the agency and the most popular among elected officials.

During my tenure at ACTION the fastest growing program was the Retired Senior Volunteer Program. I tried to identify President Gerald Ford with this program and on one occasion had him present the annual awards to those seniors whose service was exemplary. The president's participation in personally handing the certificates to each of the seniors was heartwarming. When the ceremony ended he gave me a double-handed handshake and said he wanted to be involved in the next award ceremony. Unfortunately, the next award ceremony was held after the 1976 election.

Following Ford's defeat, I prepared briefing papers for the Carter Transition Team that would be coming to take over ACTION. At the same time, I had to prepare a budget submission to the Office of Management and Budget (OMB) for my agency for the federal fiscal year 1978, well in advance of the president's budget submission to

Congress. All agency heads have tense relationships with OMB during negotiations over agency budgets for the coming year. My deputy, Jack Ganley, a consummate professional and career government official for some forty years, was dealing with OMB staff and always dealt with OMB bureaucrats during budget negotiations. He assured me that we would have no problems.

Early in December 1976, Ganley came into my office and said, "Boss, we have a problem. Don Derman, an OMB senior staffer, called me just now and said that the president is going to submit a zero budget for the entire agency." With any other staffer I would have said, "Jack, you're joking." Not with Jack Ganley. I assembled my senior staff and included Emerson Markham, another career budget officer. No one could recall such any precedent. I called OMB Deputy Director Paul O'Neill, who generally said no to any request I made, to ask if the OMB request was real. He responded that it was and that I could appeal the OMB request but the appeal had to be made directly to the president at a Cabinet Council meeting. He also warned that before Jerry Ford left office on January 20, he would be ready to terminate any official who refuses to accept OMB's decision (technically known as a "mark"). I told Paul that the entire administration had been terminated on Election Day, so I had nothing to lose by appealing OMB's ruling.

On the day of the appeal I brought Jack Ganley and Ron Gerevas, ACTION's director of international operations, with me to the White House. We entered the cabinet room, which, but for the three seats reserved for us, was completely filled with career OMB bureaucrats.

President Ford sat in his chair, his back to the Rose Garden. Jim Lynn, the director of OMB, sat directly across from the president with Paul O'Neill at his left, backed up by OMB staff who sat behind them. The president had an unlit pipe in his mouth as he thumbed through my appeal booklet on the table before him.

Jim Lynn opened the conversation with a very clear statement for the reason that OMB was advocating a zero budget for the ACTION agency. As he talked, I pondered my decision to appeal the mark. The agency had undergone a complete transformation under my directorship. Poor people, who were the agency's constituents had better access to the agency's services, because we had decentralized staff from Washington to the states where the services were close to the centers of poverty. The decision to decentralize met with challenges from many quarters. Some employees whose jobs were transferred sued me, yet I won in court. I had to defend my decision before House and Senate committees that unsuccessfully sought my removal as director. National newspapers such as *The Christian Science Monitor* [68] carried stories that the Congress was going to dismantle the agency and send the component programs of the agency back to the other agencies from whence they came to protect the programs from me. By contrast, a few years later, *Government Executive*, a magazine dealing with management issues in the federal government, ran a major story [69] on the innovations and accomplishments that the agency had achieved over the four years of my tenure.

The real turning point in the congressional hearings occurred when key members of the Congressional Black Caucus weighed in to defend the decentralization of ACTION, because it improved services to blacks in both cities and rural communities. Prominent black politicians like Augustus Hawkins, Shirley Chisholm, Louis Stokes, and Andrew Young heard black mayors from large and small cities testify on the drastic improvement in both quality and volume of services they experienced.

As Jim Lynn told the Cabinet about runaway inflation and cost of living problems in the country, I recalled Gerald Ford's firm commitment to the Retired Senior Volunteer Program award recipients and the genuine affection he had for the older American volunteer programs. I concluded that a zero budget for the agency was not in President Ford's interest. As I sat there, Mike Balzano from Wooster Street took over.

The president interrupted my thoughts, "Mike," he said, "Do you want to respond to Mr. Lynn's analysis?"

I looked at him and at first didn't answer. "Mike," he repeated.

Very softly, but firmly, I said, "Mr. President, you lost the election." The entire room gasped, *"You can't tell the president he lost the election"* was audible in their gasps.

I answered their gasps with, "We did. We lost the election." Ganley grabbed my hand as he often did to silence me in congressional hearings where I spoke my mind. I ignored him.

"Mr. President," I said, "the polls show that older Americans voted for you in large numbers. A zero budget will send a message to them that your opponents were correct, you don't care about the people."

Jim Lynn interrupted, "Mr. President, from a purely political perspective, Mike is correct but we have to focus on Republican strength. They say Democrats are more creative in creating programs but we have the reputation of being good managers. We have to manage and we have to responsibly manage this government."

While Lynn talked, the president and I stared at each other. You couldn't help but like Jerry Ford. I waved my left hand in a hold gesture at Lynn never leaving my eyes from Ford. "Mr. President," I said, "I don't believe this is your idea. You are responding to the advice of the people in this room." I looked around the room and recognized many of the people who I had fought with on most of the decisions I made to improve the programs in my agency.

I then stepped off the cliff. "Mr. President," I continued, "these people are career bureaucrats. In less than fifty days they will be in this room singing "Hail to the New Chief" and telling him how insensitive you were when you cancelled all of the senior citizen programs. They will not tell President Carter this was *their* idea; they will blame you."

I could feel the tension I created all around me including in Ganley and Gerevas, my own deputies. Everyone was pale except Gerald Ford who nodded to signal to me, 'I hear you.' Ford then said that he would consider my appeal and moved the booklet to the left.

As I passed the line of seated officials heading for the door, the president called my name. "Mike," he said with a serious face, "you are a good man. I respect your honesty. But as president I have to make hard choices. The goal of this exercise is to point the way for the next administration to deal with inflation. So I have to do what is necessary to offer the appropriate government policy. Thank you, Mike." He stared at me, smiled, put the unlit pipe back in his mouth and opened the next folder.

The president submitted a zero budget for ACTION and was immediately criticized as being insensitive to the elderly volunteers and the recipients of the social services these volunteers contributed. Of course I was accused of wanting to dismantle my own agency. Worse still, all Republicans were seen as being completely insensitive to seniors who had survived the Great Depression.

Contrast President Ford's behavior with that of Jimmy Carter: Following President Jimmy Carter's inauguration, his mother, Lillian, herself a former Peace Corps volunteer who served in India at the age of sixty-eight, went to ACTION to meet and greet the staff in a widely televised reunion.

President Carter will be remembered as a champion of senior citizens even though his policies which ballooned interest and inflation rates practically bankrupted the country. But Gerald Ford will be remembered for attempting to zero out an agency that operated the popular Retired Senior Volunteer Program. That's what I mean by not being political. Ford was being postured to either look presidential or as an enemy of old people; a situation that he couldn't win. His senior advisors talked Ford into selecting an unobtainable public policy option that made him look callous toward seniors.

After our White House meeting with Gerald Ford and OMB, Jack Ganley and I returned to my office. I was obviously disappointed that we could not stop the president's proposed decision. Jack said, "We shouldn't be disappointed. After all, Republicans are only visitors here."

Although Jack was a Republican, he was really a career civil servant who floated in and out of government at his pleasure. I asked him why he came and went from government. He said he came back to keep the system straight. He said that a touch of career professionalism was needed from time to time. Jack said many things about the politics of the town, but there were two things he said that took me decades to understand. Before he passed away, I visited with Jack in a nursing home in South Carolina. I thanked him for his guidance and reminded him of the two crucial observations he gave me.

"First," he said, "Washington is a Democratic town. They own the District of Columbia. Look at the *Washington Post* society page. Look at who is throwing parties, hosting receptions, cutting ribbons at museum openings, and attending the symphony. If you look for

Republicans on the society page you won't find them because this is not a Republican town."

I was too busy to analyze the Style section of the *Post* so I took him at his word. Over the next forty years I learned that he was absolutely right.

Jack's second observation was extremely important for the Republican Party. "When it comes to governing," he said, "Republicans are visitors in Washington. Republicans win elections; they come to Washington because they win a presidential election. They serve out their term and then leave. They *all* leave, the appointed as well as elected officials." He continued, "The older, more established appointees such as the undersecretaries and assistant secretaries leave, as do the Schedule C political staffers in the White House and in the agencies."

Jack pointed out that after the Ford administration, the big guys went back to their law firms and major corporations. George Shultz, for example, went back to Bechtel. But, he argued, Democrats who had come to town during and after the Roosevelt administration had never left. Many became career civil servants who managed the agencies during Republican presidencies. Jack was right. It is a Democratic town with a Democratic newspaper, Democratic radio stations and a Democratic national press corps.

Two other issues are worth noting: Labor Secretary Brock's attempt to repeal Davis-Bacon and the attempt by the Department of Defense to implement a new personnel system at the department called the National Security Personnel System (NSPS).

In chapter 8 we discussed Secretary Brock's breaking Reagan's promise not to adjust or repeal Davis-Bacon. This debate extended into national security issues, specifically, the construction of the MX missile defense system.

I spoke with Governor Pete Wilson, Senator Dan Quayle, and Secretary of Defense Caspar Weinberger who all agreed that building the MX missile silos was a massive construction project. These silos would employ the building and construction trades as well as the Teamsters, who would be required to move megatons of concrete as well as all of the equipment and wherewithal to the centers where the silos would be constructed. The building trades unions, as well as the Teamsters, were fully aware that the Democrats were not supporting the MX program. The union leaders were feverishly working Democrats to vote for the project. In fact, the building trades unions and the Teamsters were the *only* unions still supporting the president's MX missile defense program.

During Brock's move on Davis-Bacon I had warned him that the attempt to repeal the Act could undermine a priority that was more important to a defense-oriented Reagan administration, namely, the MX missile program.

As Heinz predicted, the repeal effort on Davis-Bacon failed. But the goal of the building trades union in the 1986 Senate elections was to recapture Democratic control of the Senate in order to end Republican attempts to repeal Davis-Bacon. At a building trades convention held later that summer Democratic Congressman Jim Wright told the labor gathering: "We forgive you [for voting for Reagan]. We knew all you wanted was jobs. You wanted to build those missile silos for Reagan's MX program. But," he said through his signature smile showing all of his teeth, "Reagan didn't tell you he was going to kill Davis-Bacon and have you pour concrete for $5 an hour, did he?"

Yes, the Republicans lost control of the Senate that year, but more importantly union support for the MX missile program evaporated. The program goal of 200 MX missiles was capped at forty. Unlike Reagan, Nixon would have been more interested in obtaining the maximum number of MX missiles, *not* pursuing the repeal of Davis-Bacon. If the Republicans had been politically smart they would have looked at the missile issue as being of greater importance to the president than reforming the Davis-Bacon Act.

The second major issue that demonstrates the collision within an administration over competing policies occurred when the Department of Defense in the George W. Bush Administration attempted to institute the National Security Personnel System (NSPS), while at the same time they were engaged in an effort to modify the "Buy America" provisions in the defense bill.

As I indicated earlier, Jerry Jones had joined Rumsfeld at the Defense Department in the early days of the Bush/Cheney administration.

Ever conscious of the need for Republicans to keep an open dialogue with labor unions, Jones arranged a meeting between leaders of the National Industrial Base Workforce Coalition, Vice President Cheney, and Chief of Staff Andy Card two days before the 2001 Inauguration. Jones convinced Rumsfeld to begin a series of meetings with the AFL-CIO general presidents whose members produced defense weapons. At the same time, Rumsfeld agreed to hold a series of meetings with the presidents of local unions in the workforce coalition. Rumsfeld also arranged for the local unions to meet with the secretaries of the Air Force, Navy, and other Defense Department officials including two- and three-star generals involved in the war in Afghanistan. The goal was to cement a relationship between the Secretary of Defense and organized labor at the local and national level.

The strategy was working well. Rumsfeld met with each of the labor groups and tasked the leadership of the Pentagon to meet with the unions. The unions received briefings on the war in Afghanistan and other important issues. Some of the union leaders had children serving in combat in Afghanistan and Iraq.

In addition to the industrial base unions who attended meetings, we also included public sector unions who were federal employees working in the Defense Department. In one of those meetings I set up an individual photo op for Greg Junemann, president of the International Federation of Professional and Technical Engineers (IFPTE). Junemann had, for many years, been an active member of the workforce coalition supporting defense programs and made many visits to Capitol Hill on behalf of defense workers. Junemann's son was stationed in Afghanistan at the time of the meeting with Rumsfeld. (He later served in Iraq as well.)

A few weeks later Junemann called with a problem he had at the Defense Department that involved the department changing its personnel system. I met with Greg to try to understand the issue. Then I went to Jerry Jones, who was not familiar with the issue, but arranged a meeting with Dave Patterson, the Principal Deputy Undersecretary of Defense (comptroller), who already had met with union leaders when he interviewed most of them for the Department of Defense's Defense Acquisition Performance Assessment project. This was the first time that the unions had been allowed to participate in any such study. Patterson inquired within the Defense Department about the National Security Personnel System (NSPS) and told me that the program came under Undersecretary of Defense for Personnel and Readiness David Chu. Chu was in charge of creating an entirely new personnel system for DoD. Patterson thought it would be a good idea for us to meet with Chu. Jerry thought it would be wiser to go to Pete Geren, who was an administrative aide to Rumsfeld and who had been involved in creating the labor meetings with the secretary.

Geren, a former Democratic congressman from Texas who had worked for Senator Lloyd Bentsen, was a team player and was eager to resolve any conflict between the Defense Department and the unions. At the same time, Geren cautioned that there was another issue important to both DoD and the unions, namely the Buy American Act.

The Buy American issue emerged because a growing percentage of the components of American defense products were manufactured by foreign countries. This put the United States at risk of having critical components withheld from a defense system if a foreign manufacturer opposed US military strategy on political, philosophical, or religious grounds. This occurred during the Iraq War when a Swiss company supplying a crystal used in the Joint Direct Attack Munition (JDAM) guidance system held up delivery of this critical component while waiting approval from its government, which opposed our policies in Iraq. In this instance, the JDAM prime manufacturer, based in the United States, was forced to buy the parts from an American supplier. Luckily we were able to get these parts to help our soldiers engaged in combat.

In the summer of 2003, workforce coalition leaders learned that a wide-sweeping Buy American provision was attached to a House FY04 Defense Authorization Bill that was entering conference deliberations. Language added to this bill by Rep. Duncan Hunter (R-California), then-chairman of the House Armed Services Committee, would have greatly expanded these restrictions, so much so that no foreign product or materials, no matter how small, could be used in a US defense system.

Here was a Republican championing an issue vital to every union in America. That said, the wide scope of Buy American provisions as originally proposed would have had some unintended consequences. Hunter's amendment would have required every defense contractor to immediately switch to American suppliers. Under the Hunter amendment, the machines used in the manufacture of component parts had to be made in the United States, as well. The unions were ecstatic. The law would have begun to immediately reverse America's shrinking industrial base. However, there was no way the law, as written, could be implemented in the time stated in Hunter's amendment. President George W. Bush said he would veto the entire defense bill if the Hunter amendment passed.

I attempted to get our workforce coalition to appear before Congress and ask for a more reasonable time frame to approach the implementation of the Buy American provisions. We were asking the unions to support something that was against one of their most important goals: expanding the job base. I was personally torn on this issue because it was time that Congress understood that many machine tools were no longer made in America as they had been in the two world wars. We as a nation were now vulnerable because we could not manufacture our own defense products. Suddenly, like Davis-Bacon and the MX Missile System, we had an issue important to both the Defense Department and US manufacturing unions. The Buy American program was about to be derailed by the National Security Personnel System.

On the surface, the problem emanated from the DoD attempt to implement a pay-for-performance plan already authorized by Congress. At the same time, NSPS was to replace the General Schedule (GS) system used throughout the federal government. The automatic pay increases under the GS system would no longer exist under NSPS. But, the department could argue that they would reward employees with cash bonuses based on performance. The concern from the unions was that the department might engage in favoritism that would result in an employee charge that bonuses were given for reasons other than job performance. The unions believed that Congress had given them the right to represent the aggrieved employees. The unions also believed that NSPS challenged the right of unions to represent federal employees. This issue united all of the unions in the AFL-CIO.

A coalition of thirty-six different unions emerged to challenge what appeared to be the Defense Department's attempt to dismantle the unions. In an interview for this book, Greg Junemann, president of the IFPTE, noted that it was essential to manage such a large collection of different unions in the coalition. The problem from the outset was that it appeared that the Defense Department had already decided what they would propose to the Congress about replacing the GS schedule with the NSPS. Junemann said that member unions in the coalition attended what became known as the "no-go negotiations." He said, "We would propose something and they would study it." Greg advised the coalition not to leave the table, lest the Defense Department report to Congress that the unions were uncooperative.

In this instance, Junemann played a key role in keeping the unions in the negotiations. Junemann, who represented unions in both the public and private sector, such as the engineers and scientists at Boeing, maintained that he was not opposed to pay for performance, which was a major bone of contention with many of the other unions in the coalition. But Junemann had negotiated pay for performance contracts in the past. Greg also said that the IFPTE was interested in obtaining the efficiencies that the Defense Department sought. "We wanted to streamline the labor management process where we saw fit, and if they were going to have a pay for performance system we wanted to have a say on how that was going to happen."

Junemann said that it became clear to him and the unions that the Defense Department wanted to separate the members from their union. One way to do that was to eliminate the time that union stewards get on the clock to handle union matters. This would diminish the unions' ability to have the time to represent the workers.

As they moved through the six-month period that Congress set for the Defense Department and the unions to "work cooperatively," it was clear that the Defense representatives were not bargaining in good faith, and four months into the process they had not shared any of their initial conclusions with the unions.

This was difficult for Junemann because his personal philosophy is, rather than fight over differences, to focus on the areas where there is agreement. But months into the process the Defense Department would not share with the unions their analysis of union number-crunching. Four months into the process Junemann asked for my help. I explained the situation to Jerry Jones who was able to get Pete Geren to agree to an off-site meeting with Junemann.

Jerry and Pete met with Junemann and two of his union officials for almost four hours in my conference room in Arlington, Virginia to try and resolve the conflict. As I walked with the delegation out of the building, Greg said that the Department of Defense was putting the union in a position where the unions would no longer be able to represent their own members. I asked Greg to give me some more time to work it out.

I later sat down with Jerry Jones and Dave Patterson and went through what had transpired. Dave was very concerned that we not lose sight of the importance of union support on the Buy American issue. David said these were competing issues, and it would be important to get the Department's legislative director, Powell Moore, involved because he was representing the Defense Department on the Hill during the conference committee deliberations. It appeared to all of us that the union's right to represent its members came from a congressional act establishing a collective bargaining agreement under which employees voted in elections monitored by the Department of Labor that gave the unions the sole authority to represent its members in a grievance procedure.

A seasoned Washington insider, Powell Moore was the former congressional liaison in the Nixon White House. His view of the NSPS situation was purely political. "We have to fix this," he said. "We cannot lose the union support on Buy American." Moore concluded that a meeting with David Chu was now necessary. Chu, the Undersecretary of Defense for Personnel and Readiness, was regarded as *the* intellectual among Rumsfeld appointees.

On July 7, 2003, Powell Moore, Jerry Jones, and I met with David Chu and his human resources specialist on the issue. Moore made the case for resolving the NSPS issue as amicably as possible. Chu, who seemed very reasonable to me, said that the unions were overreacting on the representation issue. Moore made the point that House and Senate Republicans had a close working relationship with the unions on the Buy American issue. He mentioned that Congressmen Duncan Hunter (R-California) and Tom Davis (R-Virginia), as well as Senator Susan Collins (R-Maine), were eager to satisfy the union's legitimate demands.

As the conversation progressed, my mind went back to my conversation with Labor Secretary Brock and Sen. John Heinz on the Davis-Bacon issue. Chu was pursuing an issue from his perspective; Moore was talking about Rumsfeld's concern over labor's support for Buy American. It was Davis-Bacon versus the MX missile all over again.

I cautiously spoke up at the meeting on the issue of federal statutes governing union representation in a grievance procedure. I asked Chu, "Do you think that Congress will deny unions the right to represent their own members?" Before Chu could respond, his staff assistant said, "Yes, we can!"

It was clear that I was being perceived as a union representative rather than as an individual trying to avert a conflict between the union and the Defense Department. Such a conflict would have caused the department to lose union support on the Buy American issue, just the way trying to adjust Davis-Bacon lost the union support for the MX missile.

Chu asked me what I thought he should do. I said I thought it would be important for him to meet with a key union leader to try to resolve this issue so that everyone felt they were being heard. He agreed to set up the meeting. When we left the room, I told Powell Moore that I should not be involved in the meeting between Chu and the union.

Greg Junemann and his legislative/political director, Matthew Biggs, met with Chu and, to avoid any political posturing, did not bring any representatives from any other union of the coalition with them. Chu was working based on the background briefings he received from his team, but had not personally attended any of the meetings. Greg told me that Chu spoke in broad general terms about the need to reform the personnel system but gave no indication what proposals the Defense Department would make either to the unions or the Congress. Junemann told Chu that his major concern was that the unions did not lose the right to represent their members in the event of a grievance. At that point, Chu tried to assure him that there would be no personnel favoritism at the department concerning employee grievances. He told Greg the department would set up something similar to a "court-martial proceeding" to assure that the employees were treated fairly.

Junemann and Biggs left the room dazed. Greg asked Biggs, "Did he say court-martial?" Biggs replied, "Well that's what I heard." Both men returned to their office and began analyzing the meaning of the words "court-martial proceeding," which they knew was used to prosecute a uniformed offender but wondered how such a proceeding would have anything to do with representing aggrieved employees. They wondered whether Chu was saying that the managers applying favoritism would be court-martialed, or that the employees would be court-martialed by managers determining employees' guilt and punishment.

In the interview with me, Junemann reiterated that the six month time allotted by Congress was quickly coming to an end and that the Defense Department had not shared a single conclusion on implementing the NSPS with the unions. Around this same time I began receiving calls from William "Chico" McGill, director of government employees for the International Brotherhood of Electrical Workers. Chico said that the NSPS included language about "issuances" that superseded discipline and performance reviews and that even if a case went to arbitration, the secretary of defense could overrule the arbitrator!

I told Geren and Patterson that NSPS would never stand: that the Congress would eventually repeal the law, which was already being challenged in federal courts. We were risking Buy American for nothing.

In October 2009, the Congress repealed NSPS. But the damage was done. Buy American legislation disappeared when the unions refused to do anything to help the Defense Department on the Hill.

In the Davis-Bacon/MX and the NSPS/Buy American examples the issues involved public policies that were in contention. Davis-Bacon and Buy American were public policy objectives that were clouded by someone inserting their own agenda into the administration's agenda.

It would have been politically smart if someone in the Republican White House or in the Department of Defense could have taken the appropriate steps to identify the overriding political advantage of avoiding the damage caused by seeking to reform Davis-Bacon or colliding with union allies over NSPS.

There are several recent examples of Republican office holders abandoning their principles to attack their own party. For example, Florida's Republican Governor Charlie Crist announced in May of 2009 that he would run for the US Senate seat being vacated by fellow Republican Mel Martinez. Also running for that seat was Republican Marco Rubio. Prior to the primary election, Governor Crist said that he would abide by the decision of the voters as to who they would select for the Senate. Since Crist had served as education commissioner in Florida, the state teachers unions knew him and many registered as Republicans so that they could vote for him in the primary. It didn't matter. Rubio won the primary.

After Crist lost the primary he decided to run as an independent against Rubio in the general election. After losing the senate race to Rubio in the general election, Crist changed parties, and spoke at the Democratic Convention supporting Obama. He ran as a Democrat against Republican Governor Rick Scott in 2014 and lost.

Still another example: Senator James Jeffords from Vermont served as a Republican until 2001 when he switched parties, in the middle of a term, to become an Independent. Jeffords's move from the Republican Party changed the Senate makeup to fifty Democrats, forty-nine Republicans, and Jeffords as the lone Independent. As an Independent, Jeffords promised to vote for Democratic control after being promised a committee chairmanship.

My point is that Republicans engage in actions that *hurt* their own party while the Democrats go out of their way to *protect* their party at any cost. For example, Democratic Senator Robert Torricelli from New Jersey was involved in a series of personal indiscretions months before an election that sabotaged any chance he had of winning. The Democrats in New Jersey simply replaced him on the ballot for the Senate and ran former Democratic Senator Frank Lautenberg as his replacement.

Compare the Torricelli scenario with the case of Republican Congressman Todd Akin, who in 2012 ran against Senator Claire McCaskill, a Democrat from Missouri. McCaskill was in serious trouble due to her support for Obamacare and shouting matches with her constituents in town hall meetings. She actually said she was going to have to use language that she would normally use with her grandchildren to get voters to understand the reason she was supporting Obamacare. McCaskill was in such political trouble she wouldn't even go to the Democratic National Convention. This was an easy Senate seat for the Republicans to win.

Then Akin, in a televised interview, claimed that women who were the victims of what he described as "legitimate rape" rarely got pregnant from the rape. The outrage from both parties and the voters was intense. The Republican Party pleaded with him to get out of the race. The politically smart thing would have been to honor the judgment of his party and let someone else run against McCaskill. But, despite pleas from his party, Akin hung in the race and lost.

Still another symbol of Democratic allegiance to party was seen when Supreme Court Justice David Souter stepped down from his secure seat to give President Obama an opportunity to appoint a younger justice more in line with the president's political philosophy. Justice Sonia Sotomayor happily accepted the seat to give Obama a Hispanic appointment. Yet, during the Bush administration the Democratic Senate made certain that Bush would not have the opportunity to appoint a Hispanic as a Justice to a federal court no matter how qualified the appointee. The appointment of the first Hispanic Supreme Court justice by a Republican president would have undercut the Democrat argument that Republicans do not support Hispanics. Democrats would not give Bush any credit for appointing a Hispanic. Over and over we see demonstrations of the political unity within the Democratic Party.

As an observer of Republican philosophy and decision-making at the national level, it is clear to me that there is a distinct difference between Republicans at the state and local level and those who acquire a seat in the US House or Senate. Republicans at the local level seem more in tune with their constituencies than those who actually serve in the national legislature. As I travel through the country, I see no burning passion from state legislators to repeal the Davis-Bacon Act. I certainly did not see it during the Nixon or Reagan years. So where did the impetus for Brock's decision originate? It probably came from organizations like the Chamber of Commerce, the National Association of General Contractors, and other groups who lobby to change labor laws, change, they say, that will benefit the nation.

Early in my White House tenure as labor liaison, Richard Nixon cautioned me about people who would approach me with ideas on how to save the government money. He said that at the heart of many of those ideas was the goal of giving industries an advantage over their labor force. So it was with Davis-Bacon. Conservative think tanks and trade associations most likely have encouraged the pursuit of public policy that is not in the interest of the president, the Republican Party, or the nation.

The issues of the MX and Buy American bear close monitoring by the Republican Party because they are natural channels for communicating with labor unions. But, the generation of union workers who fought in World War II and Korea and who are strongly anti-communist has quickly fading. My major concern now is the philosophical changes in the labor movement that favor the progressives.

The public sector unions that have prospered in the era of massive entitlements as well as those unions that are part of the city, county and state governments are beyond the reach of Republicans. The goal of balancing budgets or shifting government spending from massive entitlement programs to reindustrialize the private sector will be met by opposition from progressives for philosophical and political reasons, first, because they seek to create European-style socialism, and second, and more importantly, the public sector has created massive electoral support for continuing and expanding the progressive agenda.

Still another example of Republicans being apolitical is the tendency for conservative Republicans to ignore, belittle, and denigrate liberal Republicans who come from states that are not considered conservative: New York, Pennsylvania, Oregon, Massachusetts, and Rhode Island. How many times have I heard castigations concerning

Rockefeller, Packwood, Heinz, Javits, and many others to the present day. These senators were called "RINOs", or Republicans in Name Only. Missing from all of this was the recognition that these Republicans had been elected in liberal states. Nixon was always grateful for liberal New York Senator Jacob Javits's support. Javits supported Nixon on the war and was the first senator to endorse Nixon for president in 1968.

I recall a meeting I set up with Missouri Senator Kit Bond and the Missouri aerospace unions when Bond faced a tough 1992 reelection. He looked at the AFL-CIO regional officials and sternly reminded the group, many of whom knew him as governor, that he had fought Republican conservatives in Missouri when they wanted him to support a right-to-work measure. Bond noted that he had taken on his own party for the unions and was offended that he had to ask them for their support in his reelection bid. He told the unions that he earned their support and concluded: "If you go against me in this election, you better beat me." The message was clear. Bond won his reelection.

On another occasion, in 1986, during a Washington meeting that I set up for Senator Dan Quayle with AFL-CIO union officials from Indiana, I watched Quayle give the union leaders the silent treatment after I had previously told him they were under extreme pressure to support his opponent. I had arranged the pro forma meeting with Quayle while the union delegation was in Washington on one of their annual meet-and-greet lobbying trips. Quayle, who had met with many of these same union officials in meetings I had set up in Indiana to save the jobs of steelworkers, sat quietly while a non-conversation ensued. Finally, Quayle spoke up and said he was constantly in touch with the rank and file members, and that he was well informed about all of their issues. He concluded by asking if the unions had a specific reason for the meeting. No one talked. Dan left.

The head of the state federation exhaled. "He's pissed," he said. "Yes," I said. "He's done everything for you for five years and it's obvious that you're being pressured to support his opponent." I then repeated the comment that Kit Bond had made to the unions in his meeting: "If you go against me in this election, you better beat me." The Indiana state federation declared neutrality in his 1986 reelection campaign.

Both Quayle and Bond were self-assured men. They worked closely with the unions on jobs issues and knew them personally. Both were not apologetic about being Republicans.

Today, Republicans pay for TV ads that attempt to present themselves to the people as engaged and sympathetic candidates, but few get "up close and personal" with voters to convey their desire to help working people. I believe Republicans are sensitive, if not gun-shy, about being perceived as having nothing in common with the working classes. They are mindful of being identified as the party of the rich. They fear being perceived as siding with corporate America and against the worker, the party unconcerned with the poor and the downtrodden. If anything, the tendency to characterize Republicans in this manner has increased today because the leadership of the national Democratic Party has placed its hope on maintaining political power by promoting class envy, defining Republicans as "one percenters," the party of business and corporate America. Any attempt at addressing the communication gap between Republicans and the rest of the American people must deal with the perceived gap that is dividing Americans into modern day patricians and plebeians. Coming from a working-class Democratic union household, I predict this division among Americans has the potential to tear the nation apart.

CHAPTER 10

Opportunities

One month before the election of 2008 I received a letter from Chuck Colson telling me that he had recently been to the National Archives and listened to the November 19, 1972, tape from the Nixon files.[70] It was a recording of a conversation he and Nixon had concerning the New Majority and the role I played in its formation. I later told Chuck that I believed that a New Majority coalition of voters could be reassembled to support a Republican candidate because many of the issues that were important to Middle America in 1972 and in 1980 had resurfaced over the past decade. It was clear that opportunities for outreach abounded in the areas of national security, rebuilding the defense industrial base, the energy and aerospace industries, as well as the nation's antiquated infrastructure. Investments in these areas would have an immediate impact on America's economy and national security. More importantly, all of these opportunities and issues would have a significant impact on working-class Americans who are the bedrock of the New Majority.

Republicans and National Security

Republicans enjoy a reputation of being strong on national security and national defense. This gives them a major advantage over Democrats who are seen by unions as weak on both. Here the Republicans have a historic advantage. While Democratic presidents Kennedy and Johnson kept America's industrial base strong, after the end of the Vietnam War and President Ford's brief presidency, the Democrats were looking for a peace dividend which they extracted from the defense budget. But America's security rests on a strong national defense. As orders for military hardware decreased, so did the prime contractors, subcontractors, and supplier-base companies, large and small. By the end of the Carter presidency, the weakness of America's defense industry was clearly visible. Republican conservative Ronald Reagan seized on this weakness and made it the focus of his 1980 campaign.

Although defense cuts usually fall heaviest on the blue-collar workforce devoted to hands-on assembly (what economists call "touch labor"), research and development (R&D) programs are usually cut as well, thus reducing the ranks of engineers whose work often begins ten years or more in advance of production. What is more, public policy makers often fail to recognize the importance of encouraging and inspiring students to pursue studies in engineering and science in order to be prepared for the needs of the future. Some members of Congress believe that in a national emergency they can simply turn on a faucet to increase the number of engineers who can begin research and development to produce up-to-date weapons systems. It simply does not work that way.

While chairman of the Council of Engineers and Scientists Organizations (CESO), Harold Ammond testified to that effect before Congress, saying that, although the government could declare an emergency and order industry to produce military equipment, training new engineers takes approximately eight to ten years. A ten-year notice of the emergency would be needed before a cadre of trained engineers and scientists could begin work.

Late in the 1980 campaign, Nixon's New Majority resurfaced to coalesce behind Ronald Reagan. Not surprisingly, Reagan pledged to rebuild America's defense industry. The craft unions of America's industrial base went back to work. The craft and industrial base workers supported Ronald Reagan with the same passion and fervor with which they had supported Richard Nixon. Why? Because Republicans are strong on national defense that protects America and its allies and at the same time creates and maintains high-paying jobs for the entire spectrum of the defense industrial workforce. For Republicans to capture a majority of working-class voters, they should communicate with workers both union and nonunion in the defense industrial base. Here, Democrats are at a disadvantage.

Industrial union membership is now at an all-time low, even after the defense buildup of the Reagan years when there was an infusion of capital into defense programs such as the B-1 and B-2 bombers, the C-17 transport, and a 600-ship Navy. As the defense budget declines, the armed services are cutting more weapons systems from their arsenals. In 2008, the Navy truncated the first twenty-first century surface combatant ship, the Zumwalt Destroyer, from an anticipated thirty-two to three. The Navy had already invested more than $16 billion in designing the Zumwalt and effectively cancelled the program before the first of the three ships was built. The Navy also cancelled the CGX, a twenty-first century cruiser scheduled to replace the 1980s Ticonderoga-class cruisers. The CGX ships were to be built using the same hull and composite deckhouse as the Zumwalt destroyer. In October 2012, *Popular Science* [71] featured an article on the Zumwalt, as did the January 2014 issue of *Proceedings* [72] of the US Naval Institute. Both articles highlighted the advanced high-tech stealthy features of this warship, which bring to mind something out of a Jules Verne novel.

The Zumwalt destroyer and the follow-on cruiser would have employed ship builders for more than a decade. Gone are the jobs as well as the new shipbuilding technologies that would have modernized our shipbuilding workforce. Northrop Grumman and Huntington Ingalls invested $10 million to develop the most advanced composite facility in the world, which is now closed.

Here is an opportunity. Today, the pleas of the international unions, the defense and aerospace unions, as well as the shipbuilders who represent what remains of America's industrial base go unheard. I have spoken to the presidents of local unions as well as the presidents of international unions who confidentially tell me they have no future. Democrats will not fund programs that employ industrial workers who build defense systems. The defense industrial workforce will respond to Republicans if they demonstrate that they appreciate the value that these American workers provide to our economy and our national security.

The Republican Party is and always has been committed to engaging the private sector to create jobs in a variety of industries that have languished under progressive Democrats. Since the Reagan defense buildup, the defense sector has fallen on hard times, and with it, major portions of the industrial base. A significant opportunity exists for Republicans to demonstrate their support for the millions of American workers who make up the majority of what is left of America's defense-industrial base. The shipbuilding industry is a case in point. Reagan built a 600-ship Navy. Today the fleet has fallen to 273 ships. The impact has been most severe on the master craftsmen who are retiring without replacements. We need a Republican candidate ready to revive our shipbuilding industry by ordering new ships that would, in turn, trigger the creation of thousands of jobs in the prime, subcontractor and supplier base. It would be a massive stimulus program, not only for the shipyards but also for the entire machine tool industry. At the same time, it would provide for our national security. The opportunities for the Republican Party to reach out to workers in the industrial base are everywhere. Yet Republicans are not acting on this opportunity.

Some might argue that I am advocating defense spending as merely a jobs program for defense workers. I respond that the world we live in today is filled with nation states engaged in activities reminiscent of the 1930s. The Russians are engaging in open aggression in Ukraine. China is claiming portions of island reefs in the South China Sea, where they are building airstrips to expand Chinese sovereignty. At the same time, the Chinese are building nuclear aircraft carriers and submarines while the Russians have introduced a new tank that has an unmanned turret. Meanwhile, all the peace-loving Scandinavian countries are doing a land-office business as defense subcontractors to the world, including the provision of arms to our political opponents.

Today the United States is unilaterally disarming. This is not the time for America to abandon what is left of the arsenal of democracy that saved the world in two wars.

Opportunities in Energy

A similar opportunity exists for Republicans to begin a dialogue with unions on energy issues. As I have said, progressives in the Democratic Party are totally committed to renewable energy, except, of course, for nuclear power. They champion solar, wind, geothermal—anything except oil, gas, coal, and nuclear where America has a market advantage. Throughout the 1980s, Democrats railed against acid rain, which they argued resulted from coal emissions. They favored a BTU tax, which, while aimed at coal, hurt oil as well. They also attempted to pass legislation that would have created a ban on the use of solvents necessary for the manufacture of high-tech component parts, from computer chips to space vehicles. The ban would have impacted everything from sprays used on computer components and all of the coatings used in the civil space industry, as well as on all military platforms, as well as cleaning fluids used in dry-cleaning processes.

The environmentalists and their progressive allies in the Democratic Party essentially drove the ban on solvents. The nation was saved from this legislative disaster when Gladys Greene, then-president of IBEW Local 1805 representing workers in the Baltimore high-tech radar facility of Northrop Grumman, explained to Sen. Barbara Mikulski (D-Maryland) that many of her members who had come from the inner city now had high-skilled jobs working in glass booths with clean garbs spraying gold on computer chips and component parts for the defense and aerospace industry. "All of these people will be back on the street if this bill passes," Gladys told the senator. Mikulski got it and voted against the ban.

Today, there is opposition to extracting oil from shale, and opposition to the Keystone pipeline, all driven by progressives in the Democratic Party. This is an opportunity for the Republican Party to champion these sources of energy for America. Some Republicans might argue, "Well, we already support nuclear power, coal, and the construction of Keystone as well as the thousands of jobs associated with those industries." True, but Republicans are not sitting down with their shirt sleeves rolled up in the trenches, meeting and talking with the unions as opposed to being mere cheerleaders standing on the sidelines. Republicans could mobilize workers and the public on all of these energy issues by demonstrating their support for these workers and their jobs. This is a tremendous opportunity to open a genuine dialogue with the unions.

Coal miners have made a futile attempt to reach out to the Democratic Party to tell them that the current generation of coal miners may be the last in the nation's history. The United Mine Workers and their allies are fighting for their survival from a progressive-dominated Democratic Party that has once again declared war on coal miners in several states. These miners will support a Republican if that Republican reaches out to them.

Opportunities in Science

With the exception of John F. Kennedy, for the last sixty years Democrats have been as weak on science as they have been in the areas of national security and defense. Conversely, the Republican Party has solidly supported science and technology. In 1969, Nixon argued that America should invest in building a supersonic transport (SST). Labor unions also supported the SST. George Meany, then-president of the AFL-CIO, was concerned about job losses that were beginning to happen because the de-escalation of the Vietnam War and the Apollo program's completion were occurring at the same time. Democrats in the Senate were concerned about sonic booms over major cities and stratospheric pollution the large aircraft engines would produce. The House sought to revive the program. However, in May of 1971, the Senate rebuffed the move and effectively killed the American SST program.

Nixon correctly predicted that, if the United States did not build an SST prototype, other nations would and America would lose its competitive advantage and eventually market domination of the world's commercial aircraft industry. Nixon was right. The Europeans established a consortium of nation states, not private companies, to build the SST followed by expanding their collaboration to build the Airbus. At that time Boeing, Lockheed and McDonnell Douglas dominated the world's commercial aircraft industry. The competition from Airbus ended America's monopoly in commercial aircraft.

Similar objections were raised by Democrats to oppose the Superconducting Super Collider program, a major scientific research project to extract new subatomic matter from protons in near light-speed collisions. In the late 1990s, research from probes and improved telescopes revealed that during supernova explosions, stars give off new material that evolves from protons colliding at supersonic speeds. The superconducting supercollider would set protons in motion traveling at supersonic speeds in an underground tunnel where they would collide, replicating collisions in exploding stellar bodies. The collider's underground tunnel was to be filled with scientific measuring devices to study the process and advance our understanding of particle and high-energy physics. The program was a high-tech employment project that would require thousands of engineers and scientists as well as construction workers and mining crews to dig and build the tunnel that would be some fifty miles in circumference. But in 1993, the Superconducting Super Collider required too much imagination for the Congress to see its value. Focused on the claim that the project would detract from other government spending priorities, the project was abandoned in the United States, but not elsewhere. Europe went ahead with its version of the collider. Today, the Large Hadron Collider is an intra-European project located on the French-Swiss border.

On January 14, 2015, NOVA aired a documentary on the collider entitled, *Big Bang Machine*. NOVA described the collider as the largest, most complex machine ever built. As one who tried to promote the economic advantages of the Superconducting Super Collider to a disinterested Democratic Senate, I was depressed by the description of the jobs created throughout Europe that could have been created in the United States. I thought about the construction of a tunnel fifty miles in circumference and 300 feet deep, and the tens of thousands of operating engineers, laborers, and Teamsters it would have taken to move all of that earth and all of the concrete and steel it would have required to build the tunnel. The project employed tens of thousands of engineers, scientists and astrophysicists, all earning top salaries for decades, while their counterparts in America were looking for work. The Europeans now lead the world in particle acceleration research. All of the economic benefits of building an American supercollider were lost because Democrats in the Senate were more interested in funding entitlements.

Opportunities in Space

The biggest potential recovery program for America would be to revive America's commitment to manned space exploration. When President Kennedy challenged the nation to go to the moon, his words inspired a generation of students to pursue math and science education. Summing up the accomplishments of the US space program, Charles D. Walker, the first commercial industry astronaut, who flew three times in the space shuttle in the mid-1980s, noted:

> The economy exploded in every direction. Most importantly, the youth of our nation accepted the challenge, saw the adventure, and enrolled in the newly expanded universities' science, engineering, and mathematics curriculums. The number of graduate degrees in those fields soared: doctoral engineering and mathematics degrees increased four-fold in eight years, doctorates in the physical sciences were up almost three-fold in the same time immediately after Kennedy set America on the path to the moon. Collectively, aerospace companies in the private sector invested billions of dollars in R&D programs that employed engineers and skilled technicians who built the spaceships, launch and support systems. The economy was flooded—and benefited many fold—with spinoff products from the space program. We have harvested that crop. Those benefits are now behind us. There are many aerospace workers, Kennedy Democrats all, who believe that the space program died with Kennedy.

The Public Broadcast System aired a program on April 22, 2015, entitled *The Invisible Universe Revealed*. The broadcast documented John Grunsfeld's visit to the Hubble telescope on May 18, 2009. Astronaut

Grunsfeld touched the Hubble noting that no American would ever return to adjust its navigational controls to prevent its return to the earth's atmosphere where it would burn up in reentry. America launched the Hubble, serviced it, reaped its benefits, but no longer has a space vehicle to repair it. Our astronauts fly to the International Space Station on Russian rockets.

The decline in the manned space program began in the early 1970s, when President Nixon and the Congress turned their attention from space exploration to ending the war in Vietnam. By 1982 the numbers of new science and engineering degrees had dropped by almost half. While the count of graduate degrees granted by American universities in science and engineering has languished, the number of new technical degrees from European and Asian universities given each year since 1970 has steadily increased.

There were two Republican attempts to revive the space program, both of which failed. The first was when George H. W. Bush announced in 1989, on the twentieth anniversary of America's landing a man on the moon, "a long-range, continuing commitment" to establish a base on the moon from which we would launch a manned mission to Mars. Lacking Democratic support on the Hill, his effort failed.

The second Republican effort came in the third year of the George W. Bush administration. On January 14, 2004, he directed NASA to "gain a new foothold on the moon and to prepare for new journeys to the worlds beyond our own." The president envisioned the development of a crew exploration vehicle (later named Orion), and a return to the moon to establish and extend human presence, followed by a manned mission to Mars. NASA entitled the overall effort "Constellation," but it lacked the support of the Obama administration. The program was effectively terminated in 2010.

Meanwhile, both India and China are ramping up their space and defense programs, employing thousands of newly-graduated engineers, many of whom were trained in the United States. The Indian government has its own probe now orbiting Mars. The Chinese have launched more than ten astronauts, a small starter space station circling earth, and successful probes to the moon that are expected to robotically return moon rocks to China by the end of this decade.

Chinese military satellites are approaching the capabilities of those of both the United States and the resurgent Russian armed forces satellites orbiting above us.

The question is: Does the country that was the first to put a man on the moon care? American workers care. The entire labor movement has a stake in the endeavor. Every union, from those who would have dug the tunnel for the supercollider to those who would pour the concrete at launch sites and those who build and service the launch vehicles, is waiting for a president to lead the nation once again in space exploration.

From the Apollo program–that "giant leap for mankind"–came the technological spinoffs that many Americans take for granted. Charles Bofferding, an engineer and former executive director of Boeing's engineering union, testified many times before Congress and before presidential commissions concerning America's defense and space budgets. He argued that those budgets should have been termed "technology budgets" because they spawned the Internet, the semiconductor / computer / telecommunications products used today, as well as life-saving technologies that can be seen in any hospital, such as magnetic resonance imaging (MRI), computerized axial tomography (CAT), and other noninvasive diagnostic and treatment tools. All of these industries and products have been derived from research and development in our space and defense programs.

Today, programs in manned space exploration barely exist. Some time ago I interviewed Jeffrey L. Rainey, a former union business rep of the International Association of Machinists who represented NASA workers at Cape Kennedy, Florida. Like Charles Bofferding, Rainey had testified before President George W. Bush's Commission on Space Exploration. The demise of NASA's manned space program devastated the unions in Cape Canaveral. Rainey told me he had recently attended a funeral for one of his union coworkers. During the wake, the laid-off union aerospace workers spoke about what had happened to them after the Obama administration canceled the Constellation program in 2010. Many of those who had jobs are now driving trucks and working in supermarkets. Many of the union workers who once put a man on the moon are retiring with no one coming up behind them.

An excellent overview of what has happened to America's space program in the post-Kennedy years is contained in a book by Mark Albrecht that is appropriately titled, *Falling Back to Earth*. Mark, a longtime friend and colleague, served as executive secretary of the National Space Council during the term of George H. W. Bush.

By the time the 2012 campaign rolled around, even the Republicans would not make space exploration an issue. The only Republican candidate who talked about restoring the manned space program was Newt Gingrich. He made a statement to that effect during a Florida GOP debate in response to CNN host Wolf Blitzer's question about what each candidate would do about the nation's space program.[73] Gingrich was laughed at by his Republican opponents.

The Republican Party today does not understand the opportunity at hand. Reviving a manned space exploration program would create an explosion in investments and employment throughout the country and propel the economic recovery. This is fertile ground for Republicans, but it will take more than speeches of support to gain the trust of American workers. Republicans should visit the communities surrounding NASA facilities now decimated by NASA cuts and talk to the local workers, press the flesh, deliver the message face-to-face.

By supporting expanded programs in defense, space, and energy production, the Republican Party can capture a sizeable majority of the American workforce, union and nonunion. In the areas of defense and space alone there are many union members who have personally told me they want a relationship with the Republican Party now more than any other time in their history.

Rebuilding the Nation's Supply Chain

Local unions are frustrated. They assume that the money from their paychecks that goes into the union political action committee (PAC) will be used to support candidates who will support defense programs that employ union members. Often, the opposite is true. During her first run for the Senate, Barbara Boxer was asked by a reporter whether she would support the local economy by voting for programs that employed defense workers. A March 6, 1991, *Los Angeles Times* article carried her response:

> 'It is not the role of a congressional delegation to be a chamber of commerce,' said Rep. Barbara Boxer (D-Greenbrae), a San Rafael-area Democrat on the House Armed Services Committee who is fighting to reform the procurement system. 'We should make sure that California has a fair shot at getting programs, but we should not be boosters for local industry. When I took the oath of office, it did not mean supporting local contractors. It meant supporting the nation.' [74]

Local union members who read her statement were outraged, but the international unions continued to contribute to her campaigns, providing her with victory after victory. Moreover, the AFL-CIO PAC contributions continue to flow to Democrats almost without deviation, regardless of their votes on aerospace and defense issues. This has resulted in the Democrats having a near-monopoly on labor union endorsements and donations. Defense contractors in California are slowly but surely moving their corporate headquarters, as well as corporate taxes and jobs, to facilities in nonunion southern states where congressional delegations are more sympathetic to the defense programs that employ their constituents. Arguments from labor unions that those industries moved from California to get away from unions are bogus. Those companies moved to find states that appreciated their contribution to the tax base. The fact that some of these states had nonunion workers was incidental. The impact in California was devastating to the remaining aerospace labor force. According to an August 2012 report of the California Economic Development Department, *The Aerospace Industry in Southern California*, from 1990 to 2011 the state lost well over a half million high-paying direct and indirect jobs in the aerospace industry due to corporate migration out of the state.

As the defense industrial infrastructure in California steadily declined, the political powerbase in that state shifted to public employee unions. David Goodreau, then-chairman of the Small Manufacturers

Association of California, noted that the impact on the aerospace and defense supply chain has been severe. According to Goodreau, "There was a time when unions, large corporations and small businesses had common values/interests that helped put people to work and create a regional manufacturing infrastructure that was second to none. The impact from the disintegration of that alliance for a strong manufacturing base has been devastating for the supply chain. Today, we are at a competitive disadvantage, from a variety of regulations that, over several decades, has added up to an adversarial environment for manufacturers." Goodreau continued, "Manufacturing is an extension of the Industrial Arts, a field where creative people with mechanical aptitude succeed."

Five years ago, Pat Ainsworth, director of The California Technical Education (CTE) programs for the California Department of Education, testified before the California state legislature that seventy-five percent of the CTE programs had been closed between 1980 and 2008. The cultural and economic impact from a lack of mechanical skills development and career awareness has had a devastating impact on the supply chain. In 2012 there were only thirty machine shop programs left in the state and most were only funded as part time with one to two class periods a day. By contrast, in the 1970s, about 1,000 high schools in California had machine and auto shops, wood shops, welding and electric shops and drafting programs. The California Industrial & Technology Education Association stated that, as of 2013, they could not identify a single student in the California State University system preparing to get a CTE degree and/or credential for teaching in the shop trades field.

Goodreau summarized, "This collective decay of critical education policies and resources are negatively impacting those remaining aerospace and defense suppliers at a time when both opportunity and competition is intense."

The loss of jobs in the aerospace and defense sector in California can be laid at the feet of Democrats not Republicans. Local unions know that the Democrats will not reliably support defense spending. However, one Democrat who understands the problem and realizes that something must be done to reverse this trend is Senator Barbara

Mikulski (D-Maryland), who will be retiring in 2016. Throughout her public career, Barbara Mikulski has been close to the unions. She represents the steelworkers in Sparrows Point, Maryland, as well as scientific employees at NASA's Goddard Space Flight Center in Greenbelt, Maryland. As she did on the attempt to ban the use of solvents in manufacturing, Mikulski supported the unions building the space station. Mikulski had been an opponent of the space station until she visited a large facility building major components for the space shuttle. During that visit, a senior official in the United Auto Workers and Aerospace Workers union approached her on the tour and told her that his parents had been migrant workers in California. Now, one generation later, he was earning high wages producing component parts for the space shuttle that would enable the transportation of cargo including astronauts to the space station while in orbit. The meeting had an enormous impact on Mikulski.

In the early 1990s, when Senator Dale Bumpers was determined to defund the space station, calling it "technopork," Senator Mikulski made a speech on the Senate floor responding to Bumpers. [75] Her defense of the space station was a complete reversal of her earlier opposition to the program. After listing all of the job losses in various industries in her state, Mikulski asked:

> So where is our economy going to turn to? There are those who allege this is `technopork'—'technopork' to put together people in the aerospace industry, men and women whose hands I shook when I visited the space centers, many of them union labor, UAW labor.
>
> When I talked to people in the space program who are from the Hispanic origin, one generation away from being migratory workers are now working as space techs making good wages and at the same time creating an infrastructure that will take us into the 21st century.

Mikulski's speech on the Senate floor saved the space station that is now in low orbit around the earth. Furthermore, her speech was so effective that Senator Bumpers never introduced his amendment again.

Republicans must, like Senator Mikulski, articulate their appreciation and respect for blue-collar hourly workers and high-tech scientists and engineers who perform a great service in preserving both our economic and national security.

Outreach to Hispanics

While Republicans, especially business-focused groups like the US Chamber of Commerce, want to open the floodgate for Hispanic immigrants to take the jobs Americans are loathe to take, Republican opposition to *illegal* immigration leaves them open to the charge that they oppose *all* immigration. Former California Senator and Governor Pete Wilson is a case in point. During his 2000 presidential campaign he advocated strong measures for dealing with illegal immigrants, but he was accused of being anti-immigrant, which was far from the truth. Wilson kept insisting that he was opposed only to illegal immigration but no one listened to him.

I have previously described the ways in which the Democratic Party connected with non-English speaking European immigrants in the early days of the twentieth century. They did so by helping these immigrants navigate daily life in a variety of ways and, significantly, register to vote. Today, of course, we have a whole new wave of immigrants from Mexico and Central and South America. Because Democrats are strongly and visibly in favor of immigration reform, these Latinos are disposed to view Democrats sympathetically. More importantly, the Democrats are replaying their strategy from the earlier era. Like the precinct workers who were clever enough to infiltrate the ethnic communities with surrogates to "help" recently arrived immigrant Italians, Poles, Slavs, and Greeks settle into community life and register as Democrats, the Democrats are actively engaged in Hispanic communities. Absent a coherent Republican outreach, I predict the result will be the same as it was for the earlier European immigrants. Over the decades they worked their way into the middle class out of a dependency on the party machine. They worked hard, succeeded, and many became part of the business community and many even became Republicans. However, because of their deep historic ties to the Democratic Party, many remain reflexively Democratic.

When my wife and I first moved into our suburban home a young Hispanic came to our door offering to cut our grass. He had one mower in the trunk of his car. He became our regular lawn mower. One day he showed up in a truck. Soon he had two trucks and had expanded into general landscaping services. Later, he came in the winter and plowed the snow off our driveway. Eventually he was able to operate at least two full-time crews year-round. One day he came by my house to pick up a check. He was driving a white BMW. I said, "Wow, Ramiro, you're doing well."

He became apologetic and said, "Well, Mr. Balzano, I work very hard."

I interrupted him and said, "Whoa, whoa. Don't apologize for your success. You are living the American Dream. Through hard work and sacrifice you have earned the right to drive any car you want."

He then offered, "Well, I'm a businessman and a Republican."

That he is a Republican is, I'm sure, an anomaly but not without a great deal of logic. He, like most immigrants, wants to partake of the American Dream. They are entrepreneurial, many will start businesses, and they will move up the economic ladder by virtue of hard work. In this way they are natural Republicans. The Nixon administration realized this more than forty years ago when it brought in Alex Armendaris to organize outreach to Hispanics. In Nixon's second term, Alex became head of the Office of Minority Business Enterprise and helped launch many Hispanic small businesses. Several other Republican state and local organizations developed successful outreach programs and Republicans did relatively well with Hispanic voters in the 60s, 70s, and 80s.

So why does the Democratic Party continue to attract more and more Hispanic voters? To be sure, it is, in part, because they have effectively demonized the Republican Party as anti-immigrant. But I would argue it is also because they have very effectively used grassroots outreach to bring Hispanics into the fold.

It doesn't have to be this way. Republicans can reverse this tide and regain some traction among Hispanic voters. But they will need to take a page out of the Democrat's playbook. They will need to get out of their comfort zone and build an army of precinct workers and surrogates to help these immigrants navigate their daily lives, obtain driver's licenses, enroll in English classes, locate jobs, find housing and, most importantly, register to vote. They will need appropriate surrogates, including Hispanic businessmen and women who can convince them that a business-oriented party can offer them a path to prosperity and help them realize their dreams.

CHAPTER 11
Republicans and Organized Labor

The opportunities cited in the previous chapter would create millions of jobs for working-class Americans, both union and non-union. Thousands of engineers and scientists would be needed as well as craftsmen throughout the industrial base. There would be an added benefit through the creation of new curricula in universities that would offer the science, technology, engineering, math, chemistry and physics programs to educate the next generation of engineers. Reviving our aerospace industrial base would also mean the creation of apprenticeship programs for the touch-labor workforce to build the hardware and mechanical systems for the modern age that would employ millions of working-class Americans with high-paying jobs. The Republican Party could follow the lead of Nixon, Reagan and George H.W. Bush and mobilize a New Majority of working-class Americans on the issues of careers and jobs. But to do so, the Republican Party will have to reach out to the working classes, especially the unions that dominate the defense, space, transportation, and energy industries.

Right about now my Republican readers will be saying, "There goes Balzano again with his advocacy for labor unions." To which I respond, "Hear me out." There are unions, and there are unions, and Republicans do not know enough about them to understand that many unions would support Republican candidates if they make an effort to reach out to them. I am referring to those unions who *build* things, both the engineering and the touch-labor force.

Given the opportunities for outreach to the broad base of

America's working classes, how should Republicans reach out to them? Republicans see the millions of dollars in PAC funds that unions give to Democratic candidates. They see thousands of union members volunteering for Democrats, driving voters to the polls, etc., and they are frightened. To avoid rejection, most Republican candidates do not make a sincere outreach to unions. However, in my experience those who try are often successful.

There are a few basic facts about labor unions that Republicans should bear in mind. First, it is important to understand the organizational structure of the American labor movement. The AFL-CIO is a trade association made up of member unions, just as the membership of the US Chamber of Commerce is made up of American businesses. To the untrained eye, the AFL-CIO and organized labor appear as a granite monolith. It is not. It is a mosaic made up of individual tiles that consist of different unions representing people with different skills who work in different industries. A Republican candidate wanting to speak with a business leader would *not* go to the state's chamber of commerce. The candidate would go directly to the CEO of the corporation or business. The corresponding office in a labor union is the president of the local or the directing business agent. The candidate does *not* have to go to the AFL-CIO headquarters in Washington, DC. Properly approached, most union presidents at the state and local level will talk to any candidate if the meeting concerns jobs and if the meetings are private.

Even without a union president accompanying a candidate, properly introduced, any candidate can visit a plant or a worksite. Usually, candidates are treated very well. On tours, workers take the measure of a candidate very quickly. A visit can do much to dispel the negative propaganda thrown at candidates. The unions that are most open to Republicans are the craft unions in the basic trades. These unions make up the heart of America's industrial base. They are found in the prime contractors, subcontractors, and supplier chains of a variety of industries.

Industrial workers, especially the skilled craftsmen, are extremely proud of the work they do and are delighted when candidates or legislators visit their work site to observe the skills the workers have mastered. In the mid-1980s, I toured the submarine base at Mare Island, California, with then-Senator Pete Wilson. Prior to the tour, I briefed him on some of the machines he would see at the facility as well as some of the craftsmen who would be performing highly intricate operations required to assemble critical components. In this instance, a master craftsman was assembling two halves of a valve unit that required zero tolerance when closed.

To achieve the zero tolerance required, the craftsman had to file the two connecting surfaces of the valve assembly by hand. As he filed, he would rub his hand in a circular motion over the surface of the valve, feeling for the slightest variation in the flat surfaces that were to be joined together. The senator leaned close to my ear and whispered, "What is he doing?"

I answered, "He is feeling for what could be a variance of a thousandth of an inch."

Pete then said out loud, "With his hand?"

I responded, "Yes. There is no machine that can measure that tolerance. It's all in the feel of the hand of a master craftsman."

Pete then engaged the worker, expressing his marvel at what he was watching. The workman beamed with pride as he could see that the senator visibly appreciated the skill required to perform what Wilson later described as "artistry." When I asked the worker if there was anyone else at the base that could perform the task, he said no.

When we left the base, Wilson remarked, "That man was in his late fifties. What happens if he gets hit by a car? What would we do?"

That is the problem facing the industrial sector. We need a country committed to preserving the industrial base. One way Republicans can champion the preservation of the industrial base is by encouraging young people to join apprenticeship programs. We need to train the next generation of master craftsmen.

Mare Island is now closed, like many other shipyards. The situation industry-wide has not improved. I recently brought a colleague to an East Coast machine shop at another shipyard. We watched a man standing on a ladder holding his hand on a massive shaft turning on a lathe. As it turned, he rubbed his hand across the steel surface as though he were polishing a surface made of gold. Out of the tens of thousands of workers in that facility, he was the only craftsman capable of performing that task, and he was in his early seventies.

To appreciate the role of a master craftsman, Republican candidates must visit workers at the jobsite. Talking with workers is an opportunity for Republican candidates to close the gap between themselves and the union workers in the basic trades. It also sends a message about the importance of training the next generation of master craftsmen.

It is also essential for Republicans to have a fundamental understanding of the basic terms used to describe union representation in individual states. Some states have passed right-to-work laws. Right-to-work laws outlaw the union shop, where union contracts force all workers to join the union and pay dues whether they want to or not. In the heyday of union power, there were union shops where the union could prevent a company from hiring an individual worker without the union's permission. Right-to-work laws simply allow workers not to pay union dues; they still receive the benefits of union-negotiated contracts. It does not mean that unions are prohibited from organizing companies in those states.

On one occasion, I tried to convince a Republican senator to visit a shipyard in his state to meet with workers whose jobs the senator championed. He refused, because he said his state is a right-to-work state, and he did not want to appear to his fellow Republicans that he was promoting unions. I explained that there were thousands of union members in that shipyard who supported him. Believing that he already had a relationship with the workers because he supported their programs and that they would vote for him, he chose not to reach out them. He was not re-elected.

Candidates should also remember that there are industrial workers who are not unionized and who would welcome *any* candidate who supports their jobs. The key is for Republican candidates not to be frightened by what appears to be a monolith of organized labor.

The changing profile of the labor movement today has shifted from the industrial unions to federal, state and local workers in the public sector. Unions in the public sector represent teachers, fire and police associations, as well as city and state road maintenance workers. The fire and police unions are more conservative and generally friendlier to Republicans. From my experience, public sector unions in state and local bureaucracies are less likely to support Republicans. In fact, these unions have become a major constituency of the Democratic Party.

It is important to remember some of the issues I discussed in the preceding chapters. Some union issues are sacred cows. Attempting to repeal the Davis-Bacon Act or pass a national right-to-work law are two issues that have caused Republicans to lose Senate seats on more than one occasion. Any effort to amend the Jones Act would also hurt Republicans.

Nixon's instructions to me were, "Stay out of labor issues promoted by business and trade associations; they are all trying to leverage their workforce. Let them fight their own battles. Leave the administration out of it." At the time that he gave me that admonition I was a neophyte and had no idea why he felt that way. But more than forty years of experience have taught me exactly what he meant. If Republicans want to run on a platform to reduce the cost of government, fine, but taking on work rules for unionized industries in the private sector is a third rail for Republicans. In the private sector, work rules are the business of the human resources departments of the companies that hire the workers. It is not the business of the Republican Party to negotiate contracts or set wages. The Republican Party would never dream of setting the compensation for corporate executives; why do they continually interfere with the wages of hourly workers? Nixon understood there was nothing to be gained by getting involved in collisions between management and labor, so he stayed out of them.

Republicans should be aware that local unions often will not get close to Republicans because they might be subjected to retaliation either by Democratic officials at the district level or from the Democratic-controlled AFL-CIO international.

In August of 2004, George W. Bush toured the tilt rotor helicopter facility in Ridley, Pennsylvania. At that time, Boeing was my client, so I was asked to help facilitate an event with the union. The UAW International had already endorsed the Kerry/Lieberman ticket and advised the local not to cooperate on the tour. John DeFrancisco, the local UAW president, a Democrat himself, was in his first term as president of the local. He did not want to alienate the UAW district leadership who originally supported John's opponent in the election, so John decided to go on vacation the day of the president's visit.

I called John, urging him to attend the event and lead the tour through the plant. I told him that Boeing had received enough orders for the next ten years because of the 9/11 attacks and that it would be an insult to the local and the company if the union president were obviously hiding out. John agreed to lead the tour.

On the day before the tour, Andy Card, Bush's chief of staff, asked if we could present the president with a jacket bearing the UAW logo. DeFrancisco was successful in acquiring the jacket. Despite the anger of both regional and national UAW leadership over the jacket, DeFrancisco ran for a second term. and was reelected.

Republicans need to understand that when a union president agrees to participate in any event with a Republican candidate, he or she invites expulsion from the union and receives condemnation from the international leaders and the AFL-CIO. There are risks for union leaders who deal openly with Republicans, but many are willing to do so not only for the jobs of their members but also because they support a strong national defense.

In my experience, Republicans do not recognize that some Washington-based international unions advocate policies that will directly harm their own members. Republicans expect that unions want to protect their workers and that unions would not want to harm their own dues-paying members by proposing to shut down production facilities in order to transfer funding to domestic social programs.

Republicans believe that it would be counterintuitive for labor unions to destroy the jobs that employ union members. But some of the international unions have done just that. This sounds unbelievable, but the facts bear this out. Take the case of what happened when a union local involved in building a large section of the B-2 bomber in Texas discovered that their international union's Washington lobbyist was opposed to the B-2. When the local union president and secretary treasurer learned this, they brought a delegation of angry local union officers and shop stewards to the headquarters of their union's international in Washington, DC, to make it clear to the lobbyist that their members were paying the salaries of the Washington international officials. There was an immediate policy change in that office. However, the only reason the international changed its position was because the local found out, was livid, and took action.

On another occasion, a Republican conservative who first observed this phenomenon moved to protect the dues-paying members from their own international officers. I was called by then-Senator Pete Wilson who showed me a letter to him from the international president of a major industrial union representing thousands of aerospace workers. The letter transmitted *The Empty Pork Barrel,* a study by Employment Research Associates that had been sent to all the members of Congress. The study concluded that, "our economy is being undermined by a sustained emphasis on the military" and that "the military build-up generated fewer jobs, less investment capital, and less money for state, local and civilian federal government than comparable civilian expenditures." The study recommended "a cut of $50 billion in the Pentagon's budget."

The letter to Senator Wilson from the international president stated that his union had more members engaged in the production of military goods and services than any other union in the AFL-CIO. He then wrote:

> . . .but that doesn't mean we approve of current runaway military budgets and rambo militarism, nor does it mean we should keep silent about the devastating consequences and economic and social distortions such militarism *is* causing.
>
> We suggest the time is long overdue to forget about such military fantasies as real spending increases; 'force symmetry;' Space Defense Initiatives; and 'broad' interpretations of the ABM treaty. It is time to return to the rational jargon of reductions in weapons and force levels in a context of mutual preservation. Then wasteful, runaway military spending can be converted into rehabilitating and reindustrializing our sagging civilian sectors of the economy. [76]

Pete sat back in his chair, shook his head, his mouth open in disbelief, and said, "I don't get it. Do his members know what he is doing? He's trying to put them on the street!" Pete said that he was contemplating a press conference to release the letter. I advised against it, because the locals were voting for candidates who supported a strong defense.

The international union did not stop sending letters to the Congress. It began working with community organizations to bring their campaign to the shop floor. On one occasion a group of women went to Cass Williams' IAM office in St. Louis and announced that they were nuns (wearing regular dresses and pantsuits) from an unspecified religious order who wanted to talk about *The Empty Pork Barrel*. They sought his help in reaching the defense workers on the shop floor to promote a peace dividend. Cass was polite but told them that the international president proposing that idea was crazy. Later Cass sent copies of the letter to Senator Wilson to other union locals whose members worked in the defense sector. The word spread like wildfire. Regional directors said that the international president was misunderstood and that he was only trying to create more civilian union jobs.

Cass was called to Washington to meet with the international union president and was told that the international would be pursuing a strategy to expand membership by organizing workers in the fast-food industry. He was told that there were more potential members making McDonald's hamburgers than there were making jet fighters. Cass was dumbstruck. He returned to St. Louis and told his members what he had heard and gave an order to stop all money from his members to political action committees that would be used to support anti-defense Democrats. Cass broke with his union's national PAC, which was managed in Washington, DC, and which supported candidates hostile to the defense industry. He set up his own PAC supporting any candidate who supported the defense industry. Enormous pressure was put on Cass Williams, who was driven out of the union a few years later.

On another occasion the president of a large defense local in California went to Washington to lobby Pete Wilson for a program that employed his members. He called the senator whom he had met during the senator's visit to the aircraft facility in Burbank, California. Wilson called then-Secretary of Defense Cheney and set up a meeting with several union leaders about the program that was threatened with cancelation. When the international found out about the meeting, they backed an insurgent candidate for president of the California local. The election was won by the insurgent, despite the irregularities involved in that election. Following the election, the defeated union president appealed to both the district leadership and the international to investigate the irregularities. Both declined to investigate. Senator Wilson went to the Department of Defense but it did not have jurisdiction to intervene in a labor dispute. The defeated president went back to his previous job as a security guard and was assigned to the front gate of the plant so that all the members would see what happens to someone who is opposed to the international on defense policy.

When Senator Wilson heard about the way the former union president was being treated, he was outraged. With me still in the room, he called the CEO of one of America's largest defense contractors, who was only too happy to speak with the senator who supported all of his California programs. Wilson told the CEO that this defeated union leader was a soldier, a soldier who was now being put on a cross in front of the building to serve as a warning to anyone who did not follow the orders of an international bent on destroying high-paying defense jobs. "I am a Marine," Pete said. "You don't leave a wounded soldier on the battlefield. I would be personally grateful if you would bring this man into the company. Surely you can find a place for this hero." The CEO was polite but noted that the company could not interfere with union politics.

Later in 1990, Pete Wilson was governor of California and appointed that defeated union leader to a position of special assistant to the director of the department of industrial relations where he served as liaison between the department and the Division of Workers' Compensation, Occupational Safety and Health, and served as Labor Standards member of the OSH Board of Appeals (OSHAB).

The story of Pete Wilson standing behind this defeated union leader swept through the ranks of organized labor. I am confident that if Pete Wilson had received the Republican nomination for president, local union members who knew of his loyalty to a fallen worker would have supported him.

The preceding examples are offered for Republican candidates to understand the risk that union leaders take when they try to help a Republican. Union presidents invite retaliation when they depart from the AFL-CIO's unstated but ever-present warning not to endorse or in any way help a Republican candidate.

Having said all this, there are still numerous ways in which Republicans can reach out to unions in the industrial base. Candidates can contact local union officials to begin a dialogue. They can set up informal sessions to obtain labor's views on manufacturing issues.

There is absolutely no question that the Republican Party can capture a sizeable majority of America's unionized workforce right now, if they approach these unions with a sincere desire to work with them. The major problems that Republicans will encounter will be the lack of trust that has developed over the decades.

Over the years, Republicans have told me that Democratic unions will only support liberal Republicans. They point to past Republicans like John Heinz, Bob Packwood, Nelson Rockefeller, Jacob Javits, and Mark Hatfield. It must be remembered that all of these men were Republicans from liberal states, and as such had to be aware of their constituencies. However, Heinz, Rockefeller, and Javits spent a great deal of time courting union leaders and rank and file members. Senator Jacob Javits always got the endorsements of the labor unions in New York. The endorsement of these liberal Republicans by labor unions has reinforced the belief that only liberal Republicans can secure union support. But that is simply not true. Labor unions supported Richard Nixon and Ronald Reagan.

In many of the Senate races in which I was engaged, Democratic labor union members supported conservative Republicans such as Pete Wilson, Dan Quayle and Paul Laxalt. Well, you will say, these men were powerful Senators. True, but then how does one account for labor support for Pat Buchanan, a Nixon speechwriter and conservative columnist? Pat was considered an extreme right-winger when he won the New Hampshire presidential primary in 1996. Following that primary, he went to Wheeling, West Virginia, and was endorsed by the independent steelworkers in Weirton. This endorsement was particularly embarrassing to Jay Rockefeller who tried unsuccessfully to stop the union endorsement. Steelworkers from the surrounding mills in Ohio, Pennsylvania, and West Virginia joined the unions in Weirton.

Buchanan has always been a champion of the industrial unions, whom he sees as victims of America's free trade policies. Calling free trade the leading cause of the deindustrialization of America, Buchanan cited, in his column, the job losses in the industrial base that have, he argued, created unemployment worse than had occurred during the Great Depression. He noted that America is dependent on other countries to build its essential component parts for jet fighters, helicopters, and other defense systems. "This is our reward for turning our backs on the economic nationalism of the men who made America, and embracing the free-trade ideology of economists and academics who never made anything."[77]

Predicting the bankruptcy of Detroit long before it came, Buchanan exonerated the United Auto Workers, the traditional culprit for US automakers market share losses. Instead he placed the blame on the free traders in both parties. In November 2008, Buchanan wrote an article in his syndicated column entitled, "Who Killed Detroit?" [78] He argued that the autoworkers were harmed by taxes, regulations and air quality standards.

A few days after this article appeared, a UAW union leader called me. He was excited about the article and asked if Buchanan would allow him to share the article with his members. Coincidentally, Pat and I were boarding the same flight to Los Angeles and I handed Pat my cell phone to speak with the union leader personally. This resulted in copies of Pat's article being distributed to union members at a rally.

Given the support Buchanan had in Ohio, West Virginia, Pennsylvania, and Michigan, I believe he would have carried the unions in all of these states and probably carried the states as well had he run in 2008. The point is that conservative Republicans can secure union support if they work with the unions on jobs issues, especially blue-collar jobs.

Republicans' cultural distance from the working class and its fear of rejection discourage them from reaching out to unions. What is worse, the progressives have convinced the working class that Republicans side with management and industry against workers. Republicans are blamed for the shifting of our economy from one that employed hourly workers to one that caused layoffs due to globalism and free trade.

Republicans should not be afraid to make an outreach to labor unions. As I have said, American labor is not monolithic; it is a mosaic made up of state and local unions that are approachable. The key to reassembling the labor component of a New Majority is to reach out to the individual tiles (locals) that make up the mosaic of organized labor, and put aside the notion that labor is a monolithic structure.

Republicans offer one excuse after another for not approaching the unions. I often hear Republicans say that the unions are no longer relevant because they have lost members and electoral significance. The unions are not important if you expect to win by a landslide, but the tighter the margin the more important the union vote. I remind these Republicans that even though union members have been laid off or are retired, they are still union members who vote in large numbers and will still vote their pocketbook. In my experience, unemployed union members closely monitor Republican candidates and will vote for a candidate who appears to be pro-jobs and at least not anti-union. In the last two presidential elections, steelworkers whose mills have been closed for more than a decade voted Republican in Ohio.

It is important for Republicans to reach out to labor union workers *now*, because unions that once supported the free enterprise system and our market economy have fallen under the influence of the progressives and are increasingly aligning themselves with those who attack our system of capitalism.

Earlier, when discussing Nixon and the hard hat confrontation of 1970 with the Vietnam protesters on Wall Street, I argued that the construction trade unions that defended Nixon on Vietnam did so out of a sense of patriotism. This was the most significant event in the birth of the New Majority because it created the initial bond between a Republican president and Democratic union members.

On May 12, 2010, Kevin Whiteman, an independent writer on an

Internet news blog, marked the 40th anniversary of the New York City Hard Hat Riot. He noted that when the anti-war Marxist-led protestors burned and urinated on the American flag at the George Washington statue on Wall Street, construction workers jumped off their scaffolds and physically tangled with the protestors. He also noted that these workers were joined by white-collar workers from the New York Stock Exchange.[79]

Writing in that same week, Kathy Shardle noted, [80]

> The 'hard hats' briefly came to represent Nixon's 'silent majority,' the Archie Bunkers whose sweat (and taxes) built the very nation which the ascendant Left seemed determined to destroy.
>
> That same Left later more or less erased the Hard Hat Riots from the historical record. Photographs of the event are particularly rare.[81]

Fast forward, to the 2011 Occupy Wall Street movement. A large group reminiscent of the hippies of the 1960s took over Zuccotti Park near Wall Street. They camped out in tents and demanded money. One spokesman who appeared on multiple network channels kept repeating, "It's my money and I want it now!"

Unlike in 1970, when the hard hat unions dispersed those "college students," in 2011 the following unions began protesting *with* the Occupiers: National Transit Union, United Steelworkers of America, Amalgamated Transit Union, United Federation of Teachers, National Nurses United, Communication Workers of America, Operational Weather Squadron, New York Transit Union, United Pilots Union, Teamsters Union, Local 802 American Federation of Musicians NYC, AFL-CIO President Richard Trumka, and Los Angeles County AFL-CIO. The unions also joined the Occupy Wall Street movement in protests in Oakland, California.

October 29, 2011, Jeff Brady of National Public Radio wrote about AFL-CIO President Richard Trumka's speech on Wall Street, stating that Trumka said, "Our economy falters and people suffer, but the richest one percent—they're living high on the hog." [82]

In San Francisco, unions joined ACORN in a clash with police. In California, unlike New York, the Occupy Wall Street movement spread to seventy-three cities. The protests receiving the most attention were in Oakland and San Francisco.

What happened over the last forty years to cause the unions to ally with the occupiers? The labor unions blamed the country because their jobs were outsourced. But I blame congressional support for globalism, free trade, and our tax policies that are so punitive that domestic businesses relocate manufacturing jobs overseas. The worst part is that the workforce, especially the unions, blames the Republican Party. It is also clear that a good portion of younger Americans, especially those with college degrees, have become alienated from our market economy and the free enterprise system on which it is based. This phenomenon is set against a constant media drumbeat of a class war now taking place in America.

In my experience many, if not most, of the union workers I know are church-going, God-fearing people who pray before meals and are as red, white and blue as our flag. They may be registered and vote Democrat but that is the fault of the Republican candidates who refuse to try to win them over.

I believe that Republicans also avoid reaching out to working-class voters, both union and non-union, because they fear they will be rejected because of their association with wealth. They are uncomfortable being seen as the party of big business. Republicans must understand and accept the fact that they will be viewed as pro-business candidates. But pro-business candidates also seek investments that create jobs and hire working-class Americans. The working class understands that men of means, like Rockefeller and Heinz, will seek public office. Both of them were friendly to the working class.

In 1972, I attended an event in Pittsburgh sponsored by the Italian Sons and Daughters of America. I was a White House speaker at this event. At the event, John Heinz announced his candidacy for a congressional seat in Pittsburgh.

The moderator told the crowd, "We don't need a lengthy introduction for Johnnie because every time we put his ketchup on our hamburger we see John Heinz." The crowd laughed. I didn't see sneers among the largely Democratic audience in reaction to an obvious reference to Heinz's wealth. The crowd was there to hear this young man talk about his ideas and how these ideas would affect their lives. No one in the crowd felt uncomfortable that Heinz was a fabulously rich man. Moreover, when John Heinz, accompanied by Lefty Scumaci and Fred Gualtieri, went to jobsites at steel mills and factory gates, he demonstrated that he truly liked the workers and they knew it.

The same was true of Nelson Rockefeller's run for governor of New York. In the heart of the Great Depression not only did the Rockefeller family decide to build the Rockefeller Center, but they also stipulated that it should be built by union labor. This was the beginning of a relationship between one of the richest men in America, Nelson Rockefeller, and organized labor that continued until Rockefeller's death. The labor unions did not curse him for his wealth. They knew he would fight for union jobs.

In my more than forty years of dealing with both the business and labor communities, there has always been tension between labor and management, usually surrounding contract negotiations. Yet, there has always been an unwritten understanding among the unions in the private sector, especially in the skilled trades, that if the boss did not make money the worker would not have a job. As my mentor, Lefty Scumaci, always said, "No poor person ever hired anybody." Class envy was not a factor in our thinking through the 1960s.

There are two problems that Republicans must overcome. First, is the characterization that Republicans only care about rich people. The only way this negative characterization of Republican candidates can be neutralized is to do exactly what Nelson Rockefeller and John Heinz did: establish a close relationship with working-class Americans. Workers know that there will always be rich and poor in all societies. The goal of wealthy Republicans should be to demonstrate to the working classes that Republicans seek to unleash the power of entrepreneurs to create jobs. Republicans cannot accomplish this through television commercials and printed materials alone. Nixon, Reagan, and George H.W. Bush made every effort to meet with American workers.

A second problem emanates from a press corps and network

television barrage that vilifies the Republican candidate as the "candidate of the rich." The press continues to amplify the class envy we see today. The only way for Republican candidates to overcome the partisan media is to get as close to American workers as possible to show them that their goal is to expand the pie so everyone can participate in the American Dream.

The Founding Fathers envisioned a free press as a positive check on government. The Founders saw the press as an umpire ready to attack corruption or any form of partisanship that would cloud the vision of the public. Journalism today is decidedly partisan. The public understands this as well as the Republican candidates who are constantly presented negatively.

Republican candidates must interact with working Americans, directly and personally. They must let the people hear from them, their vision for raising the standard of living, creating jobs, and creating wealth for workers. Republicans need to make the case for their vision directly to the people, not through television commercials. Remember, Nixon, Reagan and George H.W. Bush faced an extremely hostile press and still won elections.

Let's return to the 1970s. As America's industrial base shrank, the public sector grew. The AFL-CIO and some of the international unions in the public sector began to see the organization of the public sector as a way to replace the loss of union dues payers in the industrial base sectors. These trends have heightened in the last thirty years. A 2014 Department of Labor report states that, "In 2014, public-sector workers had a union membership rate of 35.7 percent. That was more than five times the rate for private-sector workers, 6.6 percent." [83]

Union leaders, of course, want to reverse the decline in private-sector union membership. I have repeatedly asked labor leaders who would be their ideal candidate for either party. They consistently say, Nixon on the Republican side and John Kennedy on the other. We have said enough about Nixon to understand why the unions would choose him as the ideal Republican; but why Kennedy as a Democrat? They respond that Kennedy was a Democrat who stood in the Roosevelt tradition. He respected people who worked with their hands. He was an anti-communist who was strong on defense. Many of them even cite

Kennedy's criticism of Nixon for not being strong enough to pledge to attack China if it tried to invade the islands of Quemoy and Matsu. In his inaugural address, Kennedy warned the Soviets:

> Let every nation know, whether it wishes us well or ill, that we shall pay any price, bear any burden, meet any hardship, support any friend, oppose any foe to assure the survival and the success of liberty.

Most importantly, Kennedy saw the relationship between lower taxes and investing in blue-collar industries that were essential to our national security:

> It is increasingly clear that no matter what party is in power, so long as our national security needs keep rising, an economy hampered by restrictive tax rates will never produce enough jobs or enough profits.

Kennedy's comments, given during a question and answer period at the Economic Club of New York on December 14, 1962, were thoroughly consistent with his war record and his view that the blue-collar workforce that makes up the industrial base is the moral backbone of what made America great.

Kennedy also reduced corporate taxes, which created opportunities for new businesses and new jobs. While he was sympathetic to the poor, Kennedy also believed that entitlement programs should be reserved for the elderly and the truly needy. He also believed that all Americans, rich and poor alike, had a responsibility to help their country. In his inaugural address he stated, "And so, my fellow Americans: ask not what your country can do for you--ask what you can do for your country."

In the progressive Democratic Party of today, Kennedy could never get the nomination of the Democratic Party. He, like Reagan, John Connally, Jeane Kirkpatrick, and the rest of us who were once Democrats, would conclude that the party left him.

CHAPTER 12

Building a New Majority

Two days before the election of 2008, I wrote to Chuck Colson to explain why, in my view, the New Majority fell apart. Many of the reasons I have explained in this book. I also told Chuck that I believed that a New Majority coalition of voters could be reassembled to support a Republican candidate because many of the issues that were important to Middle America in 1972 and in 1980 had resurfaced over the last decade.

The Republican Party can recapture a winning majority in national elections if it has a message that clearly states what the party stands for. The Republican Party must also create a mechanism to transmit that message to the party faithful and the nation. To accomplish this, the Republican Party must transform itself from convening every four years to nominate a presidential candidate and instead begin the work of building a strong party structure from the precinct level up.

Consider the progressive Democratic Party of today, which speaks in a single voice about how entitlement programs have to be increased, the public sector has to be expanded, and taxes on the wealthy and the middle class must rise. Republicans, by contrast, do not speak with a unified voice.

Progressive Democrats also have a national machine in place to deliver their message. Their members in both the House and Senate are in lockstep whether or not they are in the majority, and over the last forty years, Democrats in Congress have been in lockstep with the progressive agenda. The progressive Democratic Party's control stretches to the local party organizations throughout the country. The support for the progressive agenda is vertical and horizontal. It extends to party members at the state and local levels, which are provided with the same position papers and talking points. These talking points are generated from progressive Democratic strategy groups, the White House, and, unfortunately, the national media, which since 1968 has unabashedly endorsed Democratic candidates by using the same talking points politicians utter. The media then distorts or simply does not report the Republican message.

The Republican Party, from my perspective, is not united except when it is engaged in a presidential contest every four years to choose the party's nominee. After years of dealing with the American workforce, union and nonunion, I can tell you that Republicans are *not* sending messages important to the working class. Further, I do not see a visible mechanism for delivering those messages either to the working class, the American people, or to local Republican organizations.

The Vision and the Message

In the Nixon campaign of 1972, Colson focused on communicating with the party's base and the constituencies that were the bedrock of the Roosevelt coalition. We had a message for each constituency, a mechanism to deliver it, and surrogates who embodied the characteristics of the people we were trying to reach. What is the Republican message today? The only consistent message we hear from the Party today is the need to lower taxes. Lower taxes? Is that the message designed to stir the hearts of the American people? Why lower taxes? Because Republicans understand that lower taxes are the linchpin for companies to become competitive, expand the economy, and create jobs.

The criticism from the Democratic Party is that lower taxes will produce profits that will line the pockets of corporate leaders, but the rewards for entrepreneurial risk-takers only happen if these entrepreneurs produce marketable goods and services at a profit. Profits create jobs.

In today's class-warfare environment, the Republican message cannot be simply to lower taxes. Republicans need a message that will resonate with working-class Americans. Ronald Reagan articulated such a message in a news conference on June 28, 1983, when the country was still suffering from the Carter administration's mismanagement of the economy. Gary F. Schuster of the *Detroit News* asked Reagan about polls that showed that sixty to seventy percent of the people considered him "a rich man's president." Reagan responded that he was frustrated by that label that had been "hung" on him; that he was raised in poverty and saw oatmeal as a luxury because his parents could not afford meat.

As I heard him say that, I remembered that my grandmother in 1939 fed us boiled cornmeal covered with a red meat sauce that contained very small strips of over-cooked chuck roast. It was cooked in a pan on the stove with red kidney beans and then baked in an oven and served as a main meal for the week. Today, this same dish is served as an appetizer in upscale Italian restaurants and given the more fashionable name of polenta. That cheap Italian soul food kept us alive as Reagan's oatmeal did for him in his household.

Reagan then addressed the reporter's question about the president's policies being designed to help the rich. Reagan's response to that question was earth shattering: "No, the rich don't need my help, and I'm not doing things to help the rich. I'm doing things that I think are fair to all of the people. But what I want to see above all is that this country remains a country where someone can always get rich. That's the thing that we have and that must be preserved."

Reagan believed in preserving an America where anyone can get rich. It is true that immigrants who have come to America have sought freedom. But freedom to do what? To live a better life. My grandparents and other ethnic neighbors in our community came to our country because they were starving in Europe. I believe that is one of the reasons that ethnic communities are so focused on food and making sure that everyone has enough to eat. My grandmother told me that in America the streets were lined with gold but you had to bend down to pick it up.

In America, going from rags to riches has been and continues to be the experience of millions of people over multi-generations. Many people became extremely wealthy. They did so by building businesses, by inventing everything from the hula-hoop to the laptop computer and the iPhone. They did so by inventing software, by playing football or other sports; by becoming entertainers or writing a hit Christmas song.

It is true that everyone did not get as rich as the Rockefellers but many, many millions made it into the middle class. They owned their own homes, automobiles, boats and campers. Their homes are filled with the electronic wherewithal associated with the good life.

Today, immigrants still come to our shores because the standard of living and opportunities in America surpass those of all other nations. Moreover, in our capitalist system the success of one person creates opportunity for others. When Henry Ford built his automobile factory, he got rich. But by making a reliable car at a low price, he opened the opportunity for thousands of workers to get high-paying jobs and own their own automobiles.

What Reagan was saying is that America is a country where anyone can *still* get rich. Reagan was arguing that everyone has the opportunity to get rich; we can all win. *That* is the message! We are a party of upward mobility, and everyone can improve their economic and social status. Reagan's message in 1983 *is* the message Republicans need to champion today. It is a message that can unify working-class Americans.

I heard Nixon deliver a similar message at a cabinet meeting in a discussion of government activities to deal with future energy embargoes and our nation's energy supply. At the cabinet meeting, he was told that his energy team was ready to print gasoline ration books for a future energy crisis. Nixon was outraged. He did not want to manage scarcity, he stated emphatically, and he contrasted his view with that of bureaucrats who so often revert to managing scarcity. Spreading his arms out wide, he emphasized that he wanted to expand the supply of energy, not to ration smaller and smaller pieces of the pie. Nixon's message was consistent with the American experience of the horn of plenty and the good life.

Americans need to hear that Republicans seek to expand the economic pie for everyone. This message must be directed to every school child, especially in the lower socioeconomic groups. Reagan did not say, we'll all be better off if we lower taxes. He said he wanted to keep America's free enterprise system in place so that "someone can always get rich" as Americans have since colonial days.

The message the Republican Party should send to attract future voters is not to lower taxes. The message should be that everyone prospers when we enlarge the economic pie, not divide it into smaller slices. In our free enterprise economy everyone can succeed if they are prepared to work hard. It is the same message my Italian grandmother and my parents gave me that I rejected for the first twenty years of my life and then turned my life around to pursue. It was the same message that Democrats gave to the lower classes before the advent of the progressive movement of the 1960s, which has come to demonize not only the rich but the free enterprise system as well.

There are variations of this message that are not only basic tenets of the Republican Party but are fundamental truths of the American experience. These truths are consistently found in the history of America since colonial times. They are rooted in the achievement ethic and the strive-and-succeed adventures written by Horatio Alger. Both political parties accepted these pro-achievement messages well before the New Deal. It is only with the progressive control of the modern Democratic Party that the time-honored advancement up the economic and social ladder has been denigrated. The Republican Party still accepts the upward mobility of Americans as commonplace and, in truth, the vast majority of our people have advanced from the lower socioeconomic ranks to the middle and upper classes.

The Mechanism

Messages are important, but equally important is a mechanism to deliver them. In the Nixon White House we had both messages and a machine to deliver them. Nixon's Office of Public Liaison created a series of messages that were clearly understood and often repeated within the White House. These messages were broadcast to the Congress and to state party officials. If you were to stop anyone on the White House staff in the Old Executive Office Building and ask, "What are the goals of the Nixon Administration?" the response would be, "a generation of peace," "peace through strength," "peace with honor," "new federalism," "law and order," "workfare, not welfare," and so on. All of these messages were written into presidential and cabinet speeches by Chuck Colson's staff and transmitted to waiting House and Senate members who used them in floor statements before their respective chambers. Equally important, these messages were then sent to state and county party chairmen.

In the Nixon White House, Office of Public Liaison staff constantly communicated with our respective constituencies. Prior to a presidential address to the nation, the relevant members of Colson's staff for each constituency contacted their groups. For example, I called labor and ethnic leaders to advise them and their constituencies to listen to the president's address. After the president's speech, we called these leaders to get their comments, which were passed on to the president. All of these were components of a mechanism capable of connecting the Republican Party, from the president to the Congress and the party faithful in the states. No matter how distant they were from the White House, the party faithful were regularly given accurate information they needed about the president's policy objectives. They were urged to contact their elected representatives to express their concerns regardless of political party. During the Vietnam War, messages about the status of the Paris Peace Accords between Henry Kissinger and the North and South Vietnamese were passed on through a variety of social networks. Foremost in all of the information that we passed to our constituencies was the status of the POWs and Nixon's determination to bring them home before the official end of hostilities.

The Surrogates

One of the reasons Nixon was successful in delivering his messages was that he had surrogates in the White House who were trusted by the people in the voter blocs they represented. Don Rodgers was truly as much a labor leader as anyone he contacted. I was as Italian as any of the Italian leaders within the labor movement or the fraternal orders. Alex Armendaris was as Hispanic as any of the Hispanic leaders he approached. We also had national counterparts in the communities who, like ourselves, had Democratic ties to their ethnic and labor communities. These people multiplied our efforts by explaining Nixon's policy agenda in the mills, factories, and in their communities. All of these people were surrogates with constituencies who knew and trusted them. As a team, we were flesh and blood, not television spots. We believed in Nixon, and he believed in our constituencies. Today, I don't know who the Republican Party's surrogates are within America's working class, which was the largest component of Nixon's New Majority.

A carefully constructed mechanism must include the selection and organization of surrogates. Surrogates are vital because they represent the party's philosophy. Early in the Chapter 2, I discussed the Heritage Division of the Republican National Committee under the direction of Laszlo Pasztor, the Hungarian Freedom Fighter who escaped with his son when Russian tanks crushed the Hungarian Revolt in 1956. Laszlo set up a network of Captive Nations Freedom Fighters living in the United States. His effort began in the Northeast and spread across the country to Illinois, Ohio, Michigan, and other states where voters had relatives still behind the Iron Curtain. To this community, Nixon was the very definition of a Freedom Fighter.

In the 1970s, traditional business groups dominated the Republican National Committee. These pro-business Republicans, while appreciative of the Freedom Fighters and their cause, were not effusive in their support for taking down the Iron Curtain until Ronald Reagan picked up the Nixon banner and told Soviet Premier Mikhail Gorbachev to "tear down this wall." In the early 1970s, the nationalities were vocal and visible. Colson saw the nationalities as both a mechanism and an inexhaustible source of surrogates. (Hispanic business people could serve a similar function today.)

Terry Szmagala's appointment as ethnic coordinator for the 1972 campaign was key to reaching out to anti-communist ethnic groups. Terry organized all of these groups and coordinated them with the White House through my office. Terry went everywhere in America to convey the White House's message to ethnic leaders and communities.

Following the election, Terry, along with Jack Burgess who worked for Laszlo Pasztor, came to my White House office and gave me a framed collection of twenty-seven campaign buttons representing the different groups Terry organized during the 1972 campaign, which included Armenians, Bulgarians, Byelorussians, Chinese, Cossacks, Croatians, Latvians, Slovenians, Ukrainians, and others. Terry had organized all of the nationalities that could be found in America to support President Nixon. The nationalities were 100 percent behind Nixon. It is clear from the list of ethnic groups that these people believed that Nixon was the supreme Freedom Fighter who defended all of them.

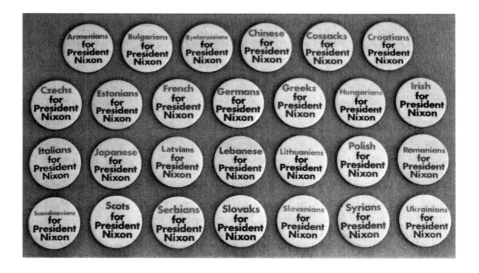

The conditions that were present in 1972 and 1980 during the Cold War have now reemerged in the twenty-first century. The Cold War ended when the Soviet Union gave up control over its satellite nations. But today, with Vladimir Putin gobbling up Crimea and eastern Ukraine, the current generation of American college students is confused by the presence of naked aggression. The nationalities that were part of the Captive Nations are not confused; they are thoroughly familiar with Russian belligerence and are not surprised to see what is happening in Ukraine today. The nationalities believe that Putin is seeking to reconstitute the Soviet Bloc and enslave the Captive Nations all over again. The nationalities are primarily Republicans and would be the first to support a hardline Republican candidate. Years ago, the nationalities would have supported a Hubert Humphrey, a Scoop Jackson or any conservative, hardline Democrat who had the backbone to resist Soviet tyranny and the naked aggression that the world had not seen since Adolph Hitler. But this history, insight and wisdom does not exist in the current generation of progressive Democrats.

The key is to find Republican surrogates who represent a broad array of constituencies. These could include successful business leaders who started their own businesses large or small but who are clearly part of a Republican entrepreneurial class, individuals who are either on their way to becoming the upper middle class or who are already there. Such people can be found in local communities in virtually every state. The operative word here is "local." The state party chairman should be in charge of this effort. They will know who would be excellent surrogates to approach the different constituencies in their communities. Over the years I have met with such chairmen who, as Nixon often said, had the "fire in their belly" and were capable of advancing the basic tenets of the Republican Party.

Colson was constantly on the phone with activist Republican chairmen in key states. On more than one occasion he referred to them as "the generals in the field" who were really in charge of delivering the vote.

In Pittsburgh during the 1972 campaign I met Elsie Hillman, an upper-class woman with solid Republican credentials who relentlessly threw herself into the Democratic labor community. She met workers in taverns, restaurants, union halls, and at job sites. Elsie told me, "Democrats outnumber us five to one in this city, and that's why we have to go where they live." I learned a lot from Elsie whom I met several times during the 1972 campaign.

During John Connally's attempt to win the Republican nomination for president, I accompanied him to meet with labor leaders in Pennsylvania and Michigan. We rode in a limousine with Elsie Hillman. As we traveled through Pittsburgh, Elsie briefed Connally on all of the intricacies of the Democratic labor population in the greater Pittsburgh area. Here was a Republican woman who was extremely knowledgeable about unions; she knew to which internationals they belonged; she knew how the laws of the state affected construction jobs; she was thoroughly familiar with Davis-Bacon, the right-to-work laws, and all of the issues that affected the unions in Pennsylvania.

Connally later said to me, "If we had party chairmen like her in every state the Republicans would be a majority party." He noted that the problem comes from the appointment of honorary chairmen who only talk to Republicans and the party faithful in what he described as a Republican "social club." On the contrary, the party chairmen who Colson constantly talked with were Republican activists who knew the strengths and weaknesses of their own party and were committed to venturing into Democratic strongholds.

Building a Republican Party at the national level will require state party officials like Elsie Hillman who are committed to courting Democrat voters where they live. As Nixon said, many of these Democrats are really Republicans. They just don't know they are Republicans. Colson's statement about the "person who drives to church on Sunday in a pickup truck with a rifle rack on the back window is our guy but he doesn't know he's our guy," still resonates today. Though a multimillionaire herself, Elsie Hillman conveyed that message in labor halls, pizza parlors, and in front of steel mills and at work sites.

We have talked about a message, a mechanism, surrogates, and the need to have strong party chairmen at the local level. We will need all these to compete with a progressive Democrat machine that is constantly on the move. We cannot engage in the competition of ideas casually. We must give it everything we have. The progressive Democrats are true believers who are out there recruiting low-information voters, people who do not understand the economic and social consequences of their political choices. They do not understand that the progressive Democratic Party seeks to undermine our market economy. Capitalism is the very reason immigrants still come over our borders. They understand opportunity. The problem is that Republicans who do offer opportunities to the working classes and even those college students who joined the Democratic Party for romantic reasons are not being approached by credible surrogates.

Republicans are not competing to persuade these voters. They must reach out to the working class.

Re-registering the Roosevelt Coalition

In Nixon's letter commending my contribution to the Hofstra University symposium on the Nixon presidency, he wrote, "Had Watergate not aborted our efforts we would have changed the political balance of power in the second term."

As I look back now, I understand why Nixon and Colson sought to enlist the working-class and ethnic communities into the Republican Party ranks. These people possessed the qualities envisioned by America's Founding Fathers, qualities that would form the bedrock of this new nation. They were people of faith who believed in the achievement ethic and who were industrious. They were people who fought in two world wars and Korea and whose patriotism was needed to preserve our liberty in a world engaged in a cold war.

During the Vietnam War the national mood changed. President Johnson was under siege and chose not to run for a second term in 1968. Nixon was subsequently confronted with protests by university students and professors who repeatedly tried to bring the war to a halt. College-age students fled to Canada to avoid the draft. Yet, the young men from ethnic and working-class communities did not abandon their county. They served with honor. These were the people Nixon referred to in his call to the Silent Majority to support him.

Would these working-class Democrats have changed parties over the next four years if Nixon had not resigned? We'll never know, but it was certainly not possible after Watergate and the judicial witch-hunt of prominent Democrats identified with Nixon's New Majority.

In 1980, Reagan had the opportunity to re-cement the relationship with prominent Democratic labor leaders who broke ties with the Democratic Party to vote for Reagan. All the conditions for converting Nixon's New Majority of 1972 into a permanent Republican majority were present when that same New Majority coalesced behind Reagan in 1980. That opportunity was lost when Reagan, who was a great president, never made an attempt to expand the base of the Republican

Party by persuading "Reagan Democrats" to become Republicans. This was especially true for the labor unions that supported Ronald Reagan.

I believe Republicans do not win elections. I believe Democrats lose them. They lose them by abandoning the traditional values that Roosevelt Democrats hold dear, as did McGovern, and as did President Carter did by granting amnesty to those who fled the country during the Vietnam War. They also lose them by projecting weakness in the international arena, as Carter did, inviting the takeover of the US Embassy in Iran, and by mismanaging the economy. In such elections, Democrats will vote Republican, but they are unlikely to change their party registration.

In Chapter 1, I recalled the experience of Democratic precinct workers helping the immigrants in our Italian neighborhood to become citizens. Republicans never showed up in the neighborhood. Hence, immigrants barely able to speak English believed that the Democratic Party precinct workers were agents of the American government and made the connection, rightly or wrongly, that it was the Democratic Party that made them citizens. I know my family believed that, and so did all the other families in the neighborhood.

Democratic Party surrogates are now engaged in the same tactic with both documented and undocumented immigrants, helping them fill out forms, get driver's licenses, find housing, enroll in English classes, touching as many as they can in all those cities where immigrants reside. They are steadily bringing in new generations of Democratic voters. Among the foreign-born, non-English speaking population, many of whom are hiding in the shadows, these Democratic Party workers assume the mantle of a parish priest. For this reason, I believe that party registration takes on an almost religious significance and that asking working-class people to change parties and vote Republican is asking them to commit something close to a sin.

On the other hand, we have seen in the elections of 1968, 1972, and 1980, that Democrats lost because their party was championing social behaviors that contradicted the morality and beliefs of millions of pro-achievement Americans. Jeane Kirkpatrick identified these

Americans as "the masses." She argued that in the elections of 1968, 1972, and 1980, the Democratic Party began to champion behaviors that contradict the deep moral belief of Middle America. In such elections the masses will not only get closer to their religion, their guns, and their flag, they will vote Republican, and the Republicans will win.

Following Nixon's victory, I had an extended luncheon in February 1973 with Jeane Kirkpatrick at her Bethesda home. For hours we talked about the philosophy of George McGovern and the consequences of the 1972 election. She began by stating that in her view Nixon won the election, but McGovern won the war. Before I left, Jeane gave me a pre-publication draft of an essay entitled, "The Revolt of the Masses: George McGovern and the New Class Struggle." (This essay was later published in the February 1973 issue of *Commentary* entitled, "The Revolt of the Masses." Significantly missing from the title was "George McGovern and the New Class Struggle.") [84] Jeane said she did not see Nixon's 1972 victory as a political realignment where Democrats who voted for Nixon would become Republicans. She saw that election as a revolt by traditional Roosevelt Democrats against everything that McGovern stood for. But she also warned that McGovern's constituency of antiwar activists and protestors would not disappear but would become an elite generation that would destroy the party of Roosevelt.

Jeane foresaw the emergence of the progressive leadership that has become today's Democratic Party. She argued that the Roosevelt Democrats sought to move the lower socioeconomic classes of the Democratic Party into the middle class by adhering to the time-honored mechanism of hard work and sacrifice. Jeane saw a generation of progressives who did not extol the virtues of the achievement ethic as the essential ingredient for upward economic and social mobility. She predicted a counter-culture leadership that would argue that the poor were poor because the wealthy class held them down. A student of revolutions, Jeane was always concerned that revolutions are preceded by class conflicts followed by class war.

Jeane's published essay in *Commentary* does not include some statements contained in the original draft that she gave me at the luncheon. Specifically, the original includes the following:

It is not difficult to understand why cultural conservatives should seek to protect their vested interest in traditional America. One is, after all, one's culture. Cultural revolution is the most painful kind of social change. Worse than losing one's property, one's job, one's family is the loss of confidence in one's relevance to the significant events of the times.... Cultural revolution threatens to declare millions of American living relics. Superannuated. Irrelevant. Superfluous. No one can be expected to collaborate in his own annihilation.

She went on to say,

Working class Americans, middle class Americans, upper class Americans – portions of each share middle class values, middle class ways, a middle class preference for short hair, clean clothes, patriotism, and self reliance. Like all cultures, their's embodies disciplines. It demands deferring the pleasure of leisure and lying late a-bed for the long range gratifications associated with a steady job; it demands at least serial monogamy or a reasonable facsimile thereof; it demands the assumption of responsibility for others, especially the young. As in all cultures 'middle class' culture offers rewards to those who have paid the price. A degree of physical well being and comfort, a degree of security. Above all, it offers respect – for work, for experience, for shouldering one's responsibilities.

Her draft essay also centered on the perception of the masses during times of cultural upheaval. During the heyday of the 1960s the progressive elite saw a culture in transition. The American electorate saw something quite different. They saw an attack on the culture that was a threat to their very survival.

Only the completely dispirited will fail to defend their 'way of life' against an enemy. That middle America

perceives the counter culture as an enemy has been reflected in public opinion polls for at least half a decade.
Middle America did not see Chicago as a 'police riot.'
It did not view university disorders as understandable
– if misguided – expressions of the idealistic young. It
does not view America as a sick or a repressive society. It does not view crime as a quasi-legitimate form
of political protest. It does not even view Vietnam as
a moral crime. Neither does it view the achievement
ethic as the cultural artifact of a past era.

Jeane also feared the influence of counter-culture advocates in
the universities where liberal professors were already telling students
that America was a country where the lower classes could never rise
to middle-class status. She foresaw a country forever divided by class
conflict of rich and poor. She predicted teachers who were taught by
tenured leftist professors would promote this class war in elementary
and middle schools. Jeane also believed that a class war mentality
would permeate the next generation of lawyers and journalists who
accepted McGovern's philosophy.

Forty-two years later we are witnessing Jeane's predictions with
a media-driven public anger over a society falsely divided by a di-
chotomy of "the 1 percent versus the 99 percent" that is dangerously
dividing our country. In the draft essay Jeane handed me, it was clear
that she believed that the Democratic Party that she grew up with in
the 1930s and 1940s was gone.

Today Republicans have an opportunity. From my dealings with
Democratic labor unions and working-class constituencies, I believe
they are still conservative on social issues. They do not support the
policies of counter-culture progressives and the elitist Democrats
who actually hold them in contempt or, as Jeane Kirkpatrick said, as
"low-life Archie Bunkers." Progressives remain in power because they
have captured leadership positions in the Democratic Party and in
both the electronic and print media that either distorts Republican
messages or does not report them at all. The Republican Party can
still win elections by appealing to the millions of disenchanted

Democrats who are not represented by the Democratic Party as it exists today.

Republicans do not understand that many labor union rank-and-file members are very conservative. If Republicans were to pay attention to these workers, it would result in more Republicans being elected. Two examples make this case. First, over the past twenty years, I have traveled numerous times to Steubenville, Ohio, which was, like Johnstown, Pennsylvania, a center of the steel industry. In the last two presidential elections, the unions in Steubenville's Jefferson County voted Republican. I always winced when I heard Rush Limbaugh attack unions. Does he not know that in the steel mills, union members listen to the conservative messages of his daily radio program?

Second, during the election of 2012, I was meeting at 4:30 pm with a prominent union official at a New Hampshire restaurant to discuss her role in our workforce coalition to save jobs in the defense sector. We were suddenly surprised to see former governor and White House chief of staff John Sununu, Sr., enter the restaurant. He was dining early because he was scheduled to appear via satellite hookup on the Sean Hannity show, on Fox television, for a discussion concerning the upcoming election. Marlene Anderson, my associate on that trip, recognized Sununu when he came into the restaurant and called him over to our table. As he made his way, I grabbed the hand of the union president and pleaded with her to believe that I had not set her up for a meeting with a major Republican operative. Sununu explained what he was doing that evening and, after I had introduced him to the union leader, Sununu told her about the years he and I had worked together battling for the Seabrook Nuclear Power Plant. Then he asked if I was involved in the Romney campaign. I told him that I was not because client commitments made it impossible.

As I sat there, I thought to myself, *"My accidental meeting with Sununu is going to kill my relationship with this union president."* As Sununu got up to leave, the union leader asked him for his card, saying that she wanted to show the card to her husband because he might not believe she really had dinner with Sununu. She then shocked everyone by saying that she and her husband watched Fox News every night and that she would call her friends to tell them that she had met with Sununu before the show.

Progressive Elites and the Working Class

The greatest opportunity Republicans have is the fact that today the progressive Democratic Party no longer represents America's working classes. Beginning decades ago, the Democratic Party began turning its back on the blue-collar workforce. Thomas B. Edsall, in his November 27, 2011, *New York Times* opinion piece [85] noted that Democrats over the years have lost the large majorities of "white working-class" voters they captured during the Roosevelt era. He reports that in 2011 key Democratic political strategists decided to officially abandon the "white working-class" vote. Instead, the party would pursue a "center-left coalition made up, on the one hand, of voters who have gotten ahead on the basis of educational attainment – professors, artists, designers, editors, human resources managers, lawyers, librarians, social workers, teachers and therapists – and a second, substantial constituency of lower-income voters who are disproportionately African-American and Hispanics."

What do these strategists believe are the priorities that should be pursued on behalf of the educated members of the coalition?

> The better-off wing, in contrast, puts at the top of its political agenda a cluster of rights related to self-expression, the environment, demilitarization, and, importantly, freedom from repressive norms—governing both sexual behavior and women's role in society— that are promoted by the conservative movement.

The progressives see a Democratic Party composed of a yuppie class of professionals who are non-churchgoers, if they identify with any church at all, and the sexually adventurous who are free from repressive norms promoted by society and conservatives. The progressives see a party of white-collar professionals and government bureaucrats combined with low-income voters who are highly dependent on government entitlements. At the same time, the new Democratic coalition voter will support demilitarization, and oppose defense spending essential to national security. The progressives will reduce the ability of the working classes to earn a living and pay the taxes that support the progressive elitist superstructure.

Jeane Kirkpatrick predicted this strategic shift. Today's progressives do not view working-class Americans as the future of the Democratic Party. They see them as "Archie Bunkers," just as Kirkpatrick noted in her 1973 essay.

Of particular significance in Edsall's article [86] is the quote of Ruy Teixeira, a senior fellow at the Center for American Progress, asserting that "the Republican Party has become the party of the white working class." However, there is no such thing as the "white working class." There is only the working class. Enter any shipyard, aircraft plant, electronics assembly for radar, sonar, missile or anti-missile assembly, and you will find blacks, Asians, Hispanics and women who are "the working class." This is both class warfare and race-baiting.

However, Teixeira is correct in one respect. The *working class*, those God-fearing people who work with their hands, believe in America, and believe achievement is gained by merit, has more in common with the Republican Party than the progressive elitists who control today's Democratic Party. While working-class voters generally distrust Republicans, they supported Nixon and Reagan because they were viewed as more sympathetic to American workers than the leadership of the Democratic Party. With the exception of the expansion of some parts of the welfare state, the progressive wing of the Democratic Party has totally ceded the working class to the Republican Party and envisions a nation controlled, not governed, by an elitist society of well-to-do intellectuals. The authors of this strategy advocate that the Party of Roosevelt should "jettison" the working class, i.e., throw out, abandon, discard, and dump these people from the Democratic Party.

Returning to the statement I made that "Republicans don't win elections, Democrats lose them," I do not mean to indicate that Republicans will always lose elections. To be sure, Republicans will have victories in presidential races and they will carry with them on their coattails enough senators to win a majority in the Senate, as we saw in Reagan's 1980 election and in the off-year elections of 2014. But these victories have not resulted in a permanent realignment. Reagan brought with him a majority in the Senate, but that majority was swept out in the next election. In the off-year election of November 2014, the Republicans amassed an impressive victory with some eight senators elected. The question is, will these senators survive in their next election? Will the people who voted them in reelect them six years from now, making it a true realignment? History shows that Republicans cannot resist the temptation to attack those issues of importance to their newly-won Democratic constituencies. Republicans do not nurture voters who cross party lines to support them. In fact, as we have seen over the last forty years, Republicans have gone out of their way to drive the labor unions back into the Democratic Party.

The key for Republicans to preserve electoral majorities is to address the concerns of these Democratic constituent groups who put them in office rather than attacking them. With respect to the labor unions, I cannot stress this too strongly. When union members abandon the Democratic Party to vote Republican, they do so because they suffered under Democratic polices that not only ignored them but harmed them as well. In such cases, labor union rank-and-file members voted Republican in desperation. That does not constitute a solid base of support. I liken it to attending a church of a different denomination because you are uncomfortable with the sermons of the minister in your current church. Generally, attending a new church produces the same discomfort, which then drives a parishioner back to their original church. Changing parties is equivalent to changing one's religion. It's that serious.

The driving force behind Nixon's 1972 victory was not re-registered Democrats voting Republican; rather, they were Democrats impatient with the issues of crime in the streets, protests on college campuses, and the breakdown of law and order across our society. Those discontented Democrats, called "Reagan Democrats" in 1980, are still with us. Blue-collar and industrial unions know that they have helped to create a political environment that puts them at a disadvantage. If they vote Democrat they will lose the jobs of their members in the defense and industrial base. While the Democratic Party wants their money, it no longer represents their interests. On the other hand, if they vote Republican they could lose their union. If Republicans reach out to these union members and show they have addressed the issues important to the workers, they can create a permanent majority.

The Achievement Ethic and the American Dream

Throughout this book I have made many references to the achievement ethic, which I believe is the glue that has held together the different components of our pluralistic society. The achievement ethic is widely accepted by immigrants who come to our shores. And why not? By what other formula would wealth, honors, and benefits be distributed—by birth, height, or the weight of individuals? In America we chose merit, and consistent majorities over the last 225 years have accepted those criteria. In my graduate studies, I analyzed the public acceptance of a meritocracy as the mechanism to distribute honors and riches. During the Hofstra symposium on the Nixon Presidency, I identified the relationship between the achievement ethic and the different members of the New Majority, i.e., ethnics, labor, and working-class Americans. I concluded that the achievement ethic held the people together and was a cohesive force embedded in the soul of the nation. In America everyone has a chance to win.

Weeks before my doctoral oral exams, Jeane Kirkpatrick and I got into a deep discussion. I argued that the achievement ethic was the DNA of the American people. Jeane insisted that the subject should be tabled until I completed my orals. But I could not resist referring to the ethic during my doctoral orals.

On the morning of my orals I faced a panel of faculty members who asked questions from each of their respective fields. Dr. Karl Cerny, chairman of the government department; Dr. Ulrich Allers, a classical scholar; Dr. Howard Penniman, an expert on American elections; Dr. George Carey, whose expertise lay in the American political system, especially the intellectual underpinnings of the Revolution and the Federalist era, and Jeane, whose intellectual range covered both the classics and the modern era.

After I had weathered a barrage of questions from the pre-Socratics through the Hegelian and Marxian dialectics, as well as questions on the history of the primary system in American elections, Dr. Carey asked a question. "Where would one go to identify the fundamental nature of the American character?"

I responded to Dr. Carey that I knew that he wanted me to trace and discuss the documents that underlie the foundation of our Constitution from Locke through the Federalist Papers, which I did, to the delight of the panel. But then I added that, in addition to these documents, there were other places where one could find expressions of the American character. They could be found in our literature and our music.

Dr. Allers did not smile. Jeane softly inhaled and closed her eyes. I could see her saying, "No, no."

"Music," Carey repeated. "Give me an example of a piece of American music that depicts the American character."

I suspected that Carey thought I was referring to our national anthem, "The Star Spangled Banner," as the French would refer to "La Marseillaise" or the British to "God Save the Queen." That was not what I meant. I paused for a moment, and then responded, "Rudolph the Red-Nose Reindeer." The entire group dropped their jaws.

"Rudolph, the Christmas song?" Carey asked in a serious tone of voice.

"Yes," I said. "Look at the narrative in the lyrics behind the music. Here's Rudolph, with a shiny nose that makes him different from all the other reindeer. He's ostracized and mocked by the other reindeer that will not even play with him. But because their Christmas mission was interrupted by a foggy night, Rudolph leads the other reindeer through the fog with his bright red nose. Look at the punch line in the song: 'Then, how the reindeer loved him.' Why then? The other reindeer accepted Rudolph because of the value of his contribution. His contribution to the group was the determining factor in the success of the mission. His reward was acceptance. In America all rewards are distributed by merit. This Christmas song has been popular since Gene Autry recorded it in the 1940s. The philosophy underlying this song would not fit in any other society. It fits in America because there is universal acceptance that the achievement ethic is an unconscious myth that underlies our society."

I continued that in the 1960s, it was clear that the achievement ethic was under assault and that as a nation we would regret its loss. I told the group I believed that the achievement ethic was as meaningful to our understanding of who we are as a people as any of our other founding documents. Coupled with our free enterprise system and market economy, the achievement ethic made the distribution of honors and riches available to all Americans. America is a democracy but one that rests on the foundation of merit that makes our pluralistic society cohesive.

The group stared at me and said nothing. Then Dr. Cerny, the department chair, said, "Well I think we've all heard quite enough." I really thought I had blown it, but after the group adjourned, I was awarded a doctorate with distinction.

I continue to believe today, as I did in 1971 when I was defending my dissertation, that the achievement ethic is a core belief of the American people. But it is under assault from many quarters. Since 1620, generation after generation of Americans have climbed the economic and social ladder of our society. While some in America were born wealthy, most often one generation stood on the shoulders of their parents to reach the next step up the ladder. At the same time, as in every society in world history, there has always been poverty, and many people who tried hard were not successful. Still, an overwhelming percentage of our population has moved from the lower to the middle and upper classes, with some having become extremely wealthy.

While I was still in college, I began hearing arguments that the economic deck was stacked against the lower socioeconomic groups, especially minorities. Those arguments have intensified today. The difference is that many university professors as well as many in the media now insist that individuals are prevented from climbing the economic and social ladder because our capitalist system favors the rich. This view has become more pronounced over the last forty years.

With the rise of the progressive movement we see an emphasis on the division between the "haves" and "have-nots," the classes of rich and poor being set against each other, and the rhetoric of class envy being elevated to class war. Educators, from grade school to our universities large and small, are telling students that the economic deck is stacked against them. For example, an economics professor recently authored a study in which he concluded that the American Dream does not exist: "America has no higher rate of social mobility than medieval England or pre-industrial Sweden." He argues, "The truth is that the American Dream was always an illusion." [87] Reading his comments, I am reminded of the French entomologist who concluded from an engineering study that bumblebees cannot fly. The point is that such professors are instilling in generations of students a message of hopelessness. The people who influenced my life instilled in me a belief in the American dream and gave me hope for the future. The current generation of college professors will condemn the next generation to hopelessness unless we rescue them from this kind of thinking.

Ours is a nation of immigrants who came here for equality of opportunity and, for the most part, immigrants continue to come here for that reason. They still believe, like my grandparents, that in America the streets are lined with gold. While the achievement ethic and our market economy are denigrated by progressive Democrats and liberal professors, Republicans and Roosevelt Democrats, of which there are millions, still believe in the achievement ethic. It is still a central tenet of their worldview. From my view, this is where hope lives.

It is important for Republicans to demonstrate why they support a market economy: because a market economy enables individuals to climb the economic and social ladder to success. Moreover, they need to bring the message that the Republican Party wants to help everyone climb that ladder and share in that prosperity.

It is true that Republicans promote a business agenda. We should not apologize for our business orientation, because it is entrepreneurs who create the companies that hire workers. Opportunity is all about entrepreneurial risk-takers who create jobs. The Republican Party must have as a core belief expansion of the economic pie. This will not be difficult, because most of the Republicans I meet in the business and political world really want to see a nation of entrepreneurs creating more opportunities for everyone. We can all win. This is a vision capable of rallying a nation.

The cover of this book depicts the stars on an American flag that are fading and must be restored. I believe that the working class can catch the falling flag and restore America's greatness. Here, the working class and the Republican Party share the same values and have the same aspirations.

The major theme of this book is that Republicans can win elections if they reach out beyond their comfort zone, especially to the working men and women of America. The Republican Party has a lot to offer America. It is founded on the principles of Adam Smith and John Locke. We are the party of Lincoln that ended slavery. We are the party of Horatio Alger. We want everyone to prosper. We want everyone to have a chance at a bigger piece of the pie. We are the party of the American Dream.

Endnotes

Chapter 1

1   William Delaney, "Garbage Man to Ph.D.," *Evening Star,* June 9, 1971.

Chapter 2

2   May 24, 1972, White House Memo Chuck Colson to Mike Balzano. For an analysis of how this quotation has been misconstrued, see Paul F. Boller and John George, *They Never Said It: A Book of Fake Quotes, Misquotes and Mislabeling* (New York: Oxford University Press, 1989), 31-32.

3   August 28, 1972, White House Memo Chuck Colson to The Staff

4   James P. Gannon, "President Nixon Finds a Real Garbage Man to Woo Garbagemen," *Wall Street Journal,* June 21, 1972.

5   Hugh Sidey, "The Coalition of Work, *Life*, October 6, 1972.

Chapter 3

6   James P. Gannon, "President Nixon Finds a Real Garbage Man to Woo Garbagemen," *Wall Street Journal,* June 21, 1972.

7   Seymour M. Hersh, *The Price of Power: Kissinger in the Nixon White House,* (New York: Summit Books, 1983), 344-347.

8   Ibid.

9   Joseph A. McCartin, *Collision Course: Ronald Reagan, the Air Traffic Controllers, and the Strike That Changed America* (New York: (Oxford University Press, 2011); Victor Riesel, "The President and Waterfront Labor Chiefs Make a Revolutionary Deal," syndicated column distributed November 8, 1971.

10   Homer Bigart, "War Foes Here Attacked by Construction Workers," *New York Times*, May 9, 1970.

11 January 5, 1973 Staff Memo to Ken Cole.

12 January 23, 1973 Memo Charles Colson to Ken Cole

13 Charles Colson, *Born Again* (Grand Rapids, Michigan: Chosen/Baker, 2008), 81.

Chapter 4

14 Edward Schreiber, "Most Aldermen Supporting McGovern," *Chicago Tribune,* October 22, 1972.

15 Michael Kilian, "Vote Vignettes: Human Nature Adds Fillip to Serious Day," *Chicago Tribune*, November 8, 1972.

16 For reporting on Marzullo's trip to Washington, see George Tagge and Edward Schreiber, "Won't Seek Collins' Seat, Marzullo Says," *Chicago Tribune*, December 13, 1972. Edward Schreiber, "Nixon Thanks Vito, Calls Daley great" *Chicago Tribune*, December 16, 1972.

17 November 16, 1972, Memo Charles Colson to Michael Balzano

18 December 8, 1972 Memo Michael Balzano to Charles Colson

19 December 8, 1972 Memo Charles Colson to Fred Malek.

20 Cartoon by Henry Archacki appearing in *Zgoda*, January 1973.

21 January 2, 1973 Memo Charles Colson to Fred Malek, Jerry Jones, Rob Davison, Stan Anderson, Frank Herringer (The original onion-skin document reflects 1972, a typo which should have read 1973.).

22 January 2, 1972 Memo Charles Colson to H. R. Haldeman (The original document reflects 1972, a typo which should have read 1973.).

23 January 4, 1973 Memo Fred Malek to H. R. Haldeman.

24 January 8, 1973 Memo Charles Colson to Larry Higby.

25 September 30, 2008 Letter Charles Colson to Michael Balzano

26 January 5, 1973 Staff Memo to Ken Cole.

27 May 1, 1989, Letter Richard Nixon to Michael Balzano

Chapter 5

28 September 1980, Pamphlet Reagan Presidential Campaign, Elect a Former Union President, President.

29 September 15, 1980, White House Issue Paper, A Program For The Development of an Effective Maritime Strategy.

30 Clyde H. Farnsworth, "Vote Near on Senate on Exports," *New York Times*, February 27, 1984; "Japanese Assault on Alaska Oil," *American Marine Engineer*, April 1983.

31 Speech by Ronald Reagan to the National Maritime Union, St. Louis, Missouri, October 9. 1980.

32 Ibid.

33 1980 Booklet published by the Marine Engineers' Beneficial Association, Reagan-Bush, A New Beginning for America's Maritime Industry.

34 October 20, 1980, Letter of Understanding PATCO endorsing candidate Ronald Reagan, from PATCO counsel of Leighton, Conklin, Lemov and Jacobs Law Firm to Michael Balzano, Ph.D, Reagan-Bush Campaign Headquarters, Arlington, Virginia.

35 J.J. O'Donnell was president of the Air Line Pilots Association. Lane Kirkland was president of the AFL-CIO.

Chapter 6

36 US Department of Transportation, Bureau of Transportation Statistics, *National Transportation Statistics, Table 1-24: Number and Size of the US Flag Merchant Fleet and Its Share of the World Fleet.* http://www.rita.dot.gov/ bts/sites/rita.dot.gov.bts/files/publications/national_transportation_sta-tistics/html/table_01_24.html_mfd

37 October 20, 1980, Letter of Understanding to Michael Balzano of Reagan-Bush Campaign Headquarters, Arlington, Virginia, from Richard J. Leighton, General Counsel, PATCO, "relating to the endorsement of Governor Ronald Reagan by the Professional Air Traffic Controllers Organization".

38 October 20, 1980 Letter Ronald Reagan to Bob Poli, President PATCO, pledging, if elected President of the United States, to work with air traffic controllers to bring about a spirit of cooperation.

39 October 20, 1980, PATCO Letter of Understanding.

40 John J. Seddon, 1990 Master's Thesis, PATCO - A Perspective – Who Were They? What Were They, and What Could Have or Should Have Been Done?.

41 "Calhoon Backs Bill to Block Alaskan Oil Sales to Japanese," *American Marine Engineer*, March 1983.

42 "Senate Approves Alaska Oil Export Ban," *American Marine Engineer*, April 1984.

43 April 3, 1985, Library of Congress, 99th Congress (1985–1986) S.883 - Export Administration Amendments Act of 1985.

44 September 15, 1980, President Ronald Reagan's white paper entitled A Program for the Development of an Effective Maritime Strategy.

45 October 9, 1980, Reagan Address to National Maritime Union.

46 December 1981, Booz Allen Hamilton study, Civilian Contract Manning of Government Ships – Military Sealift Command Nucleus Fleet.

47 Jeff Gerth, "Suit Contends Navy Rigged Bidding," *New York Times*, July 14, 1983.

48 Jeff Gerth, "Navy Bidding Case Stirs US Inquiry," *New York Times*, November 27, 1983.

49 October 20, 1983, Inspector General Audit Report, <u>Evaluation of Military Sealift Command Bidding Procedures for Manning Ships</u>.

50 Barton Gellman, "Merchant Fleet Is At War With the Navy," *Washington Post,* July 14, 1983.

51 Richard E. Neustadt, *Presidential Power* (New York: Wiley, 1960), 42.

Chapter 7

52 The Joint Maritime Congress changed its name to the American Maritime Congress in 1989.

53 January 21, 1991, President George H. W. Bush note to Michael Balzano.

54 January 24, 1992, Letter Mike Balzano to Sam Skinner, Chief of Staff to President George H. W. Bush.

55 January 24, 1992, Personal Note, Vice President Quayle to Sam Skinner regarding Mike Balzano as labor liaison.

56 July 22, 1992, Memo Mike Balzano to Secretary of Defense Dick Cheney, <u>Defense and Aerospace</u> <u>Workforce Constituency</u>.

57 August 5, 1992, Letter Michael Balzano to Craig Fuller on need to set up union meeting with president

58 Federation of American Scientists, "US Client Arms Sales—Saudi Arabia," http://fas.org/asmp/profiles/saudi_arabia.htm

59 August 13, 2008 email exchange Michael Balzano and Chris Koch.

Chapter 8

60 April 30, 2013, Phone call interview by Michael Balzano with Everett Alvarez, Jr.

61 1986 Memo Mike Balzano to Senator Jeremiah Denton's campaign manager re Alabama's labor vote.

62 Like the Davis-Bacon Act, the McNamara-O'Hara Service Contract Act requires employers who have federal contracts in excess of $2,500 to pay prevailing wages to the service employees covered in the contract.

63 Pension Benefit Guaranty Corporation, http://www.pbgc.gov/about/who-we-are/pg/history-of-pbgc.html

64 October 9, 1980, Ronald Reagan speech to the National Maritime Union, St. Louis, MO.

65 Owen Moritz, "Survival of the Fittest: The End of Westway, 1985," *New York Daily News,* November 20, 1998.

66 August 7, 1986, Letter Secretary Bill Brock to Senator Pete Wilson.

Chapter 9

67 In 1993, ACTION merged with another agency to form the Corporation for National and Voluntary Service or AmeriCorps.

68 Louise Sweeney, "Why Storm Signals Fly Over ACTION," *Christian Science Monitor*, April 2, 1975.

69 "Action: A Case of Mismanagement Hard at Work," editorial, *Government Executive*, October 1980.

Chapter 10

70 September 30, 2008, letter Charles Colson to Michael Balzano

71 Clay Dillow, "The Most Technologically Advanced Warship Ever Built," *Popular Science*, October 2012.

72 Thomas H. Copeman III, "The Future Surface Fleet," *Proceedings of the US Naval Institute*, January 2014.

73 Zach Carter, "Newt Gingrich Defends Space Exploration, Moon Colony During GOP Debate in Florida," Huffington, Post, January 26, 2012.

74 Ralph Vartabedian, "Political Moves in Defense," *Los Angeles Times*, March 6, 1991.

75 July 17, 1991, C-SPAN Video Library Transcript Viewer, Senate Session, position on S. 323, as Amended (Senate-July 17, 1991), discussing VA HUD-IA funding. http://www.c-spanvideo.org/videoLibrary/transcript/transcript.php?id=13732&fullscreen

Chapter 11

76 February 25, 1987, Letter from William W. Winpisinger to Sen. Pete Wilson

77 Patrick Buchanan, *Suicide of a Superpower: Will America Survive to 2025?* (New York: Thomas Dunne/St. Martin's Press, 2011), 17.

78 Patrick Buchanan, "Who Killed Detroit?", syndicated column distributed November 21, 2008.

79 Kevin Whiteman, "Hard Hat Riots Turn 40," examiner.com, May 12, 2010.

80 Kathy Shaidle, "The Hard Hat Riot: 40 years Later, Rare Photographs Emerge," examiner.com, May 7, 2010.

81 Kathy Shaidle, "New Photos Emerge of Forgotten Chapter of 'The Sixties,'" newrealblog.com, May 7, 2010.

82 Jeff Brady, "Unions Assume a Support Role for Occupy Movement,' npr.org, October 29, 2011.

83 Bureau of Labor Statistics, US Department of Labor. The Economics Daily, "Union Membership Rate in Private Industry was 6.6 percent in 2014; Public Sector 35.7 Percent."

Chapter 12

84 Jeane Kirkpatrick, "The Revolt of the Masses," *Commentary*, February 1973.
85 Thomas B. Edsall, "The Future of the Obama Coalition," *New York Times*, November 27, 2011.
86 Ibid
87 Gregory Clark, "The American Dream is an Illusion," ForeignAffairs.com, August 26, 2014.

Index

Derwinski, Edward 39, 42
Dole, Elizabeth 109, 128-129, 134,
    135, 142, 214
Duesterberg, Tom 138
Dukakis, Michael 165, 167, 184
dyslexic 14

E

Eder, Gary 168
Edsall, Thomas B. 295, 296, 308
Ehrlichman, John 27, 67, 68, 75, 79,
    91-96
Eisenhower, Julie Nixon 97
Empty Pork Barrel 267, 268
entitlement(s) 213, 240, 250, 277,
    297, 295
ethnic(s) 3-4, 6, 9-10, 15, 17, 22, 23,
    25, 29, 32-34, 36-43, 46, 56, 58-
    59, 63, 64, 66, 68-74, 77, 80-88,
    90-91, 94-95, 102, 106, 110, 120,
    135, 165, 169, 257, 281, 284-286,
    289, 298
Evans, Bud 28
Evening Star 20, 21, 303
Export Administration Act 54,
    139, 150

F

Federal Aviation Administration
    (FAA) 115-119, 126, 128, 139,
    141, 142, 144, 145, 146, 170-178,
    212-213
Feklisov, Alexander 29
Ferry, Christian 185
Fitzsimmons, Frank E. 125
fleet support (civilian manning) 113,
    125, 139, 151, 153, 161, 209, 213-
    217, 305
Ford, Gerald R. 97, 98, 208, 218,
    224-228

Fosco, Angelo 135, 136
Fuller, Craig 128, 138, 139, 140, 141,
    148-151, 158-159, 165, 167, 168,
    175-176, 177, 179, 213, 215, 217

G

Ganley, Jack 225-228
Gannon, James P. 46, 49
Garrick, Robert Rear Admiral (Bob)
    114, 117-120, 125-126, 129,
    140, 144
Gellman, Barton 160
Georgetown University 6, 19, 20
Georgine, Robert 135-136
Geren, Pete 232, 235, 237
Gerevas, Ron 225, 227
Gerth, Jeff 159
Gibson, Andrew E. (Andy) 123
Gingrich, Newt 253
Gleason, Teddy 52
Goodreau, David 254, 255
Government Executive 226
Gray, Ed 140
Greene, Gladys 247
Gualtieri, Fred 42, 99, 121, 275

H

Haldeman, H. R. (Bob) 52, 67, 73, 88-
    90, 93-97
Halsey, Ash 65
Hard Hat Riot 50, 55, 91, 194,
    272, 273
Harlow, Bryce 50
Harper, Ed 158, 159
Hart, Karen 70
Heinz, John III 151, 212, 230, 236,
    241, 270, 274, 275
Helms, J. Lynn 144, 213
Hersh, Seymour 51, 52, 53, 75
Higby, Larry 90

Skinner, Samuel K. (Sam) 175
Snyder, Al 31
Society of Professional Engineering
    Employees in Aerospace
    (SPEEA) 188, 199
Sorzano, Jose 149
St. Michael's Catholic Church 8-9, 14
Statue of Liberty Museum 68-71, 122
Steubenville, Ohio 42-43, 100, 110,
    121, 122, 294
Stone, Roger 107
Strategic Arms Limitation Talks
    (SALT) 51
Sununu, John H. 169, 171, 172, 174-
    175, 182-183, 187-188, 198, 294
Superconducting Super Collider 249
Szmagala, Taras (Terry) 42, 69, 72-
    73, 285-286

T

Teixeira, Ruy 296
Timmons, William E. (Bill) 105-106,
    107, 109, 112
Torricelli, Robert 238

U

United Automobile, Aerospace
    and Agricultural Implement
    Workers of America (UAW)
    256, 265-266, 271
United Steel Workers (USW); steel-
    workers 42-44, 62-63, 78, 98,
    110, 120-122, 199, 212, 241, 256,
    271-273
University of Bridgeport 19

V

Vander Jagt, Guy 142-143
Volpe, John 37-40, 42, 80

W

Walentynowicz, Leonard F. 69, 98
Walker, Charles D. (Charlie) 250
Walker, Ronald H. (Ron) 69-70, 73,
    105-106, 122-123
Wall Street Journal 18, 46, 49, 148
Wall, Shannon J. 123, 124
Wallace, George 31, 65
Warren, Gerald L. (Jerry) 4, 69-70, 74
Watergate 28, 76, 97-98, 101-102, 122,
    204, 206, 289
Weidenbaum, Murray 136-137
Weinberger, Caspar (Cap) 92, 162,
    213-214, 229
Westway Highway 110, 120-121,
    209-210
Whiteman, Kevin 272
Williams, Cassell (Cass) 166, 172,
    176, 177, 198, 268
Wilson, Pete 153, 169, 176, 184, 211,
    229, 257, 263, 267-270
Winchester Repeating Arms
    Company 11
Woerth, Captain Duane 171, 177
work ethic 15, 22, 47, 88
working class; working class voters
    6, 9, 13, 21-22, 24, 25, 58, 63,
    77, 121, 242, 243, 245, 261-262,
    271-272, 274-275, 280-282, 285,
    288, 290, 292, 293, 295-296, 298,
    301-302
work to rule 147
Wright, James C. (Jim) 230

Z

Zgoda 74
Ziegler, Ronald (Ron) 3, 74
Zumwalt destroyer 245

CPSIA information can be obtained at www.ICGtesting.com
Printed in the USA
LVOW11s1730210716

497247LV00003B/546/P